法律文本英汉互译简明教程

聂玉景 编著

苏州大学出版社

图书在版编目(CIP)数据

法律文本英汉互译简明教程/聂玉景编著.—苏州：
苏州大学出版社,2020.12
ISBN 978-7-5672-3446-8

Ⅰ.①法… Ⅱ.①聂… Ⅲ.①法律-英语-翻译-高等学校-教材 Ⅳ.①D9

中国版本图书馆CIP数据核字(2020)第263619号

法律文本英汉互译简明教程
聂玉景　编著
责任编辑　王　娅
助理编辑　万才兰

苏州大学出版社出版发行
(地址：苏州市十梓街1号　邮编：215006)
镇江文苑制版印刷有限责任公司印装
(地址：镇江市黄山南路18号润州花园6-1号　邮编：212000)

开本787 mm×1 092 mm　1/16　印张14.25　字数312千
2020年12月第1版　2020年12月第1次印刷
ISBN 978-7-5672-3446-8　定价：48.00元

若有印装错误,本社负责调换
苏州大学出版社营销部　电话:0512-67481020
苏州大学出版社网址　http://www.sudapress.com
苏州大学出版社邮箱　sdcbs@suda.edu.cn

前言

　　法律文本英汉互译不仅仅是两种语言的表达转换，还涉及对两种法律文化和法律观念的理解。有法学专业背景的翻译初学者对中国法律知识比较了解，也熟悉英美法系的相关情况，在法律专业知识方面面临的挑战不大，但必须提升自身的英语理解和表达能力；有英语专业背景的学习者，对于不同法系的运行机制、司法实践等基本法律知识则缺乏足够的知识储备，也不熟悉中英文法律文本的基本格式和表达特点，翻译起来显得步履维艰。

　　本教材主要面向对法律翻译感兴趣的英语专业学习者。前三章的内容分别为"法律翻译职业现状""法律语言的特点""法律职业和法院结构"，讲述中国和主要英美国家的法律翻译职业的入门资格和发展现状，以及法律翻译的宏观背景知识。后七章依照法学专业的部门法体例编排，介绍相关领域的基本知识和翻译，包括民法、民事诉讼法、仲裁、刑法、刑事诉讼法、行政法等领域。从第四章开始，每章按照"常用术语""核心术语的理解和表达""常见句型结构""翻译实例分析"结构编写。其中"常用术语"部分提供常见法律术语的中英文表达以供参考学习，而"核心术语的理解和表达"部分则选取较难理解或者在不同法系中内涵有较大差异的术语，不仅给出参考表达，还进行详细阐释。"常见句型结构"部分提炼了重复度高但又具有难度的句式结构，同时辅以例句供初学者研习。"翻译分析"部分选取有代表性段落，从宏观和微观的视角进行阐述，尽量将段落文本翻译过程中可能遇到的困难和疑惑呈现出来以供参考。

　　在本教材编写过程中，正逢《中华人民共和国民法典》颁布和生效，因此民法部分直接参照《中华人民共和国民法典》，将原计划编写的"民法的基本知识和翻译"和"合同法的基本知识和翻译"统一到民法主题下，分上、下两部分进行讲解。

　　本教材的编写参考了近二十年发表和出版的法律英语和法律翻译方面的论文、教材和专著，还援引了国内外有较大影响的起诉书、答辩状、判决书等法律文书，在此我对原作者们表示衷心感谢。此外，本教材受南通大学教材项目资助，我一并表示感谢。

聂玉景

目 录
CONTENTS

第一章　法律翻译职业现状　/ 1

　　第一节　中国的法律翻译职业现状　/ 1
　　第二节　主要英语国家的法律翻译职业现状　/ 3
　　翻译练习　/ 6

第二章　法律语言的特点　/ 9

　　第一节　法律英语的词汇构成　/ 9
　　第二节　法律术语和特定句型　/ 15
　　第三节　程式化的法律篇章结构　/ 18
　　第四节　法律语言的准确性和模糊性　/ 20
　　翻译练习　/ 24

第三章　法律职业和法院结构　/ 26

　　第一节　法律职业　/ 26
　　第二节　法院结构　/ 30
　　翻译练习　/ 35

第四章　民法的基本知识和翻译(上)　/ 36

　　第一节　常用术语　/ 37
　　第二节　核心术语的理解和表达　/ 43
　　第三节　常见句型结构　/ 52
　　第四节　翻译实例分析　/ 57
　　翻译练习　/ 63

第五章　民法的基本知识和翻译(下) / 65

第一节　常用术语 / 66
第二节　核心术语的表达和理解 / 69
第三节　常见句型结构 / 77
第四节　翻译实例分析 / 92
翻译练习 / 100

第六章　民事诉讼法的基本知识和翻译 / 102

第一节　常用术语 / 102
第二节　核心术语的表达和理解 / 106
第三节　常见句型结构 / 113
第四节　翻译实例分析 / 117
翻译练习 / 122

第七章　仲裁的基本知识和翻译 / 124

第一节　常用术语 / 126
第二节　核心术语的表达和理解 / 128
第三节　常见句型结构 / 132
第四节　翻译实例分析 / 135
翻译练习 / 142

第八章　刑法的基本知识和翻译 / 144

第一节　常用术语 / 145
第二节　核心术语的表达和理解 / 149
第三节　常见句型结构 / 153
第四节　翻译实例分析 / 162
翻译练习 / 164

第九章　刑事诉讼法的基本知识和翻译 / 166

第一节　常用术语 / 166
第二节　核心术语的表达和理解 / 170
第三节　常见句型结构 / 177
第四节　翻译实例分析 / 182
翻译练习 / 187

第十章　行政法的基本知识和翻译　/ 189

　　第一节　常用术语　/ 190

　　第二节　核心术语的表达和理解　/ 192

　　第三节　常见句型结构　/ 196

　　第四节　翻译实例分析　/ 198

　　翻译练习　/ 203

翻译练习参考答案　/ 205

参考文献　/ 219

第一章
法律翻译职业现状

第一节　中国的法律翻译职业现状

中国有文献记载的翻译活动最早可以追溯到周公居摄六年（公元前1 000多年）。周武王死后，周成王年少继位，由周公摄理朝政。《后汉书·南蛮西南夷列传》载："周公居摄六年，制作礼乐，天下和平，越裳以三象重译而献白雉。"交趾（今越南北部）南面的越裳国为表示友好，派出三位翻译官向周公献珍禽白雉。因为路途遥远，并且没有人既懂汉语又懂越裳国语，所以要先将越裳国语翻译成其他语言，最终经九次转译才能译成汉语。三位翻译官经历了一个类似"越裳国语—广东话—湖南话—湖北话—河南话……周朝官话"的过程，最终翻译成功。（辛全民，2011）当然在这个过程中，是否发生信息缺失或者误读，现已无从考证。

目前能够找到的最早的法律翻译法规见于汉律，如《二年律令·具律》中就有调整译员行为的法律规定："译讯人为非（诈）伪，以出入罪人，死罪，黥为城旦舂；它各以其所出入罪反罪之。"可见，不敬业的译者是要承担刑事责任的（冉诗洋、李德凤，2019）。"城旦舂"是中国秦汉时期的刑罚，属于徒刑。"城旦"是针对男犯人的刑罚，其意思是"治城"，即筑城；"舂"是针对女犯人的刑罚，其意思是"治米"，即舂米。对违反法律翻译法规的人员施以重刑说明当时的政府和社会已经认识到翻译的重要性。

对法律翻译译者的处罚在后代得到认同和坚持。唐代的《唐律疏议》明确约定："诸证不言情，及译人诈伪，致罪有出入者，证人减二等，译人与同罪。注曰：谓夷人有罪，译传其对者。"长孙无忌等在疏议中对"译人诈伪"的定罪量刑又做了进一步的说明："传译番人之语，令其罪有出入者……译人与同罪，若夷人承徒一年，译人云'承徒二年'，即译人得所加一年徒坐；或夷人承流，译者云'徒二年'，即译得所减二年徒之类。"如果刑名未定、司法机关尚未判决，译者翻译不实被知，会被按照"不应得为"罪处罚："译人徒罪以上从重，杖罪以下从轻。"所谓的"不应得为"罪，是指"律、令无条，理不可为者"，处罚办法是"诸不应得为而为之者，笞四十；事理重者，杖八十"。此外，唐律还在程序上要求翻译人员在自己翻译的司法文书上签字画押，以保证翻译内容的准确性。两宋时期的法律翻译立法，继续沿袭汉律、唐律的相应规定，严格规范法律翻译活动。（辛全民、高新华，2010）

法律翻译近代的发展是在鸦片战争之后。在学习西方国家的科学技术时，人们逐渐认识到法律制度的社会管理价值，开始大量翻译国外法律专著和法律法规。当时西方列强不断要求清政府签署各种不平等条约，这在客观上又增加了学习翻译西方法律的需求。从鸦片战争到五四运动期间，官方和民间都对西方法律、法学著作进行了大量翻译。（张法连，2016）这些翻译活动不仅推动了中国法制的近代化进程，也为中国翻译的发展做出了贡献。

改革开放后，不断加强的法制建设和依法治国基本国策的提出，更深层次地促进了法律翻译的发展，大量法学著作译本在国内出版，西方国家的法学发展各阶段中有影响力的著作得以传播普及。此后，随着经济全球化不断发展，无论是跨国公司在中国发展，还是中国公司走向世界，都给法律翻译的繁荣提供了沃土。同时，在民间交流方面，无论是外国人在中国留学、旅游或定居，还是中国人去国外留学、旅游或定居，其间必然会产生各种法律活动并伴随纠纷，这就需要法律翻译工作者的助力来实现有效和准确的沟通。

目前活跃在法律翻译战线的从业者可以简单地分为两类：一种是中资或外资律师事务所中以律师为主要服务对象的全职法律翻译；另一种是以翻译公司为主要服务对象的自由或兼职法律翻译。律师事务所与翻译公司所面向的客户存在差异，所以两者的业务不尽相同。前者的法律翻译业务大体紧扣各家律师事务所的业务范围，但大多涉及公司法、外商投资、并购、合规、尽职调查、企业上市、知识产权等常见的非诉讼法律业务（偶尔也涉及诉讼）；后者的法律翻译业务相对更杂，但比较典型的业务是一些格式法律文书的翻译，如合同、章程、证明、法规等。当然两者之间也有业务重叠，例如有些律师事务所会外包一些翻译业务给业内声望较高的翻译公司。

在中国，要取得翻译资格，首先要通过全国翻译专业资格（水平）考试（China Accreditation Test for Translators and Interpreters，简称CATTI），并取得翻译专业资格（水平）证书。但是，翻译资格的含金量远不及法律职业资格的含金量高。原因不在于律师在薪酬或社会地位上一定高于译员，而是CATTI的地位实际上还无法与法律职业资格考试相提并论——前者无论是在文本上还是在社会中都无立法保障，还不能被视为从事法律翻译职业的资格考试，而后者的地位得到《中华人民共和国律师法》的保证。申请律师执业，应当具备下列条件：拥护中华人民共和国宪法；通过国家统一法律职业资格考试并取得法律职业资格。目前中国尚未对翻译立法，CATTI考试缺乏相应行业资格的法律保障。

现阶段与法律翻译最相关的资格证书考试是法律英语证书（Legal English Certificate，简称LEC）全国统一考试，该考试以广大法律从业者的专业英语水平为考核目标，它旨在为从事涉外业务的企业、律师事务所提供招募国际性人才的客观标准，同时督促国内法律从业人员提高专业英语水平。

该考试每年举行两次，时间为 5 月和 11 月的最后一个周六，目前已在北京、上海、广州、重庆、杭州、济南、武汉、西安、兰州等城市设置了考点。LEC 考试的题型、考查内容与美国的律师资格考试相近，同时又突出法律英语语言运用的特色，并结合中国的实际增加了法律英语翻译测试。

第二节 主要英语国家的法律翻译职业现状

英语国家法律翻译最常见的活动是法庭翻译，它是为保障当事人的合法权益，为母语不是当地语或本国语的诉讼相关人员提供的法庭翻译活动。西方国家的法庭翻译具有较为悠久的历史。古埃及时期就有法庭翻译的文献记载，还有个说法是早在 17 世纪就有法律翻译的文献记载。1682 年，英国发生了一起凶杀案，而法庭仅仅为讲本族语的贵族提供翻译服务，显然地位的不平等直接影响了受法律保护的程度，而是否有法律翻译服务也直接影响法律平等的实现程度。这一点在 1820 年的罗琳王后通奸案中得到扭转，庭审时不仅有证人证言翻译，还有文化差异解释，这样可以在最大限度上保证法律平等。

第一次世界大战后，由于要签订《巴黎和约》而产生了英语与法语之间对译的口译需求，这是现代连续传译的开始。而同声传译则诞生于 1945 年，即第二次世界大战后的纽伦堡审判期间，那时有了第一次开始使用电子设备的口译活动。（李克兴、张新红，2006）由英、法、苏、美四国组成的盟军军事法庭要求将所有庭审程序都翻译成被告的母语，这个涉及五种语言的世纪大审判当然需要大量的法庭口译。口译员们坐在透明的玻璃房里通过电子设备把庭审过程中的话语全部传译给庭审各方。

一、美国的法律翻译职业现状

美国是移民大国，使用的语言尤为多样，造就了"一法多语"的现象。在这样的背景下，法庭翻译不仅非常重要，而且还是必不可少的。1978 年，美国开始为法庭口译立法。法庭此前审判时使用口译人员的依据只有《联邦刑事诉讼规则》（Federal Rules of Criminal Procedure）第 28（b）条、《联邦证据规则》（Federal Rules of Evidence）第 604 条、《刑事审判法》（Criminal Justice Act）、《联邦民事诉讼规则》（Federal Rules of Civil Procedure）第 43（f）条等，并以前两部法律为主。为进一步完善法庭翻译制度，美国联邦法院于 1978 年制订了《法庭口译员法案》（Court Interpreters Act of 1978），要求法庭口译员必须完整准确、一字不差地翻译，不得修饰和省略源话语的任何信息，不得更改源话语的语体和语域。该法令还要求美国法院管理办公室制定联邦法庭口译人员认证标准。经认证合格的口译人员全部被录入专门的合格口译人员信息库，供地方法院挑选。

1988 年，美国联邦法院对该法案又进行了修正完善，对译员认证、安保、同传等特定情况做出了更加明确的规定。该法案明确阐明：忠实和准确是法庭口译的最基本要求。为达到忠实和准确的标准，译员要完整地、一字不差地传译说话人的话语，不得随意增加、删减、解释、改述，也不能有遗漏、曲解、误传等现象。哪怕证人说的是脏话，翻译时也不能用委婉语代替。中立、保密是法庭译员的职业道德。回避原则是使法庭译员保持中立的有效方法。该法令规定：法庭口译人员和控辩双方不应有任何私人关系或其他能够影响译员中立立场的特殊关系。法庭译员是透明的，在任何场合，都应当自己不存在，所说的话只依据讲者的意思。第一人称是证人专有的，译员只是证人的代言人。证人说"我想喝水"，译员在翻译时就要说"I need water."。当译员真正要提及自己时，应用第三人称说"May the interpreter have some water?"。

美国明尼苏达州、新泽西州、俄勒冈州和华盛顿特区于1995年成立了州法庭译员认证协会（Consortium for State Court Interpreter Certification），约40个州加入该协会。为保证所有译员都能胜任，该协会设立了准入门槛，申请者要参加一定期限的训练会议（orientation session），并通过资格考试。法庭翻译人员还必须宣誓，遵守州法律。

对于法律翻译职业来说，1980年实施的联邦法庭口译员资格考试（The Federal Court Interpreter Certification Examination）的意义更为重大。该资格考试系统引入以运用为核心（performance-based）的口译员测试概念和做法，要求考试者完成高强度针对性操练，其中包含从事法庭口译实践所需的知识、能力、技巧。考试主要包含两大模块，即笔试与口试，其中笔试部分又分为英语和西班牙语两大部分，每部分包含阅读理解、语言运用、错误辨识、同义词和词语翻译5类题型，共80道多项选择题。英语部分与西班牙语部分题型、题数相同，两大部分相加共160道题目。应考者的英语和西班牙语考试都必须及格才算笔试合格。（李克兴，2007）

美国翻译界没有很强的证书文化，除法庭口译和医疗口译需要认证外，其他行业更多地依赖试译、经验和口碑。如果从事不出庭的法律翻译，可以考虑美国翻译协会（American Translators Association，简称ATA）的证书。ATA的考试种类划分比较详细，不仅要选择语言，还要选择是"X译英"，还是"英译X"。最后的认证也只是认证选定语言方向上的翻译能力。ATA每年在美国各地有十几场考试。ATA规定试卷必须手写，不能使用网络和任何电子设备，但是允许携带纸质词典，并且不限数量，所以考场里常有人拖着一箱词典。ATA考试时间为3小时，考题是3篇字数为225~275的短文。第一篇是非专业性段落，第二篇选材自科技或医疗领域，第三篇选材自财经、商业或法律领域。第一篇必译，第二、三篇任选一篇译。考试结果只分通过和不通过两个等级，一般要等16周后才出，但偶尔也有人提前收到考试结果。

美国法律翻译需求广泛，以加利福尼亚州为例，据2018年的《洛杉矶时报》报道，加利福尼亚州所使用的语言至少有220种，44%的居民在家中不说英语，700万人称自己英语说得不好。此外，加利福尼亚州各法院每年审理的案件总数多达800万件。相比之下，合格的法庭口译人员的数量明显供不应求。纽约的相关数据显示：居住在纽约市的850万人中几乎约有1/2的人在家里使用英语以外的语言，约有1/4的5岁以上居民具备有限的英语能力，约有1/6的纽约市家庭没有14岁以上的英语熟练的成年人。随着各大州的移民数量不断增加,相关的法律纠纷也会不断出现,因此法律翻译服务需求也会随之增长,职业前景十分乐观。

二、英国的法律翻译职业现状

根据规定,英国法院必须在已经通过考试并在公共服务翻译人员登记处登记的译员名单中挑选法庭译员。法庭译员也必须遵守与美国相关条例类似的行为准则。

英国的法律翻译发展历史早于美国,也有相应的翻译资格考试机构,其中具有代表性的有皇家特许语言学家协会(Chartered Institute of Linguists,简称CIOL)。CIOL创立于1910年,是提供多语种培训、认证和服务的专业性国际机构,总部位于英国伦敦。协会中有不少大名鼎鼎的翻译专家、教授,如伦敦城市大学语言研究中心主任、威尔士大学语言学教授、萨里大学翻译教授彼得·纽马克(Peter Newmark)等。

该协会每年举办4类考试认证:翻译文凭(Diploma in Translation,简称DipTrans)、双语交流国际文凭(International Diploma in Bilingual Communication,简称IDBC)、公共服务口译文凭(Diploma in Public Service Interpreting,简称DPSI)和双语技能证书(Certificate in Bilingual Skills,简称CBS)。它们分别对应英国国家资格证书框架中的5级、4级、4级和3级。

其中与法律翻译密切相关的考试是DPSI,此文凭表示持有者的公共服务口译能力已经初步达到专业水平。考试包括4个专业领域:英国法律、苏格兰法律、卫生和地方政府事务。从考试内容可以看出其法律属性。考试使用英语和英语以外的其他任何一种国际通用语言。考试每年6月在获得授权的考试中心举行。取得该文凭的人有资格为法庭、医院和当地政府提供口译服务。

在英国的庭审翻译,译员需要提前30分钟左右到法院签到,查看案件具体在哪个法庭审判,有些法院会设置专门的译员等候室,译员抵达法院后必须在那里等候。如果法院没有专门的等候室,译员就要先在法庭传唤员处登记,然后在法庭门外等候,直到传唤员通知译员到庭。

译员在正式开始翻译之前要进行宣誓,法庭的书记员首先会询问译员选择宣读Oath还是Affirmation,前者是针对有宗教信仰的译员。誓词内容如下:

Oath:I swear by Almighty God that I will well and faithfully interpret and make true explanation of all such matters and things as shall be required of me according to the best of my skill and understanding.

Affirmation:I do solemnly, sincerely and truly declare and affirm that I will well and faithfully interpret and make true explanation of all such matters and things as shall be required of me according to the best of my skill and understanding.

三、澳大利亚和加拿大的法律翻译职业现状

澳大利亚的翻译认证机构是澳大利亚翻译认可局(National Accreditation Authority

for Translators and Interpreters，简称 NAATI），由澳大利亚官方机构负责，权威性很高。该机构成立于 1977 年，旨在为不同程度的笔译和口译人员设立专业标准，创建全国性注册和颁发职业上岗证书的系统。

认证考试由口译和笔译两个部分组成。这两个部分又包括 4 个不同程度的考试，即准口译（paraprofessional interpreter）、口译（interpreter）、会议口译（conference interpreter）、高级会议口译（senior conference interpreter）和准笔译（paraprofessional translator）、笔译（translator）、高级笔译（advanced translator）、资深笔译（senior advanced translator）。澳大利亚要求译员必须通过考试以证明其翻译能力，法庭口译员必须具备专业口译员的资格，如果案情复杂，则要求只有获得会议口译员资格证书的人才能担任法庭译员职务。即使是警察局需要翻译时，译员也需要提供相应的资格证书。

与澳大利亚的认证类似，加拿大也有专业的翻译专业认证协会，即加拿大口译和笔译工作者委员会（Canadian Translators and Interpreters Council，简称 CTIC），负责实施全国统一标准的翻译职业认证考试。CTIC 下属的认证委员会负责制定认证标准和实施考试。认证委员会成员由笔译、会议口译、法庭口译和术语学方面的专家组成。1975 年，加拿大首先设立了笔译考试，后来在魁北克地区设立会议口译考试，凡是有 200 个工作日或同等经历的口译者均可报考。法庭口译是考试的一个重要组成部分。作为移民大国，随着社会发展和外来人口的不断涌入，加拿大对法庭口译员的需求也在不断增长。

翻译练习

练习 1

Mark Janus is employed by the Illinois Department of Healthcare and Family Services as a child support specialist. The employees in his unit are among the 35,000 public employees in Illinois who are represented by respondent American Federation of State, County, and Municipal Employees, Council 31 (Union). Janus refused to join the Union because he opposes "many of the public policy positions that it advocates", including the positions it takes in collective bargaining. Janus believes that the Union's "behavior in bargaining does not appreciate the current fiscal crises in Illinois and does not reflect his best interests or the interests of Illinois citizens". Therefore, he would not pay any fees or otherwise subsidize the Union. Under his unit's collective-bargaining agreement, however, he was required to pay an agency fee of $44.58 per month—which would amount to about $535 per year.

Janus's concern about Illinois' current financial situation is shared by the Governor of the State. The Governor commenced an action in federal court, asking that the law be declared unconstitutional, and the Illinois attorney general (a respondent here) intervened to defend the law. The District Court agreed that the Governor could not maintain the lawsuit, but it held that petitioner and the other individuals who had moved to intervene had standing because the agency fees unquestionably injured them. Accordingly, "in the interest of judicial economy", the court dismissed the Governor as a plaintiff, while simultaneously allowing petitioner and the other employees to file their own complaint.

练习 3

Apple argues that Illinois Brick allows consumers to sue only the party who sets the retail price, whether or not the party sells the good or service directly to the complaining party. But that theory suffers from three main problems.

First, it contradicts statutory text and precedent by requiring the Court to rewrite the rationale of Illinois Brick and to gut its longstanding bright-line rule. Any ambiguity in Illinois Brick should be resolved in the direction of the statutory text, which states that "any person" injured by an antitrust violation may sue to recover damages.

Second, Apple's theory is not persuasive economically or legally. It would draw an arbitrary and unprincipled line among retailers based on their financial arrangements with their manufacturers or suppliers. And it would permit a consumer to sue a monopolistic retailer when the retailer set the retail price by marking up the price it had paid the manufacturer or supplier for the good or service but not when the manufacturer or supplier set the retail price and the retailer took a commission on each sale.

Third, Apple's theory would provide a roadmap for monopolistic retailers to structure transactions with manufacturers or suppliers so as to evade antitrust claims by consumers and thereby thwart effective antitrust enforcement.

First, Apple posits that allowing only the upstream app developers—and not the downstream consumers—to sue Apple would mean more effective antitrust enforcement. But that makes little sense, and it would directly contradict the longstanding goal of effective private enforcement and consumer protection in antitrust cases.

Second, Apple warns that calculating the damages in successful consumer antitrust suits against monopolistic retailers might be complicated. But Illinois Brick is not a get-out-of-court-free card for monopolistic retailers to play any time that a damages calculation might be complicated.

Third, Apple claims that allowing consumers to sue will result in "conflicting claims to a common fund—the amount of the alleged overcharge". But this is not a case where multiple parties at different levels of a distribution chain are trying to recover the same pass-through overcharge initially levied by the manufacturer at the top of the chain.

第二章
法律语言的特点

法律语言在英文中写作 legal language，有时也写作 statutory language，原指表述法律科学概念的语言，以及诉讼和非诉讼法律事务所用的语言。随着发展，它渐渐有了其他含义，包括某些具有特定法律意义的词语，并且扩展到了语言的其他层面。法律语言具有自身的特殊性。法律长期在人们的政治、经济、科学和文化生活中发挥着强大的规范和调节作用，因此法律语言在不断发展和完善中也形成了一系列的独特性。从狭义上理解，法律语言可以被看作法律共同体所倡导的法言法语。

不少学者关注法律语言的特殊性，并对其进行梳理和分析。一般认为，法律语言可以分为立法语言、司法语言和法律科学语言。法律语言不同于其他类型的文本，它是工具性的语言，对准确性要求较高，其词语、句法、表达方式和语体风格都有自己的特征。本章以法律英语为例，从其词汇构成、法律术语和特定结构、程式化的法律篇章结构、法律语言的准确性和模糊性角度出发，解析法律语言特征，为法律翻译奠定基础。

第一节 法律英语的词汇构成

作为大陆法系和英美法系这两大法系中的一支，罗马法及后来的法国法律在促进世界法学的发展方面功不可没，因此法律英语大量引入了拉丁语和法语词汇。此外，法律英语表达中还保留了很多古英语和中世纪英语。

一、拉丁语

拉丁语是在公元 597 年传入英国的，随后大量渗入英语中，主要集中在法律等领域，至今仍在使用。法律文本中常见的拉丁语见表 2-1。

表 2-1 法律文本中常见的拉丁语

拉丁语	汉语释义	英语释义或举例
actus reus	犯罪行为	the wrongful act that makes up the physical action of a crime
affidavit	证词，誓言	a sworn statement in writing especially under oath or on affirmation before an authorized magistrate or officer

续表

拉丁语	汉语释义	英语释义或举例
alias	别名	an assumed or additional name
alibi	不在犯罪现场证明	the fact or state of having been elsewhere at the time a crime was committed
bona fide	善意的，真诚的	characterized by good faith and lack of fraud or deceit; valid under or in compliance with the law; made with or characterized by sincerity 如：bona fide holder 善意持票人；bona fide purchaser 善意购买人
de facto	事实上的	in fact, whether right or not 如：de facto segregation 事实上的种族隔离
de jure	按照法律的	in accordance with law 如：de jure segregation 法律上的隔离；de jure recognition 法律上承认
proviso	但书，限制性条款	an article or clause that introduces a condition; a conditional stipulation
habeas corpus	人身保护令	any of several writs originating at common law that are issued to bring a party before the court
inter alia	除了其他事物以外	among other things
mens rea	犯罪意图	a culpable mental state, especially one involving intent or knowledge and forming an element of a criminal offence
per diem	每日地，每日的	by the day; based on use or service by the day 如：per diem compensation 日补偿
prima facie	表面的，初步的	sufficient to establish a fact or case unless disapproved 如：prima facie proof/evidence 初步证据；prima facie case 初步证据确凿的案件
pro bono	公益性的，无偿的	being, involving, or doing legal work donated especially for the public good
quasi	准的	having such a resemblance to another thing as to fall within its general category 如：quasi contract 准合同；quasi judicial 准司法的
sine die	无固定期限的，无确定日期的	no appointed date for resumption
situs	管辖地，行为发生地，财产所在地	a location that is or is held to be the site of something (property or crime or tort) and that commonly determines jurisdiction over it
stare decisis	遵从先例	the doctrine under which courts adhere to precedent on questions of law in order to ensure certainty, consistency, and stability in the administration of justice with departure from precedent permitted for compelling reasons
sui juris	有完全行为能力的	having full legal capacity to act on one's own behalf, not subject to the authority of another
veto	否决权，否决	an authoritative prohibition; refuse to admit or approve

当然还有不少拉丁语词汇在日常生活中较少出现，对理解和翻译构成较大障碍，见表 2-2。

表 2-2 容易构成翻译障碍的拉丁语法律词汇

拉丁语词汇	汉译	拉丁语词汇	汉译
ex parte	单方面的，片面的	lex fori	法院地法
ex post facto	事后的，追溯过去的	lex loci	地方法
guardian ad litem	法定监护人	lex talionis	同态复仇法
inter partes	各方之间	per stirpes	按照血缘、祖先
in locum parentis	处于代理父母的地位	res inter alios	与本案无关的第三者之行为
in rem	对某事物的	res ipsa loquitur	事情不言自明
in personam	对某人不利的	ultra vires	超越权限的
ipso facto	因以下事实	verbatim	逐字的，一字不差的

熟练掌握这些拉丁语表达后，我们就可以消除理解障碍，在翻译时做到得心应手。例如：

① Before registration, the creation, alteration, transfer or extinction of the property right of the vessels, aircraft, motor vehicles, etc. shall not be used against a bona fide third party.

船舶、航空器、机动车等物权的设立、变更、转让和消灭，未经登记，不得对抗善意第三人。

② The number of reliable dealers is growing, but the market needs bona fide collectors with the energy to do cultural research and to make commitments for sticking to their choices.

值得信任的经销商越来越多，但是这个市场需要有诚意的收藏家，他们要有精力去开展文化方面的研究并承诺坚持他们的选择。

③ Even such requirements existed in relation to domestically produced goods, those members reiterated that any less favorable treatment imposed on the imported goods, whether de facto or de jure, must be eliminated in order to ensure full conformity with the principle of national treatment.

即使对国产货物也存在此类要求，但是这些成员不断重申必须取消对进口货物施加的任何事实上或法律上的不利待遇，以保证完全符合国民待遇原则。

理解了 de facto, de jure 的含义后，翻译 de facto corporation, de jure corporation 也就简单很多。de facto corporation 意为"实际存在的公司，未注册的公司，地下工厂"，指未领取政府颁发的合法执照便开始营业或开工生产的公司或工厂。de jure corporation 则是指依法设立的公司。类似的是，de facto relationship 可译为"事实婚姻"，即未依法登记结婚的同居关系；de jure relationship 可译为"合法婚姻"。

二、法语

外来语中，除拉丁语外，法语对英语的影响也颇深。1066 年法国诺曼人征服英国后，法国人登上了英国王位。在英国宫廷中，法语地位很高；在宫廷外，许多人也把会说法语视为身份和地位高的象征。这一现象持续了 300 年之久，很多法语词汇大量进入英语，因此法律英语中也少不了法语。法律文本中的法语词义比较纯粹，使用频率高，但与普通英语的意思有所区别，容易引起混淆，见表 2-3。

表 2-3　法律文本中常见的法语词汇

法语词汇	汉译	法语词汇	汉译
action	诉讼	justice	正义
arson	纵火罪	legacy	遗产
assault	侵犯人身罪	pardon	赦免
alienate	让与	plaintiff	原告
accuse	起诉	plead	申辩
bail	保释	ransom	赎金
battery	殴打罪	sue	起诉
constable	警员	verdict	裁决
demurrer	抗辩	summons	传票
estoppel	禁止反言	specialty	盖印文据
esquire	……先生	saisie	查封，扣押
decree	法令	quash	撤销（判决）
bailiff	法警	save	除外
coroner	验尸官	lien	留置权
heir	继承人	voir dire	预先审查
heritage	遗产	writ de mesne	中间令状
jail	监狱	judgment roll	判决案卷
defendant	被告	fee simple and fee tail	无条件继承及限定继承的不动产

三、古英语和中世纪英语

除外来语外，法律英语中还保留了不少古英语和中世纪英语的词汇。古旧词汇在现代英语中已经很少出现，但在法律性文件中却依然常见。尽管英美国家要求法律语言简明化，提倡法律人士在撰写法律文件时尽量不用这些词语，但是为使法律文本的句子简练、严谨，更好地反映其正规、严肃、权威等特征，适当使用古英语和中世纪英语词汇确有必要。

如果要将英语法律文本翻译为汉语，了解古英语显然是有帮助的。古英语是指一直使用到公元 1150 年的英语，而中世纪英语是指公元 1150 年到公元 1500 年间使用的英语。例如：

④ Claims, if any, are payable on surrender of this Policy together with other relevant documents. In the event of accident <u>whereby</u> loss or damage may result in a claim under this Policy, immediate notice applying for survey must be given to the company's Agent as mentioned <u>hereunder</u>.

所投保货物如果出险，本公司凭保单与其他相关证明材料进行理赔。所投保的货物，如发生本保单所列出负责赔偿的损失或事故，应立即通知本公司下列打理人查勘。(陈秋劲，2013)

这份保险合同的条款中就有法律英语中常见的 whereby, hereunder 等古英语词汇，其在普通英语中比较少见。又如：

⑤ An Internet service contract is a contract <u>whereby</u> the Internet service supplier supplies Internet service to the customer, and the consumer pays an Internet service fee.

网络服务合同是网络服务提供商向网络使用者提供网络服务，使用者支付网络服务费的合同。

这样的词汇表达在法律文本中的意义和用法千百年来未发生过变化，得到很好的继承，其中比较有代表性的有 here, there, where 引导的词汇。其实只要把握好基本规则，理解这些词并不难。其规则为：here 代表 this；there 代表 that；where 代表 which / what；here / there / where + what + 介词 = 介词 + this / that / which / what。如：hereby = as a result of / by this means；thereafter = after that time。

下面我们对 here, there 引导的系列词汇分别进行举例分析。

（1）hereby 特此，由此，兹

⑥ The Buyer <u>hereby</u> orders from the Seller the undermentioned goods subject to the following conditions: …

买方向卖方订购下列商品，条件如下：……

（2）herein 此中，于此

⑦ The minimum royalty <u>herein</u> specified shall be paid by Party B to Party A.

在此规定的最低特许权使用费应由乙方付给甲方。

（3）hereof 在本文件中；hereunder 本文件规定

⑧ Both parties agree to attempt to resolve all disputes between the parties with respect to the application or interpretation of any term hereof of transaction hereunder, through amicable negotiation.

就本合同规定交易任一条款的适用和解释所产生的所有争议，合同双方同意力求通过友好协商予以解决。

（4）hereto 本文件的；thereof 它的；thereto 随之，附之

⑨ Licensed Products means the devices and products described in Schedule 1 annexed hereto together with all improvement and modification thereof or development with respect thereto.

特许产品系指在本协议附件1中所述装置和产品，以及其全部改进和修改的产品和与之相关的产品。

（5）herewith 与此，附此；thereby 因此，由此

⑩ If any one or more of the provisions contained in this Contract or any document executed in connection herewith shall be invalid of unenforceable in any respect under any applicable law, the validity and enforceability of the remaining provisions contained herein shall not in any way be affected thereby.

如果根据现行法律，本合同及与此有关的已经履行的文件中有一项或多项条款被视为无效或不能履行，本合同其余条款的效力和履行将不因此受影响。

（6）thereafter 此后

⑪ The Contract for the contractual joint venture shall continue from a period of two years thereafter.

本合作经营企业合同，此后应持续有效两年。

（7）therein 在那方面

⑫ The Leased Premises are deemed to be fit for occupation when the building therein is substantially completed.

当在那里的建筑物实质完成时，该租赁房屋才被认为适合被占有居住。

（8）therewith 以此，此外

⑬ The Employer shall indemnify and save harmless the Contractor against and from all claims, proceedings, damages, costs, charges and expenses whatsoever arising there out or in connection therewith.

业主应赔偿所有索赔、诉讼、损害赔偿、支出、收费、费用，不论因本合同产

生或与其相关，并保证承包人免于承担上述责任。

对古旧英语词汇有基本了解后，再看一例：

⑭ Whether the custom of the Port is contrary to this Clause or not, the owner of the goods shall, without interruption, by day and night, including Sundays and holidays (if required by the carrier), supply and take delivery of the goods. The owner of the goods shall be liable for all losses or damages including demurrage incurred in default on the provisions hereof.

不论港口的通常做法是否与本款规定相反，货方都应不分昼夜无间断地装货和取货，包括星期日和假日（如承运人需要）。货方对违反本款规定所引起的所有损失或损坏，包括滞期，应负担赔偿责任。

此例中，Whether the custom of the Port is contrary to this Clause or not 的意思是"不论港口通常的做法是否与本款规定相反"；the owner of the goods 的意思是"货方"；without interruption 的意思是"无间断地"；carrier 的意思是"承运人"。句中的 hereof 是修饰 the provisions 的。

第二节 法律术语和特定句型

术语是在特定学科领域表示概念的集合，是通过语音或文字来表达或限定科学概念的约定性语言符号，是思想交流的工具。正如从事科技翻译的译者需要熟练掌握科技术语，从事法律翻译的译者也需要掌握法律术语。法律术语都有明确的法律含义，能够精确地表达复杂的法律概念和关系，难以被其他词语代替。因此，理解和正确翻译专业词汇是进行法律翻译的前提和基础。

试看下例：

⑮ A person in charge of another who is a minor or subject to mental disability is liable for damage caused by the other unless the person in charge shows that he has conformed to the required standard of conduct in supervision.

监护人对其监护的未成年人和精神病人所造成的损失承担赔偿责任，除非该监护人能够证明其已经遵守监护责任的必要行为要求。

该句规定了监护人的责任，unless 引导的从句阐明免责具体要求。监护人的身份是通过修饰成分体现出来的，即 in charge of another who is a minor or subject to mental disability，其中的 minor 就属于法律术语。minor 在普通英语中多做形容词，表示"较小的，次要的"，而在此例中专指"未成年人"。

为使法律翻译学习者减少理解错误，表 2-4 列出了一些常见法律术语。

表 2-4 英语法律文本的常见术语

法律术语	汉译	法律术语	汉译
agency	代理权	force majeure	不可抗力
appeal	上诉	guarantee	担保，保证书
adjudge	裁定	grand larceny	重大盗窃案
adjudicate	判决	general jurisdiction	普遍管辖权
at issue	争论点	letters patent	专利特许证
alleged	被指控的	libel	（书面）诽谤
approach the bench	走近法官席	majority	成年的法定年龄
bail exonerated	免除保释金的	moot court	模拟法庭
cause of action	诉讼原因	no contact order	禁止接触令
common crime	普通罪	negotiable instrument	可转让文据
defendant	被告	pierce the corporate veil	揭开公司面纱
damages	赔偿金	pursuant to stipulation	根据规定
decree	判决	reverse	撤销，宣布无效
felony	重罪	review	再审
find	判决，裁定	revocation of will	撤销遗嘱
filing fees	诉讼费		

法律文本中除了上述术语会影响理解外，还有大量看起来重复的两联词（doubles 或 legal pairs）和三联词（triplets），如 null and void 就是两联词。合同、契约、交易等如果没有法律效力或者不具有当事人所期待产生的法律效力，就是无效。null 和 void 的意思都是"无效的，无法律约束力的"，在法律文本中常出现。例如：

⑯ This certificate shall be considered null and void in case of any alteration.
如有任何涂改，本证书作废。

租赁合同常常会使用 well and sufficiently repair, uphold, maintain the premises 这一说法，其中就有一组两联词 well and sufficiently，表示"充分地"，以及一组三联词 repair, uphold, maintain，表示"修缮，维护"。

两联词和三联词的出现，有人认为与文化传统有关，语言是文化的载体，必然会对文化有所反映，而英国是一个比较保守的国家。法律本身也具有保守性，新词汇不断出现时，会被直接添加到原来的术语里面，特别是英语和法语词汇的连接，由此形成了在法律英语中非常显著的词语重复现象。

两个同义词组合在一起，构成同义词组合。这样既照顾到了各方当事人的权益，也避免了出现歧义，同时还考虑到了法律文书传递信息的完整性和准确性。这种同义词组合的特殊表达形式得到同行的认可，在法律界被广泛使用。之后出现的短语既有"英—法"组合，如 fit and proper（恰当的）、rack and ruin（毁坏）；也有"法—拉"组合，如 peace and quiet（宁静的）；还有"英—拉"组合，如 will and testament（遗嘱）；当然也会有"英—英"组合，如 each and every（每一个）。在翻译时，我们原则上都可以将这些词化繁为简，即合二为一或化三为一。

下面列举出一些类似词语，供法律翻译学习者参考，见表2-5。

表2-5 法律文本中常见的同义词组合

同义词组合	汉译	同义词组合	汉译
acknowledge and confess	承认	full, true and correct	正确的
aid and abet	教唆	goods and chattels	财产
aid and comfort	支援	provisions and stipulations	条款
alter and change	更改	terms and conditions	条款
authorize and empower	授权	keep and maintain	维持
break and enter	闯入	new and novel	新的
cancel, annul and set aside	取消	save and except	除了
cease and desist	终止	request and require	请求
deem and consider	认为	sole and exclusive	唯一的
each and all	所有的	seriously and gravely	严重地
fair and equitable	公平合理的	rest, residue and remainder	剩余
fixture and fitting	附属物	convey, transfer and set over	移交
final and conclusive	最终的	give, devise and bequeath	遗赠
force and effect	有效	name, constitute and appoint	委任
fulfill and perform	履行	right, title and interest	权益
fraud and deceit	欺诈	order, adjudge and decre	做出判决
free and clear	无产权负担的	good and valuable consideration	有效对价
full and complete	全部的		

除了专业术语外，法律文本中的句法结构跟普通文本相比也稍有不同，概括起来有以下几种情形：

一是结合使用简单句和复杂长句，如"No person shall be a Senator or Representative in Congress, or elector of President and Vice-President, or hold any office, civil or military, under the United States, or under any State, who, having previously taken an oath, as a member of Congress, or as an officer of the United States, or as a member of any State legislature, or as an executive or judicial officer of any State, to support the Constituition of the

United States, shall have engaged in insurrection or rebellion against the same, or given aid or comfort to the enemies thereof."。

二是规范使用判断结构"的"字句。汉语法律文本中"的"结构通常表示假定条件，具有很强的概括性，是一个具有代表性的概念，如刑法中有关强奸罪的规定"以暴力、胁迫或者其他手段强奸妇女的，处三年以上十年以下有期徒刑"。法律英语中多用 if，where，when 等引导的句子或短语来表示，位置不固定。

三是使用复合句，包括并列复合句、递进复合句、选择复合句、目的复合句、假设复合句、条件复合句、转折复合句、解释复合句等。使用复合句可以较准确地表达较复杂的逻辑关系。

四是广泛使用被动句。与科技文本较为相似，法律文本也大量使用被动结构，主要用于规定行为人的权利义务和所要承担的法律后果，强调动作的承受者，体现法律文本的正式、庄严、客观、公正等特点，如"Representatives and direct taxes shall be appropriated among the several states which may be included within this union."。

第三节　程式化的法律篇章结构

法律语言的特点不仅表现在词汇、短语和句子结构的选择与组成上，也表现在篇章结构中。书面语和庭审语言都有极强的程式化倾向。程式化意味着规范化，是法律共同体里的从业者在长期的实践中，为了提高工作效率和规范相同行为而逐渐积累并得到共同体成员认可的格式。每个书面篇章或者口头篇章都是一个逻辑严密的整体，而不是简单的事实或法条的堆砌，能为法律法规的理解提供较为固定的语境，减少公众对法律法规的误解。

书面篇章的程式化更为显著，如法院、检察院和警察局使用的各种规范性的表格。图 2-1 是美国得克萨斯州离婚申请书的申请人信息部分，包含申请者的姓名、驾照信息及被申请人的信息。申请者只需要按要求填写或标注即可完成。

Original Petition for Divorce

My name is: ____.
First　　　　*Middle*　　　　*Last*

I am the **Petitioner**, the person asking for a divorce.

The last three numbers of my driver's license number are: ___ ___ ___. My driver's license was issued in *(State)* ______________.

or ☐ I do not have a driver's license number.

The last three numbers of my social security number are: ___ ___ ___.

or ☐ I do not have a social security number.

My spouse's name is: ____.
First　　　　*Middle*　　　　*Last*

My spouse is the **Respondent**.

图 2-1　离婚申请书填写信息一

图 2-2 要求申请者提供更多的具体信息，如配偶是否居住在得克萨斯州，如果不居住在得克萨斯州，需要进一步明确是否接受将得克萨斯州法院作为处理双方离婚诉讼的法院，之后继续填写结婚和分居的年、月、日等信息。

3C. Personal Jurisdiction over Spouse

(Check one box.)

☐ My spouse lives in Texas.

☐ My spouse does not live in Texas.

(If your spouse does not live in Texas, check any boxes that apply below.)

☐ My spouse agrees that a Texas court can make orders in this divorce, including orders dividing our property and debts. My spouse will file a *Waiver of Service* (or *Answer*).

☐ Texas is the last state where we lived together as a married couple. This *Petition for Divorce* is filed less than two years after we separated.

4. Dates of Marriage and Separation

My spouse and I got married on or about: ______________________________.
Month　　Day　　Year

We stopped living together as spouses on or about: ______________________________.
Month　　Day　　Year

图 2-2　离婚申请书填写信息二

图 2-3 所示的美国密西西比州的法院传票同样是高度程式化的，提供共性的标准表达，将个性化的信息留空，可以被重复使用，这种做法既能减少因为疏忽而出现遗漏或错误的风险，还能增加文本的正式性和严肃性。对译者而言，程式化表达也极大地减轻了他们的翻译任务和在处理文本时的认知负荷。

SUMMONS

STATE OF MISSISSIPPI

TO: ______________________________
____
____

<u>NOTICE TO RESPONDENT</u>

<u>THE PETITION WHICH IS ATTACHED TO THIS SUMMONS IS IMPORTANT AND YOU MUST TAKE IMMEDIATE ACTION TO PROTECT YOUR RIGHTS</u>.

You are summoned to appear and defend against said petition at ________ o'clock _____ .M. on the _______ day of ________________ , 20 ________, in the courtroom of the ______________________________ Court located at ______________________________, Mississippi, and in case of your failure to appear and defend, a judgment will be entered against you for the money or other things demanded in the complaint or petition.

You are not required to file an answer or other pleading but you may do so if you desire.

Issued under my hand and the seal of said Court, this the __________ day of ______________, 20 _________.

____
Clerk

图 2-3　美国密西西比州的法院传票

不仅各种书面文本中都会出现程式化的篇章，庭审过程也是高度程式化的。古今中外，庭审活动从开始到结束都会遵守严格的程序，一般可以细分为开庭准备和开庭宣布、法庭调查、法庭辩论、最后陈述。

开庭准备和开庭宣布主要是由书记员宣布庭审过程中的注意事项，查明当事人和诉讼代理人是否到场，告知当事人依法能够享有的权利，宣告合议庭的组成人员、书记员、当事人、诉讼代理人、鉴定人和翻译人员的名单，告知当事人有权申请回避，告知被告人享有辩护的权利。不同的案件有着相同的庭前准备和宣布流程，译员若多做针对性的练习，在庭审翻译时自然可以得心应手。

法庭调查是庭审的中心环节，具体包括核实证据，查清犯罪行为是否是被告人所为，被告人是否承认所指控的罪行，有无法定从轻、减轻处罚情节等。该阶段比较特殊，既有书面文本（起诉书、证人证词、司法鉴定书等），又有大量法律口头表达，法律术语较多，译员需要进行准确把握。

法庭辩论是庭审的重要阶段，是在审判员的主持下，诉讼当事人根据已经查明的事实和证据，陈述各自对诉讼争议和事实的看法及其理由和依据，以辨明是非和相关责任。该阶段的表达趋向于正式，长句和复合句较多，语言凝练、条理性、逻辑性强。这对译员的挑战很大，其应提前熟悉案情和相关的诉讼文书，此外译员可能还需要处理各种新增信息。

在最后陈述阶段，被告人针对案件事实、庭审过程、诉求等向法庭提出自己的意见、主张、申辩等。在美国，如果被告人本身没有法律专业知识，最后陈述通常会由诉讼代理人来完成。该阶段的翻译基本是重述前面提到过的主要观点，对于译员而言压力相对较小。

当然庭审活动还应该包含评议和宣判，但很多时候案件不会当庭宣判，特别是案件较为复杂时，合议庭需要时间认定案件事实、划分是非责任、准确适用法律和进行处理。宣判是对案件的审理做出公开的判决。就语言特征而言，该阶段的书面化程度较高。

庭审译员需要根据不同程式化阶段的特定特征，提前预判，做好相应准备，选择合适的表达来进行翻译。

第四节　法律语言的准确性和模糊性

一、法律语言的准确性

关于法律语言的准确性，有这样一个例子：

法官对被告人说"You have been charged with two other offences."。有个律师觉得可以表达为"There are also two charges against you."。两句话能否对等取决于 other 和 also 是否对等。other 和 also 都有"额外"的意思，但 other 是有预设的，即后面提到的事情

或人必须和前面已经提及的事情或人是一个属性；而 also 侧重于除了前面提过的事情外，还有别的事情或人。据此分析，法官的意思是被告人至少被指控三项罪名，而律师的意思是被指控两项罪名，理解出现了偏差。

严复提出的"信、达、雅"翻译三原则中的"信"要求译者要忠实于原文。其实质就是翻译要准确，最大限度地减少因为翻译而造成的信息缺失或失真。与普通文本翻译相比，法律文本翻译更强调准确性，因为法律文本是由受多年职业训练的法官、检察官、律师和法学家按照标准格式撰写的，其叙述表达、说理明法、确定责任义务等都是严谨缜密的。法律文本中每一句话、每一个词、每一个标点符号都要经过反复斟酌，一个字或标点符号的差异都可能会导致财产损失、政府或企业信誉扫地、公民的人身自由或生命权被剥夺。

法律条文如果被翻译得模棱两可、含糊其词，则会变成一个个隐形陷阱。法律翻译首先要与相关法律知识匹配，要准确和精确，而不是多样化表达。

先看一例：

⑰ ... if an order is made of an effective resolution is passed for the winding up of a Party, or a Party becomes bankrupt, insolvent, is unable to pay its debt as they fall due, stops, suspends or threatens to stop or suspend payment of all or material part of all its debts, or proposes or makes a general assignment or an arrangement or composition with or for the benefit of its creditors ...

……如存在就一方破产下达的命令或通过的有效协议，或一方破产、资不抵债、无力偿还到期债务，停止、暂停，或可能停止、暂停全部或大部分债务，与债权人或为债权人利益提出或进行整体转让、安排或和解……

该条款的逻辑性强，译员在翻译时需要在通读全段理清其中的逻辑关系后，再按照层次翻译，特别应注意英文里用到的动词和主语之间的逻辑关系。英文中的并列关系可以用逗号代替，而中文常用顿号来界定内部之间的逻辑层次，因此准确界定全段的逻辑关系后，能否恰当使用顿号、逗号和句号直接决定着该段文字翻译的准确程度。如上例中对英文中"becomes bankrupt, insolvent, is unable to pay its debt"所表达的三种情形的理解。

再看一例：

⑱ The death penalty may be imposed only for offenses of treason, piracy or setting fire to any of Her Majesty's warships or dockyards. It may not in any event be passed on a person under 18 years of age, nor on an expectant mother.

死刑仅适用于叛国罪、海盗罪或者纵火烧毁女王陛下之任何战舰或修造厂三种犯罪。在任何情况下，均不得对未满十八岁者或者孕妇适用死刑。

在此条文中，译者用三个具体罪名来确定死刑适用范围，同时又用 under 18 years of age 和 expectant mother 这两个内涵和外延都很清晰的短语对两种情况予以排除，将死刑适用范围界定得更加精确。

如果说上述例子对准确性的论证仅仅停留在理论层面，那么石家庄中级人民法院的一份有关仲裁条款有效性的裁定，则明确彰显了准确性的实际价值。

某地方法院对一份仲裁条款效力无效的裁定，使得8年纷争最终画上句号。这案件最终做出无效裁定，与中文译稿的表达密切相关。

仲裁条款关键部分原文及法院认定的译文如下：

⑲ In case of breach of any the Articles of this agreement by either of the parties, both Parties agree to put best efforts to remedy by negotiation. Otherwise, both Parties agree to arbitration as per the International Chamber of Commerce and held in CHINA.

如任何一方违反本协议的任何条款，双方同意尽最大努力通过协商予以救济。否则，双方同意按照国际商会的规则在中国进行仲裁。

按照《元照英美法词典》中的解释，as per 的意思为"按照，根据"。International Chamber of Commerce 是指总部位于法国巴黎的国际商会。在国际仲裁领域内，国际商会仲裁院是国际商会附设的唯一仲裁机构，其职责是根据国际商会仲裁规则以仲裁方式解决国际性的商业纠纷。中国国际经济贸易仲裁委员会牵头组织外语和法律专家编写的《"一带一路"沿线国家国际仲裁制度研究（一）》，将 International Chamber of Commerce 翻译为"国际商会"。翻译公司的译文增加了"的规则"就直接改变了该仲裁条款的法律效力。《中华人民共和国仲裁法（2017修正）》（以下简称《仲裁法》）第十六条和第十八条规定，仲裁条款应该选定仲裁机构，没有约定或者约定不明的，可以补充协议，达不成补充协议的，仲裁协议无效。依照译文，涉案的仲裁条款只是约定仲裁适用规则，并未约定明确的仲裁机构，直接使得该仲裁协议归于无效。该仲裁条款的翻译在翻译界存在争论，而争论的焦点恰恰就是增译法补进去的"的规则"。由此可见，译文的准确性关系重大，甚至关系着案件的胜诉与否。

此外，法庭口译特别是刑事案件的庭审口译重则关乎生命权的剥夺与否，对于译员的翻译准确性要求更高。曾有译员对庭审的准确性压力做过简单排序：排在第一位的是重罪案件庭审，译员为没有律师而自行辩护的被告人翻译。排在第二位的是重罪案件庭审，译员为被告人翻译。被告人常因紧张或其他因素而答非所问、语言上下不连贯、逻辑混乱、言辞闪烁等，准确传达更难。排在第三位的是重罪案件庭审，译员为证人翻译，如果误译可能影响庭审结果。排在第四位的是重罪罪名成立后法官在法庭宣读判决书，译员为被告人进行耳语同传。法官宣读判决书时语速快，但译员不能马虎，因为法官会留意译员有没有在翻译，而被告人急于想知道被判多重的刑罚。排在第五位的是重罪案件庭审，译员为被告人进行耳语同传。在这种情形下，错译或漏译不会影响庭审的结果，但会影响被告人的理解。排在最后的是重罪罪名成立后的量刑听证会。重罪案件保释申请听证会或上诉，以及重罪案件的提审、初审、传讯等场合中的译员的翻译精确性压力相对较小。

以上排名如将重罪案件换成轻罪案件,精确性压力与责任相对减轻。一般来说,重罪由法官和陪审团审理,轻罪只由法官一人审理。

二、法律语言的模糊性

虽然与其他很多行业比较起来,法律共同体内的从业者更讲究用词精确,但不代表法律语言没有模糊性的一面。语言本身就具有模糊性,法律语言也存在一个认知和信息解码的问题,其模糊性同样存在。模糊词语是指内涵不够精确、外延无明确界限的词语,即所指的对象范围没有一个准确的界限。在自然语言中,精确词语和模糊词语的界限是相对的。但是模糊不同于含糊不清,两者存在本质区别。含糊不清常指因语言运用不当而产生的消极结果,是尽量要避免的现象。

法律语言用有限的手段来描摹无限的现实。模糊语大多用于表述事物概念或行为的程度、性质、范围、结果等,能让人们在理解和把握时有一定的自由度,实际上模糊也是为了准确地概括、最大限度地打击犯罪和不法行为,如《中华人民共和国刑法》(以下简称《刑法》)第二十条规定:正当防卫明显超过必要限度造成重大损害的,应当负刑事责任,但是应当减轻或者免除处罚。法条对正当防卫进行了定义,其中"必要限度"中的"必要"带有很强的模糊性。对于何种限度才是必要的限度,刑法理论界一般认为:必要限度应以制止不法侵害、保护合法权益的合理需求为标准。具体到个案,要结合当时案发情况来全面分析各种因素才能确定是否在必要限度内。

法律英语中也有不少模糊表达,如 adequate(适当的)、excessive(过度的)、incidental(偶发的)、due(合理的)、more than(多于)等。因此,在翻译相关法律文本时,译者可以使用一些模糊词汇。模糊语可按照所指涉对象的范围大致分为三类(李克兴,2007),一方面表示绝对概念的词汇和短语,使受限制的事物受到更为明确的限制;另一方面为了扩大范围,使所指范围更为全面。

第一类模糊语包括 all, impossible, last clear chance, never, none, outright, perpetuity, unavoidable, unbroken, uniform, wherever, irrevocable, whoever 等。

第二类模糊语包括 and no more and no other purpose, shall not constitute a waiver, shall not be deemed as a consent 等。

第三类模糊语包括 including but not limit to …, or other similar or dissimilar causes …, shall not be deemed to limit …, without prejudice, nothing contained herein shall 等。

翻译法律文本时遇到模糊表达,译者可以根据语境大胆选择相对应的模糊表达来处理相关语句。译者只有忠实于原文的义务,没有进一步解释模糊意思的权利。例如:

⑳ The buyer is also deemed to have accepted the goods when after the lapse of a <u>reasonable</u> time he retains the goods without intimating to the seller that he has rejected them.

在一段<u>合理</u>期限后,买方保留了货物且并未向卖方主张其已经拒收货物,则同样推定买方已经接受货物。

a reasonable time 可以直接译为"合理的时间",至于这里的合理时间在司法实践中如何界定则属于另外一个领域的问题,需要结合地方情况、行业惯例等因素综合考虑和确定。

为了更好地表达立法者的意志,最大限度地打击犯罪,给法官以适当的自由裁量权,《刑法》有不少这样的模糊表达,如第一百一十五条:

㉑ 放火、决水、爆炸以及投放毒害性、放射性、传染疾病原等物质或者以其他危险方式致使人重伤、死亡或者使公共或私人财产遭受重大损失的,处十年以上有期徒刑、无期徒刑或者死刑。过失犯前款罪的,处三年以上七年以下有期徒刑;情节较轻的,处三年以下有期徒刑或者拘役。

Whoever set fires, breaches dikes, causes explosions, and spreads pathogens of infectious diseases, poisonous or radioactive substances or other substances; employs other dangerous means that lead to serious injuries or death; or causes public or private property major losses is to be sentenced to not less than ten years of fixed term imprisonment, life imprisonment, or death. Whoever commits the crimes in the preceding paragraph negligently is to be sentenced to not less than three years and not more than seven years of fixed-term imprisonment; or not more than three years of fixed-term imprisonment, or criminal detention, when circumstances are relatively minor.

英文中的 not less than ten years, not less than three years, not more than seven years 和 not more than three years 都是对中文模糊表达的精确反映。这以法条形式给出量刑的范围,将使用该法条的权利完全下放给司法人员,司法人员可根据实际情况施行自由裁量权,从而使法律更加公正。

翻译练习

练习 1

Save as described hereunder, the Sponsor does not have any duty to monitor or otherwise to ensure that the Company is in continuous compliance with the GEM Listing Rules and other relevant laws and regulations applicable to the Company.

练习 2

The distance specified in this section shall be measured in the same manner as provided in subdivision (c) of Section 11362.768 of the Health and Safety Code, unless otherwise provided by law.

练习 3

The investors do hereby form a joint venture pursuant to the laws of the State of New York in order for the Venture to carry on the purposes for which provisions are made herein.

练习 4

在解决争议期间，除争议事项外，合营各方应当继续履行合营企业协议、合同、章程所规定的其他各项条款。

练习 5

公司股东应当遵守法律、行政法规和公司章程，依法行使股东权利，不得滥用股东权利损害公司或者其他股东的利益；不得滥用公司法人独立地位和股东有限责任损害公司债权人的利益。

练习 6

除非本协议另有规定，合资方无权撤回全部或部分出资，也无权要求或收取全部或部分出资。

第三章
法律职业和法院结构

　　法律职业是指由律师、法官、检察官和公证员为代表的，受过专门的法律专业训练，具有娴熟法律技能与较强法律伦理意识的法律事务岗位从业人员所构成的共同体，他们具有一致的法律知识背景、职业训练方法、思维习惯及职业利益。狭义的法律职业主要是指法官、检察官、监察官、律师、公证员、基层法律服务工作者。广义的法律职业除包含上述职业外，还包括企事业单位中从事法律事务的职业岗位，如法务专员、法务主管、法务部门的其他岗位人员。本章的法律职业主要介绍国内和主要英语国家的法官、检察官和律师，丰富法律翻译者的背景知识。

　　法院是世界各国普遍设立的国家机关，主要通过审判活动解决社会矛盾和纠纷，惩治犯罪分子，维护公平正义。法院体系是各个国家的法院组织结构，不同国家的法院组织结构稍有区别。本章初步梳理了中国和主要英语国家的法院结构，帮助法律翻译者构建知识体系。

第一节　法律职业

一、法官

　　法官（judge, justice）是指依照法律规定的程序产生，在法院中依法行使国家审判权的审判人员，是司法权的执行者。在不同法系的国家中法官的角色不尽相同，但要求都是能不偏不倚、不受他人影响、刚正无私地根据法律判案。

1. 中国的法官

　　在中国，《中华人民共和国法官法》第二条规定：法官是依法行使国家审判权的审判人员，包括最高人民法院、地方各级人民法院和军事法院等专门人民法院的院长（president of people's court）、副院长（vice president of people's court）、审判委员会委员（members of judicial committee）、庭长（chief）、副庭长（associate chief）和审判员（judge）。

　　担任中华人民共和国法官，需要接受过与法律相关的高等教育，通过国家统一法律职业资格考试，并从事过一定时间的法律工作。目前中国法官等级分为十二级，依次为首席大法官、一级大法官、二级大法官、一级高级法官、二级高级法官、三级高级法官、四级高级法官、一级法官、二级法官、三级法官、四级法官、五级法官。最高人民法院院长为首席大法官，省高级人民法院院长为二级大法官。

2. 主要英语国家的法官

在英国，几乎所有的法官都是从各私人律师事务所的律师中选拔出来的。英国法官等级森严，由低级到高级共有七类：治安法官（magistrate / justice of peace）；支薪治安法官（stipendiary magistrate）；记录法官，即由律师兼任的法官；巡回法官；高等法院法官；上诉法官；常设上诉议员，是由上议院议员兼任的法官。英国四名最高级的司法官员分别是大法官、高等法院首席法官、档案长和家事庭长。按照 1990 年的相关法律规定，大法官要求有 10 年担任高等法院法官或辩护人的经历，高等法院法官必须有 10 年高等法院的工作经验或至少 2 年巡回法院法官的经历并且年龄在 50 岁以上，巡回法院的法官则要在巡回法院或郡法院有 10 年书记员的经历或至少有 3 年以上司法部门的专职任职期。高级法官绝大多数都是从上诉法院法官中选拔，大法官是从高等法院法官中选拔，高等法院法官则是从那些被公认为律师界带头人的高级律师中选拔。

美国联邦和州的法官产生的程序不同，因而任职资格也不尽相同。原则上，担任联邦法院的法官必须取得法律硕士学位，通过严格的考试取得律师资格，且从事律师工作 10 年以上。担任州法院的法官，特别是最高法院、上诉法院和具有普通管辖权的初审法院，一般也应具备上述条件。

联邦法官由总统提名、参议院批准、总统任命。当法官职位出现空缺时，总统提名候选人，经参议院投票表决后以简单多数通过即可任命。各州的法官选任规定不一，美国州法院法官的遴选制度有普选、州长任命、议会选举等不同程序。比如，加利福尼亚州规定，由州长向司法委员会提名法官候选人，由司法委员会任命；大选时，法官必须面对选民，如能被选上，他的任期是法定的 12 年或 12 年任期中所剩余的任期。密苏里州规定，当法院出现空缺时，由律师界选出的三名律师、州长提名的三位公民和州最高法院首席法官（任委员会主席）组成的特别提名委员会，在对有可能担任法官的人选的经历和声望进行认真调查后，向州长提交名单，由州长从中任命一人。获得任命者必须参与下一届的留任选举。

二、检察官

检察官（procurator）是对检察人员的通称。

1. 中国的检察官

在中国，检察官是依法行使国家检察权的检察人员，包括最高人民检察院、地方各级检察院、军事检察院等专门人民检察院的检察长（chief procurator）、副检察长（deputy chief procurator）、检察委员会委员（member of procuratorial committee）和检察员（procurator）。检察官必须忠实执行宪法和法律，全心全意为人民服务。检察官依法履行职责，受法律保护。

在中国担任检察官的资格与担任法官的资格较为接近，都要求接受过法律专业的高等教育，通过国家法律职业考试，并从事一定时间的法律工作。目前检察官等级分为十二级，依次为首席大检察官、一级大检察官、二级大检察官、一级高级检察官、二级高级检察官、三级高级检察官、四级高级检察官、一级检察官、二级检察官、三级检察官、四级检察官、五级检察官。

2. 主要英语国家的检察官

在英国，英格兰、苏格兰、威尔士和北爱尔兰四个区域的检察官制度并不完全相同。比如，在英格兰和威尔士，检察官须具有事务律师或出庭律师资格，即完成法律实务课程而具备事务律师资格，或通过律师专业培训课程而具备出庭律师资格。如果没有法学学位，还要接受额外的课程训练和通过考试才能取得资格。在苏格兰和北爱尔兰，取得检察官资格都需要通过考试。苏格兰皇家办公室和检察署对从其内部工作人员中招录检察官有特殊要求：第一，申请检察官职位的内部职员必须成功通过实习期，且在其现有职位上工作满2年；第二，该职员不得身负仍有效的纪律警告处分。而北爱尔兰则对担任总检察长之人有特殊要求：必须成为北爱尔兰律师协会会员满10年，或在北爱尔兰最高法院担任事务律师满10年。（郑曦，2019）

美国执行的是从地方律师中挑选检察官的制度，注重检察官的经验，即只在执业成功的律师中选任检察官。美国各州普遍要求检察官必须具备法学学位和丰富的司法实践经验，并且是一名律师或精通法律的人。实际上，某个人只有在所在州取得了执行律师执照并且参加了任何一个州的律师协会，才被认为具备了担任检察官的条件。某些州还规定担任检察官必须具备数年的法律实践经验。

美国州首席检察官和州长一样是直接民选的（选举制），所以不对包括州长在内的任何人负责；而联邦检察官的任命由总统提名，经参议院通过（任命制）。美国检察官作为政府律师在刑事案件中负责侦查、决定是否起诉、传唤证人、进行诉辩交易、根据有罪判决建议刑罚等工作，代表公众利益、国家利益。联邦总检察长是美国司法部长，州首席检察官为州司法部长。

三、律师

律师（lawyer/attorney）是指通过法律职业资格考试并依法取得律师执业证书，接受委托或者指定，为当事人提供法律服务的执业人员。按照工作性质，律师可分为专职律师（professional lawyer）和兼职律师（part-time lawyer）；按照业务范围，律师可分为民事律师、刑事律师和行政律师；按照服务对象和工作身份，律师可分为社会律师、公司律师、公职律师等。律师业务主要分为诉讼业务与非诉讼业务。

现代律师制度至少可以追溯至古罗马时期甚至古希腊时期。古罗马人发展出的复杂的成文法典及诉讼制度，包括辩护律师制度，都为近代西方法体系所继承。由于城邦社会重视法治及程序保障，古罗马时期的律师享有相当崇高的地位，常代表当事人与政府进行诉讼，并且接受与希腊地区一脉相承的修辞学及雄辩术训练。许多元老院议员都做过律师，其中最著名者当推古罗马著名政治家西塞罗（Cicero）。

律师也起源于古罗马。共和制罗马时期的诉讼必须根据执政官或法务官的告示，按法定的程序进行。由于法律和告示不断增多，日趋复杂，当事人在诉讼中特别是在法庭进行辩论时，需要熟悉法律的人协助，因此共和制末期至帝国制初期，辩护人应运而生。至公元5世纪末，辩护人须在主要城市学过法律并取得资格。他们逐渐形成行业，组成职业团体，成为专职律师。

1. 中国的律师

在中国，按照《中华人民共和国律师法》的要求，拥护中国宪法，通过国家统一法律职业资格考试（2018年以前称为"国家司法考试"），在律师事务所实习满一年后，品行良好的人可以申请律师执业。律师可以解答有关法律的询问，代写法律文书，担任法律顾问，担任代理人，参加调解、仲裁和诉讼等活动，提供非诉讼法律服务等。

2. 主要英语国家的律师

英国律师分为事务律师（solicitor）和出庭律师（barrister）两种。事务律师可以直接接受当事人委托，主要从事各类非诉讼业务；出庭律师相当于诉讼律师。两者只是分工不同。在英国取得律师资格需要经历三个阶段：接受法律学术教育、接受法律实务教育及在律师事务所实习。其中两类律师在第一阶段要满足的要求相同，在后两个阶段则因为职业发展方向不同而有所区别。

两者都要求申请人在英国获得法学本科学位（LL. B）。如果本科读的是其他学科，申请人需要取得法律研究生证书（Postgraduate Diploma in Law，简称PgDL）或通过共同职业考试（Common Professional Examination，简称CPE）。第二阶段需要完成LPC（Legal Practice Certificate）课程，以实务为导向的事务律师学习商法、民法、刑事程序法、文书写作、律师职业道德等方面的知识；出庭律师对应的课程是BVC（Bar Vocational Course），主要学习辩论技巧、法律研究能力提升等。在第三阶段，事务律师需要在律师事务所完成两年的实习期，出庭律师则需要一年的实习期。这两年中每半年要换一个岗位，一共需要轮四个岗，其中至少要涉及三个完全不相关的领域。三个阶段顺利完成后，申请人则会被英国非出庭律师协会（Law Society）或英国出庭律师公会（Bar Council）吸收为正式成员，从而成为注册执业的事务律师或出庭律师。执业满一定年限的中国律师，也可以通过英国律师执业资格转化评估项目（Qualified Lawyers Transfer Scheme，简称QLTS）的考试，获得英国事务律师资格。

澳大利亚的规定和英国比较接近，律师也分为事务律师和出庭律师，需要满足获取学位、经历实习培训、申请执业等要求。首先申请人一定要获得澳大利亚法学学士（Bachelor of Law）学位或者法律职业博士（Juris Doctor）学位。获得学位后，申请人再参加律师执业培训（Practical Legal Training，简称PLT），获得至少6个月的律师事务所实习经验。通过PLT实习培训之后，申请人便可向所在州和领地的准入委员会递交注册申请。新晋律师需要先在正式律师的指导下完成两年的工作后才能够独立执业。

美国律师执照的核准与颁发由各州掌控。一个律师只被允许在一个州执业，只有极少数律师被允许在两个及以上的州执业。各州申请执业律师资格的条件有所不同，但一般都要求申请人必须具有良好的道德品质，至少受过两年专业法律教育或者是法律院校的毕业生，并必须通过州的律师考试且成绩合格。

在美国，律师资格考试（Bar Exam）是由各州最高法院任命的主考人组成的考试委员会负责主持，主考人一般是本州具有权威的法官或律师，应考者必须毕业于美国的法学院，并具有法学学士学位。考试内容包括联邦法律和州法律。考试通过后，考试委员会颁发律师资格证书。在一个州取得律师资格，并不等同于可以在其他州执业。如要在另一个州从事律师工作还需要通过另一个州的律师资格考试。当"挂牌律师"则需要州最高法院批准。在联邦法院办案还须向联邦法院申请，经批准后方可办案。

第二节　法院结构

一、中国的法院结构

人民法院的组织体系分为四级，即基层、中级、高级和最高人民法院，并设军事、铁路、知识产权等专门人民法院。基层人民法院包括县人民法院、市人民法院、自治县人民法院和市辖区的人民法院；中级人民法院包括省、自治区内按地区设立的中级人民法院，直辖市内设立的中级人民法院，省、自治区、直辖市的中级人民法院和自治州人民法院；高级人民法院包括省高级人民法院、自治区高级人民法院和直辖市高级人民法院。目前，基层人民法院有3 000多个，中级人民法院有300多个，高级人民法院有30多个。

基层人民法院设院长一人、副院长和审判员若干人，设立刑事审判庭、民事审判庭和经济审判庭，庭里设庭长、副庭长。基层人民法院根据地区、人口和案件情况可以设立若干人民法庭。

中级人民法院的上级单位是高级人民法院，布局在除台湾地区及香港、澳门特区以外的地级行政区（包括地级市、自治州、地区、盟）以及直辖市内的人民法院。

高级人民法院是指各省、自治区、直辖市的一级审判机关，由院长（一人）和副院长、庭长、副庭长、审判员（若干人）组成。高级人民法院设刑事审判庭、民事审判庭、经济审判庭、行政审判庭和其他需要设立的审判庭，并设审判委员会。其上级人民法院为最高人民法院。

最高人民法院成立于1949年，是最高审判机关，负责审理各类案件，做出司法解释，监督地方各级人民法院和专门人民法院的审判工作，并依照法律确定的职责范围，管理全国法院的司法行政工作。

以最高人民法院的机构设置为例，大致了解中国法院内部机构及其英文表达，可使译者不犯低级错误，见表3-1。

表 3-1　中国法院内部机构及其英文表达

机构	英译
立案庭	case filing tribunal
刑事审判庭	criminal adjudication tribunal
民事审判庭	civil adjudication tribunal
环境资源审判庭	adjudication tribunal for environment and resources
行政审判庭	administrative adjudication tribunal
审判监督庭	trial supervision tribunal
赔偿委员会办公室	compensation committee office
执行局	enforcement bureau
办公厅	general office
政治部	political department
研究室	research office
审判管理办公室	trial administration office
监察局	supervision bureau
国际合作局	bureau of international cooperation
司法行政装备管理局	judicial equipment administration bureau
机关党委	party committee
离退休干部局	retired cadre bureau
新闻局	information bureau
巡回法庭	circuit court

二、英国的法院结构

英国司法组织因袭历史传统，体系比较错综复杂。法院也不是由固定配属的法官组成，而是由一定等级的法官到院进行审判。

英国的法院大致分为四级、六类，其中治安法院是英国最古老、最下位的法院，而上议院是英国最高级别的法院。

治安法院（Magistrate's Court）是最基层的法院。起源于中世纪的伦敦金融城的警长（Sheriff）办公室，专门处理金融城里的小型治安案件，于1361年正式起用治安法官（Just of the Peace，简称JP）的名称，同时治安法院诞生。除了伦敦金融城的四个治安法院，其他治安法院均内设民事和刑事审判庭。

县法院（County Court）是设在农村、乡镇的基层法院。县法院专门审理能进入快速通道的、金额不超过5 000英镑的小额债务案件，以及各类诸如遗嘱、侵权（赔偿额不超过1 000英镑）的民事案件和各类轻微的刑事案件。治安法院和县法院都是最基层的法院，但治安法院的上一级法院是高等法院和刑事法院，而县法院的上一级法院是上诉法院。

高等法院（High Court）成立于1828年，管辖英格兰和威尔士，设有三个庭：一是后座法庭（Queen's Bench Division），主要适用普通法、判例法，受理商务、金融、债务、有价证券等方面的案件；二是家事法庭（Family Division），主要处理婚姻、遗嘱、收养、家庭暴力等类型的案件；三是衡平法庭（Chancery Division），主要审理商务方面的各种纠纷案件。这三个庭都可以适用衡平法和普通法。案件开庭一般由一名法官审理。

刑事法院（Crown Court）只受理治安法院一审的刑事上诉案件及一审重大刑事案件。县法院、高等法院、刑事法院共同的上一级法院是上诉法院。

上诉法院（Court of Appeal）设有民事审判庭和刑事审判庭，分别受理不服县法院、高等法院或后座法院一审的民事或刑事上诉案件。上诉法院有35名大法官，是枢密院成员，并具有 the Right Appeal Sr. 头衔。案件开庭由3名大法官审理。

上议院（House of Lords）受理不服上诉法院判决的二审上诉或某些进入三审程序的重要案件，也是英国国内的终审法院，受理英格兰、威尔士所有案件的终审以及苏格兰民事案件的终审。上议院共由16名高级大法官（Law Lord）组成，他们也是议员。案件开庭由5名高级大法官审理。

英国法院按审理案件的性质还可以分为民事和刑事两大系统：

民事法院系统由四级法院组成：郡法院、高等法院（分为刑事庭、家事庭和大法官庭，刑事庭又分别设行政庭和上诉庭）、上诉法院（民事庭）和上议院。

刑事法院系统分为四级法院：治安法院（青少年法院作为地方法院分支，受理被告为10~17岁的案件）、刑事法院、上诉法院（刑事庭）和上议院。刑事法院系统在英格兰和威尔士按地域分为六个巡回区（circuit）：米德兰和牛津（2001年4月后改称米德兰巡回区，总部在伯明翰）、东北（总部在利兹）、北部（总部在曼彻斯特）、东南（总部在伦敦）、威尔士和切斯特（总部在卡迪夫）及西部（总部在布里斯托）。每个巡回区设置若干刑事法院，共设78个审判中心。

除上述法院外，英国还有一些特别设立的专门法院，独立于民事和刑事法院系统之外，主要有枢密院（Privy Council）、反垄断法院（the Restrictive Practice Court）、验尸官法院（Coroner's Court）、专业法庭（Tribunals Service）以及军事法庭（Courts Martial）。

三、美国的法院结构

美国法院大致分为联邦法院和州法院两大系统，它们适用各自的宪法和法律，管辖不同的案件和地域。

联邦法院系统由94个地区法院（District Court）、13个上诉法院（Court of Appeal）和1个最高法院（Supreme Court）组成。此外还有索赔法院（Court of Claims）、关税法

院（Customs Court）、关税及专利上诉法院（Court of Customs and Patent Appeal）等联邦特别法院。

联邦地区法院是联邦法院系统中的普通法院。联邦上诉法院分设在全国 11 个司法巡回区，受理本巡回区内对联邦地方法院判决不服的上诉案件，以及对联邦系统的专门法院的判决和某些具有部分司法权的独立机构的裁决不服的上诉案件。联邦最高法院由 1 位首席法官和 8 位法官组成，其判决为终审判决，并享有特殊的司法审查权。国会还会根据需要通过有关法令建立特别法院，如联邦权利申诉法院等。美国没有统一的行政法院，行政纠纷案件除由普通法院审理外，各独立机构也有权受理和裁决。

此外，美国各州均以宪法形式成立了全部或部分司法机关，或授权其立法机关成立这一司法机关。事实上，各州的司法体系在结构和名称上存在着极大的差异，但一般来说由州初审法院、州上诉法院和州最高法院组成。州初审法院是属州管辖的一般民事、刑事案件的一审法院，州上诉法院审理不服州初审法院判决的上诉案件，州最高法院是州的最高审级法院。下面简单介绍州法院的具体情况。

治安法官（Sheriff）被称为"县官"或"乡绅"，虽然是州司法系统中最低的一级，但历史十分悠久。他们通常由选举产生，但有时也由任命产生；他们通常在县、市镇、乡镇等辖区任职，任期一般为 2—6 年。治安法官受理轻微民事纠纷和刑事轻罪案件。

市法院（Municipal Court）也被称为"交通法院""小数额法院""夜间法院""警务法院"。市法院是一审初级法院，并且是州立的第一个有诉讼记录的法院。其收案范围相对有限，民事案件的标的因州的不同而有差异；也可受理轻微刑事案件；其基本管辖权因州而异。

郡法院是州司法体系中的第三级审判机关，其收案范围相当广泛，因为其宽泛的初审管辖权被限定于一个或几个郡中，所以被称为郡法院。这类法院通常会采用陪审团制度。与郡法院相关联的审判机构还包括季审法庭、中级民事及刑事法庭、刑事法庭、孤儿法庭、遗产检验法庭、家事法庭、少年法庭、衡平法院、代理验证法院、大法官法庭等。

上诉法院通常被称为上诉法庭或高等法院。在许多州，案件直接由郡法院上诉到州最高法院，后者的工作压力使中级上诉法院产生。中级上诉法院的体制类似于联邦上诉法院，根据立法规定，它是下级法院案件上诉的第一站，往往也是最后一站。

几乎所有州的司法系统的最高一级都被称为最高法院，但也有例外：纽约和马里兰州称为上诉法庭（Court of Appeal）；缅因州和马萨诸塞州称为最高司法法院（Supreme Judicial Court）；西弗吉尼亚州称为最高上诉法院（Supreme Court of Appeal of West Virginia）。尽管名称各异，但其判决对下级法院来说都是终极的。

四、澳大利亚的法院结构

澳大利亚法院分为联邦法院和州法院两大系统。

联邦法院系统主要包括联邦法院、高等法院、联邦专门法院。澳大利亚各州的法院都是独立的，不同的州法院的设置和名称不尽相同，大致可以分为州高等法院（Supreme Court）、地区法院（District Court）和地方法院（Local Court/Magistrate's Court）。

高等法院是设陪审团的最高一级法院，负责审理谋杀、企图杀人、叛国罪、严重的毒品案件等刑事案件。它也审理民事案件，如个人或公司将另一方告上法院以解决争端，但金额需在25万澳币以上。同时，高等法院还审理行政法方面的案件。所有的刑事案件和一些民事案件设陪审团。高等法院的决定由法官和陪审团做出，法官负责法律的执行并在陪审团做出是否有罪判决后公布处罚结果。上诉法院是高等法院的一部分，只听取上诉，不对案件进行初审，不设陪审团。上诉法院有三位来自高等法院的法官，由上诉法院的庭长总负责，他们听取上诉理由。

地区法院是比地方法院高一级的法院，设陪审团，能审理各种严重的刑事案件，如破门行窃、人身伤害、危险驾驶、持械抢劫、性骚扰等。地方法院可以处理个人、企业和政府间标的在15万~75万澳币的民事纠纷，还能受理地方法院的上诉。

地方法院审理地方法官依法能够审理的各类民事和刑事案件，包括刑事轻罪案件，如拒付交通违规罚款，以及不严重的违法行为，包括拒付旅店或餐馆的账单、恶意破坏他人的财产等。审案人员一般为地方法官。

五、加拿大的法院结构

加拿大《1867年宪法法案》第91条和第92条对联邦和各省的管辖权进行了具体划分。联邦法院除有权审理涉及外国使领馆人员、海事或海商案件，以及邮政、移民、著作权案件外，对两个或两个以上的省之间、联邦政府与省之间的争执也有管辖权。它也复审联邦政府任命的行政裁判做出的决定，比如移民上诉委员会和国家假释委员会的决定。

现行联邦法院体系实行三级制，即联邦最高法院、联邦法院（上诉级）和联邦法院（审判级），另外还设有税务法院等专门法院，税务法院对税收及与税收有关的事务拥有专门管辖权。联邦最高法院是加拿大的最高审判机关，受理对所有的省和地区上诉法院所做裁决提起的上诉，以及对联邦上诉法院所做裁决提起的上诉。它的决定是最终的裁决。联邦法院现共有9位最高法官，有资格成为联邦最高法院的法官是省法院的法官或拥有律师执业牌照10年以上的人。

加拿大各省或区均有独立的立法权，因而各省和区都有自己的独立法律制度。比如，魁北克省是法语区，属于大陆法系，有自己的民法和民诉法。不列颠哥伦比亚省等4个省区同属英美法系，都沿袭英国法律。与此相适应，加拿大各省、区都设有独立省、区法院。以阿尔伯塔省为例，法院分为三级，从高到低分别是阿尔伯塔上诉法庭（Court of Appeal of Alberta）、阿尔伯塔皇座法庭（Court of Queen's Bench of Alberta）和阿尔伯塔省立法庭（Provincial Court of Alberta）。

翻译练习

练习1

The percentage of minority lawyers hired at the big firms may not tell the whole story. The number of minorities allowed to enter the prestigious partner ranks was even lower. The 1982 *National Law Journal* survey found that there were no black partners in 106 firms and no Hispanic partners in 133. While the doors may be opening, minorities continue to be relegated to lower positions of power, prestige and economic rewards.

练习2

The regulation of the legal profession primarily is the concern of the states, each of which has its own requirements for admission to practice. Most require three years of college and a law degree. Each state administers its own examination to applicants for its bar. Almost all states make use of the Multistate Bar Exam, a day-long multiple choice test, to which the state adds a day-long essay examination emphasizing its own law.

练习3

联邦法院体系中共有13个联邦上诉法院,也被称为联邦巡回上诉法院。联邦上诉法院有12个巡回区,包括哥伦比亚地区。这些法院负责审理位于各自巡回区域的联邦地区法院的上诉案件。第13巡回审判区的上诉法院叫作联邦巡回法院,该法院对某些类型的案件——诸如专利权案件和美国联邦政府作为被告的案件——具有国家的上述管辖权。

练习4

最高人民法院审理下列案件:① 审理法律规定由它管辖的和它认为应当由自己审判的第一审案件;② 审理高级人民法院、专门人民法院判决、裁定的上诉、抗诉、申请再审与申诉案件;③ 审理最高人民检察院按照审判监督程序提出的抗诉案件;④ 核准本院判决以外的死刑案件。

第 四 章
民法的基本知识和翻译（上）

民法是一切调整平等主体之间的财产关系和人身关系的法律规范总称。它是法律体系中最为重要的部门法之一，也是三大实体法（substantive law）之一。基于不同角度，人们使用民法时赋予其不同含义。

民法可分为形式意义上的民法与实质意义上的民法。所谓形式意义上的民法，是指编纂成文的民法法典。所谓实质意义上的民法，是指一切具有民法性质的法律、法规及判例法、习惯法等。比如，《中华人民共和国民法典》颁布以前的《中华人民共和国民法总则》是基本的民事立法文件，而《中华人民共和国合同法》《中华人民共和国担保法》《中华人民共和国继承法》等则是民事单行法规。在我国宪法及其他部门法或法规中，凡是涉及民事问题的法律规定都是民法的组成部分。

民法也可分为狭义的民法与广义的民法。狭义的民法是指部门法意义上的民法，不包括商法典及商事特别法；广义的民法的范围相当于传统私法的范围，即商法典及商事特别法（如公司法、票据法、海商法、保险法、破产法等）均是民法的组成部分。

美国民法包括的范围很广，除若干州单独的民法典外，一般包括许多契约、侵权、财产、继承和婚姻家庭方面的制定法和判例，统称为私法。比如，多数州援照英国旧法，胎儿即具有民事权利能力，但应设财产管理人。多数州规定年满 18 岁的公民即具有行为能力，未及此年龄者可就生活必需订立契约，成年时可单方解除。

2020 年 5 月 28 日，十三届全国人民代表大会第三次会议通过了《中华人民共和国民法典》（以下简称《民法典》），自 2021 年 1 月 1 日起施行。原来的民事单行法规，如《中华人民共和国民法总则》《中华人民共和国婚姻法》《中华人民共和国继承法》《中华人民共和国合同法》《中华人民共和国物权法》《中华人民共和国担保法》和《侵权责任法》等同时废止。《民法典》共 7 编、1 260 条，各编依次为"总则""物权""合同""人格权""婚姻家庭""继承""侵权责任"。

本章以《民法典》中的表达为基本参照，结合英美法系的相关民法法律文件、诉讼文书等，分"常用术语""核心术语的理解和表达""常用的句型结构""翻译实例分析"四部分讲解相关法律文本的翻译。

第一节 常用术语

民法的常用术语见表 4-1。

表 4-1 民法的常用术语及其英文表达

术语	英译
民事权益	civil rights and interests
平等主体	civil subjects with equal status
等价赔偿	making compensation for equal value
无国籍人	stateless person
承担责任	be held responsible for
故意	deliberate intention; intention; willfulness
过失	negligence
重大过失	gross negligence
疏忽大意的过失	careless and inadvertent negligence
损害事实	fact of damage
过于自信的过失	negligence with undue assumption
有形损失	tangible damage/loss
无形损失	intangible damage/loss
财产损失	property damage/loss
人身损失	personal damage/loss
代理民事活动	be represented in civil activities by
住所	domicile
经常居住地	habitual residence
居民委员会	the neighborhood committee
村民委员会	the village committe
民政部门	the civil affairs department
法定监护人	legal guardian
法定代理人	agent ad litem
合伙人	partner
农村承包经营户	leaseholding farm household
存款保证金	guaranty money for deposit
收款担保	guaranty of collection

续表

术语	英译
重大误解	gross misunderstanding
显失公平	obvious unjust
停止侵害	cease the infringment
排除妨碍	exclusion of hindrance; removal of obstacle/impediment
消除危险	elimination of danger/peril
返还财产	restitution of property
恢复原状	restitution of original state
赔偿损失	compensate/indemnify (sb.) for a loss
支付违约金	payment of liquidated damages
消除影响	eliminate the adverse effects
恢复名誉	rehabilitate one's reputation
赔礼道歉	extend a formal apology
诚实信用原则	good faith principle
逾期利息	overdue interest
透支利息	overdraft interest
利息回扣	interest rebate
解释准则	interpretation criterion
连带负责	jointly liable to
擅自变更或解除（民事法律行为）	alter or rescind one's act arbitrarily
以欺诈、胁迫的手段	as a result of cheating or coercion
乘人之危	take advantage of one's unfavorable position
掩盖非法目的	conceal illegitimate purposes
恶意串通	conspire maliciously
有过错的一方	the erring party
附条件的民事法律行为	conditional civil juristic act
优先购买的权利	right of pre-emption
埋藏物或隐藏物	buried or concealed object
财产继承权	the right of inheritance
继承法	inheritance law
共同侵权行为	joint infringement
侵犯商标权	infringement of a trademark

续表

术语	英译
查封、扣押、冻结、没收	seal up, distrain, freeze or confiscate
按照出资比例	in proportion to one's respective contributions to the investment
解释权	authority for the interpretation
主要办事机构	the main administrative office
入伙	join in partnership
退伙	withdrawal from partnership
隐名合伙	sleeping/dormant partnership
私营企业	private enterprise
企业集团	group of enterprise
关联企业	affiliate enterprise
个人独资企业	individual business establishment
中外合资企业	Sino-foreign joint venture enterprise
中外合作企业	Sino-foreign contractual enterprise
法人型联营	association of legal persons
合伙型联营	coordinated management in partnership
核准登记的经营范围	within the range approved and registered
企业法人分立、合并	the division and merger of an enterprise as a legal person
办理注销登记	cancel the registration
取得法人资格	be qualified as a legal person
企业法人被撤销	the dissolution of an enterprise as a legal person
企业法人解散	disbanding of an enterprise as a legal person
设立、变更、终止民事关系	establish, change or terminate civil relationship
给付定金	leave a deposit with the other party
双倍返还定金	repay the deposit in double
买卖、出租、抵押、转让	be sold, leased, mortgaged or transferred
按照确定的份额分享权力	be entitled to rights in proportion to his proper share of the credit
享有连带权利的每个债权人	each of the joint creditors
有权向债务人追偿	have the right to claim repayment from the debtor
绝对权	absolute right
相对权	relative right
优先权	right of priority

续表

术语	英译
不当得利	unjust enrichment
无因管理	voluntary service
救济权	right of relief
提供一定的财产作为抵押物	offer a specific property as a pledge
支配权	right of dominion
请求权	right of claim
物上请求权	right of claim for real thing
形成权	right of formation
撤销权	right of claiming cancellation
代位权	subrogated right
中断请求	interrupt request
解除权	right of renouncement
抗辩权	right of defense
一时性抗辩权	momentary right of defense
永久性抗辩权	permanent counter-argument right
不安抗辩权	unstable counter-argument right
同时履行抗辩权	defense right of simultaneous performance
期待权	expectant right
人格权	right of personality
生命健康权	right of life and health
肖像权	right of portraiture
名誉权	right of reputation
探视权	visitation right
荣誉权	right of honor
公力救济	public protection
私力救济	self-protection
自物权	jus in re propria; right of full ownership
所有权	dominium; ownership; title
所有权凭证	document of title; title of ownership
占有权	dominium utile; equitable ownership
使用权	right of use; right to use

续表

术语	英译
收益权	right to earnings; right to yield
处分权	right of dispose
善意占有	possession in good faith
恶意占有	malicious possession
一般留置权	general lien
特别留置权	special lien
原物	original thing
天然孳息	natural fruits
法定孳息	legal fruits
流通物	res in commercium; a thing in commerce
限制流通物	limited merchantable thing
禁止流通物	res extra commercium; a thing out of commerce
特定物	res certae; a certain thing
种类物	genus; indefinite thing
动产	movables; chattel
不动产	immovable property; real estate
固定资产	fixed asset
流动资产	current asset; floating asset
可分物	divisible thing
不可分物	indivisible thing
物权分类	classification of right in rem/real right
他物权	right over the property of another
用益物权	real right for usufruct
按份共有	several possession
共同共有	joint possession
永佃权	jus emphyteuticum
地役权	servitude; easement
人役权	servitus personarum; personal servitude
担保物权	real right for security
经营权	managerial authority; power of management
承包经营权	right to contracted management

续表

术语	英译
相邻权	neighboring/related right
地上权	superficies
质权	hypotheque/pledge right
物的瑕疵担保	warranty against defect of a thing
婚姻、家庭、继承、收养	marriage, family, inheritance, adoption
包办婚姻	arranged marriage
财产分割	partition; dismemberment of property
重婚	bigamy
非婚生子女	illegitimate child
婚生子女	legitimate child
夫妻共同财产	community property
夫妻分居	divorce a mensa et thoro; divorce from bed and board
复婚	resumption of marriage
感情破裂	incompatibility
婚后财产公证	notarization of postnuptial property
婚姻登记	marriage registration
买卖婚姻	mercenary marriage
拟制血亲	blood relation in fiction of law
旁系血亲	collateral blood relation
涉外婚姻	marriage with foreign elements
事实婚	de facto marriage
诉讼离婚	divorce by litigation
无效婚姻	void marriage
协议离婚	divorce by agreement
一夫一妻制	monogamy
直系血亲	lineal descent
自然血亲	natural blood relation
收养法	adoption law
收养协议	adoption agreement
收养人	adoptive parent
送养人	person or institution placing out a child for adoption

续表

术语	英译
涉外收养	adoption with foreign elements
法定继承	legal succession
无遗嘱继承	intestate succession
遗赠继承	succession by devise
自然继承	natural succession
代位继承	representation; succession by subrogation
世袭继承	hereditary succession
共同继承	joint succession
单独继承	single succession
继承人	heir; successor
第一顺序继承人	successor first in order
第二顺序继承人	successor second in order
继承参与人	succession participant
遗产继承人	heir to property; inheritor
遗言	last will and testament
遗赠	bequest; legacy
遗赠抚养协议	legacy-support agreement

第二节 核心术语的理解和表达

1. fundamental principles of civil law

fundamental principles of civil law 可译为"民法基本原则",是指效力贯穿整个民事法律制度的根本准则,是民事立法、民事司法和民事活动的基本准则。《民法典》从第四条开始有相应的规定,分别是第四条的平等原则(principle of equality)、第五条的自愿原则(principle of voluntariness)、第六条的公平原则(principle of fairness)、第七条的诚信原则(principle of good faith)、第八条的公序良俗(principle of public order and good morals)、第九条的绿色原则(principle of green)。其中,公序良俗是从法国民法中借鉴过来的概念,法文为 ordre public et bonnes moeurs。

2. civil person

civil person 可译为"民事主体",也称 civil subject、civil body,也有版本将"民事主体"简单译为 the parties。民事主体又被称为民事法律关系主体。参与民事法律关系,享受权利和承担义务的人,即民事法律关系当事人。民事主体资格由法律规定,根据

《民法典》的规定，能够作为民事主体的有自然人（natural person）、法人（legal person）和非法人组织（unincorporated organization）。

3. the capacity for civil rights

the capacity for civil rights 译为"民事行为能力"，有时也可称为 civil status（高凌云，2017）。民事行为能力是指民事主体以自己独立的行为去取得民事权利、承担民事义务的资格。有民事权利能力而没有民事行为能力的民事主体要想享有民事权利、承担民事义务就只能通过他人代理。自然人的行为能力分为三种：完全行为能力（full capacity for civil conduct/full civil capacity）、限制行为能力（limited capacity for civil conduct/limited civil capacity）、无行为能力（no capacity for civil conduct/no civil capacity）。法人的行为能力由法人的机关或代表行使。

4. civil legal act

civil legal act 译为"民事法律行为"。民事法律行为也可译为 civil act，juridicial act。《民法典》第一百三十三条规定：民事法律行为是民事主体通过意思表示设立、变更、终止民事法律关系的行为。民事法律行为可以采用书面形式、口头形式或者其他形式。法律规定用特定形式的，应当依照法律规定。

民事法律行为可以进一步分为：单方民事法律行为（unilateral civil legal act）、双方民事法律行为（bilateral civil legal act）和多方民事法律行为（joint civil legal act）；有偿民事法律行为（civil legal act with consideration）和无偿民事法律行为（civil legal act without consideration/civil legal act without award）；实践性民事法律行为（practical civil legal act）和诺成性民事法律行为（consental civil legal act）；要式民事法律行为（formal civil legal act）和不要式民事法律行为（informal civil legal act）；要因民事法律行为（causative civil legal act）和不要因民事法律行为（noncausative civil legal act）；主民事法律行为（principal civil legal act）和从民事法律行为（accessory civil legal act）；附条件民事法律行为（conditional civil legal act）和附期限民事法律行为（civil legal act with term）；生前民事法律行为（civil legal act before death）和死后民事法律行为（civil legal act after death）；准民事法律行为（quasi civil legal act）、无效民事法律行为（ineffective civil legal act）、可撤销民事行为（revocable civil act）等。

5. guardianship

guardianship 意为"监护"，《民法典》第三十六条规定了监护人（guardian）监护资格的撤销，并按照最有利于被监护人（ward/the person under guardianship）原则（in a way that is in his best interests）依法指定监护人。

6. agency

agency 的意思是"代理"，是指代理人（agent）以被代理人（principal）的名义，在代理权限内（within the scope of authority）与第三人（又称"相对人"）实施民事行为，其法律后果直接由被代理人承受的民事法律制度。

按照规定，代理可以分为委托代理（entrusted agency/agency by entrustment）、法定

代理（statutory agency/agency by operation of law）、指定代理（appointed agency）、代理（original agency）、复代理（subagency）、有权代理（authorized agency）、表见代理（agency by estoppel/apparent agency）、律师代理（agency by lawyer）、普通代理（general agency）。

其他相关的表达还有委托代理人（an entrusted agent）、共同代理（joint agency）、独家代理（sole agency）、全权代理委托书（general power of attorney）、行使代理权（exercise the power of agency）、授权委托书（power of attorney）、授权行为（act of authorization）、代理行为（act of agency）、超越代理权（beyond the scope of one's power of agency）、代理权终止（the expiration of one's power of agency）等。

7. declaration of disappearance, declaration of death

declaration of disappearance 的意思是"宣告失踪"，是指经利害关系人（an interested person）申请，由人民法院对下落不明（can not be located）满一定期限的人宣告为失踪人（make a declaration identifying such natural person as a missing person）的制度。为消除因自然人长期下落不明所造成的不利影响，法律通过设立宣告失踪制度，宣告下落不明人为失踪人，并为其设立财产代管人（custodian），由代管人管理失踪人的财产，以保护失踪人与相对人的财产权益。

declaration of death 表示"宣告死亡"，是指自然人离开住所，下落不明达到法定期限，经利害关系人申请，由人民法院宣告其死亡的法律制度。

8. legal person, legal representative

法人（legal person）是具有民事权利能力和民事行为能力，依法独立享有民事权利（civil law right）和承担民事义务（civil law obligation）的组织。学界有"法人不是人，实是法律上拟制人"一说。

《民法典》规定了捐助法人（donation-based legal person），以区别于营利法人（for-profit legal person）。另外还有一类特别法人（special legal person），具体包括机关法人（government agency）、农村集体经济组织法人（rural collective economic organization）、城镇农村的合作经济组织法人（urban-rural cooperative economic organization）、基层群众性自治组织法人（community-level autonomous organization）。其中，法律对捐助法人的设立要求尤其严格，要求依法制定法人章程（articles of association/the bylaws of the legal person），设立理事会（council）等决策机构、执行机构，以及监事会（supervisory）等监督机构。

同时《民法典》还规定了法人人格否认制度（disregard of corporate personality）。这一制度在普通法系下又常被称为"刺破公司面纱"（pierce the corporate veil），主要是指在营利法人中滥用法人独立地位和出资人有限责任（the limited liability of the investor）、逃避债务、严重损害法人的债权人利益的出资人，应当对法人债务承担连带责任（bear joint and several liabilities）。

legal representative 是法人代表，是法人的法定代表人，必须是法人组织的负责人，能够代表法人行使职权。《民法典》第六十一条规定：依照法律或者法人章程的规定，代表法人从事民事活动的负责人，为法人的法定代表人。

9. creditor's right

creditor's right 的意思是"债权"。债权还可译为 jus in personam，right to give or orprocure，claim 等。与债务相对，债权是指在债的关系中权利主体具备的能够要求义务主体为一定行为或不为一定行为的权利。债权和债务一起共同构成债的内容。债权与物权相对应，成为财产权的重要组成部分。债权是一种典型的相对权，只在债权人和债务人之间发生效力，原则上债权人和债务人之间的债之关系不能对抗第三人。

债的分类：法定之债（legal obligation）和任意之债（voluntary obligation）；简单之债（simple obligation）和选择之债（alternative obligation）；主债（prime / principal obligation）和从债（accessory obligation）；单一之债（single obligation）和按份之债（several obligation）；连带之债（joint obligation）和特定之债（certain obligation）；种类之债（indefinite obligation）和合同之债（contractual obligation）；侵权行为之债（tort obligation）和损害赔偿之债（obligation of compensation for injury / obligation of damages）。

跟债有关的术语还有"债务的偿还"（payment of debt）、"债务的偿清"（discharge of debt）、"债务的担保"（guarantee of debt）、"债务的合并"（consolidation of debt）、"债务的给付日期"（debt maturity）、"债务的免除"（exemption of debt）。

10. mortgage

mortgage 的意思是"抵押"，是指抵押人（mortgagee）和债权人（creditor）以书面形式订立约定，不转移抵押财产（estate under mortgage）的占有，将该财产作为债权的担保。当债务人不履行债务时，债权人有权依法以该财产折价或者拍卖、变卖该财产的价款优先受偿（priority of mortgage）。

跟抵押有关的术语有"抵押权的设定"（creation of right to mortgage）、"抵押权的次序"（sequence of right to mortgage）、"抵押权的抛弃"（abandonment of right to mortgage）、"抵押权的让与"（alienation of right to mortgage）、"抵押权的实现"（materialization of right to mortgage）、"抵押权的消灭"（extinction of right to mortgage）、"抵押物登记"（registration of estate undermortgage）等。

11. rem

rem 译为"物权"。物权还可译为 property right，real right，right of the thing。它是指权利人依法对特定的物享有直接支配和排他的权利（directly and exclusively control a special thing by the obligee），包括所有权（ownership right）、用益物权（usufructuary right）和担保物权（secured interests）。

或者说，物权是指自然人、法人直接支配不动产（immovable / real property）或动产（movable / personal property）的权利。不动产是指土地及建筑物等土地附着物；动产是指不动产以外的物。

12. negligence

negligence 译为"过失",是英国现代侵权法中一种重要的侵权形式,类似于中国的过失侵权。过失侵权是对行为不符合法律但为保护他人免受不合理的受损风险而做的规定。如果行为人做出的行为违背了一个理性谨慎的人在同样的情况下理应做出的行为,那么他便会构成过失侵权。

过失侵权有三个要件:被告有注意义务(the defendant owed him a duty of care);被告没有履行该义务(the defendant was in breach of that duty);原告所遭受的损失与被告的过失行为之间存在因果关系,且该因果关系有足够的原因力(the claimant suffered damage caused by the breach of duty, which was not too remote)。

13. lien, pledge, mortgage, security

美国法律中,lien 的含义非常广泛,相当于担保物权的统称,兼具中国抵押权、质权和留置权的性质。

possessory lien 类似于中国的留置权,《美国统一商法典》(Uniform Commercial Code)第 9-333 条(a)将其定义为除担保物权之外的以下权利:该权利担保某人在其正常经营活动中提供的与有体动产相关的服务或装备该有体动产的材料所产生的偿付请求权或者履行请求权;该权利是法律为该人的利益所创设;该权利的生效取决于对该人有体动产的占有。

pledge 的意思是"担保",被广泛应用于商品及有价证券,如黄金、股票及各种权证的担保。出借人实际占有这些担保物,直到借款人偿还所有欠款。一旦债务逾期,出借人可以出售这些担保物以收回自己的本金和利息。相关表达有"抵押"(hold in pledge)、"出质资产"(pledge asset)、"动产质权"(chattel pledge)、"股权质押"(share pledge)。

mortgage 的意思是"抵押贷款",是指出借人和借款人之间约定,由出借人借钱给借款人购买房子或者其他不动产,如按揭买房。在借款人到期不偿还债务时,银行可申请拍卖该房产或者其他不动产收回借款;如果该房屋被查封或被出借人出售,那么就以该房屋的收益偿还借款。

guarantee 一般指的是担保的法律文件,它规定了担保人债务逾期时必须承担借款人还款义务的条件。出借人希望确保担保人能够履行担保义务,但担保人希望尽可能确保借款人将履行其还款义务。

14. property settlement

property settlement 的意思是"财产分割"。财产分割多见于离婚案件,包括两种情况:依据双方的协议并经法院批准;依据法院的判决。

财产分割协议包括分割配偶双方在婚姻存续期间所拥有或取得的财产,以及配偶一方向另一方定期支付或一次性支付的生活费或一次性财产转让。

15. trespass

trespass 的意思是"侵害",是英格兰中世纪的一种诉讼形式,是指因自己的身体、财产、权利、名誉或人际关系被侵害而索赔的诉讼。巡回初审（nisi prius）制度建立起来后，这种诉讼形式在14世纪才被普遍应用起来。

后来又发展出间接侵害之诉（trespass on the case）的诉讼形式：一方的损害行为与另一方的损失或伤害之间有直接或间接的因果关系（causal relationship）。

16. tort，infringement

tort 最初源自拉丁文 torquere，其英文含义为 twist/tortus，原义为"扭曲，弯曲"。它通常是指侵犯法律规定而非合同约定的权利，并导致诉权产生的不法行为或损害行为。tort 有"错误，过失"的意思。只有存在错误或过失，才能构成侵权。

侵权责任包括故意侵权责任、过失侵权责任和绝对侵权责任或无过错严格侵权责任。与 tort 相关的常见表达有 tort feasor（侵权行为人）、tort liability（侵权责任）、Tort Law（侵权法）、tortious（侵权的，违法的）。

infringement 较多地用在侵害知识产权方面。《布莱克法律辞典》更简洁地直接指出"It especially involves intellectual property; namely, an act that interferes with the exclusive right of a patent, trademark or copyright."，说明 infringement 尤指侵害知识产权，即侵害了专利、商标、版权的排他权。英美法系国家的法院认定 infringement 时，从来不需要去找过错、实际损失这类要件，只要有侵权事实即可。常见的相关表达有 infringement of trademark/patent/copyright（侵犯商标权/专利权/著作权）、infringer（侵权人）。

17. will

will 的意思是"遗嘱"，是指某人处分其动产和不动产且在其离世之后生效的意思表示，或指显示该意思表示的书面法律文件。该意思表示（或法律文件）可在行为人生前被撤销或废止。

will 与 testament 都指遗嘱。18世纪以来两者之间的区别逐渐消失，故在法律用语中两者可以相互替代，但前者的使用较多。

will 在广义上包括遗嘱、补充遗嘱（codicil）以及其他各种遗嘱性处分（testamentary disposition），但在严格意义上仅指以完整形式做出的遗嘱文件。在英格兰的法律中，遗嘱设立人（testator）在设立遗嘱时应具备遗嘱能力，因此未成年人和精神病人不能设立遗嘱。

口头遗嘱（nuncupative will）是指遗嘱设立人在足够人数的证人面前所宣布的遗嘱，但无任何书面形式。自英格兰1677年《防止诈骗法》（Statute of Frauds）制定以来，英美等国的法律都认为遗嘱设立属于要式行为，须以书面形式为之。

在苏格兰，口头遗嘱或口头遗赠所处分的财产不得超过8.33英镑。除此之外，须有书面形式。此外，根据法定继承权原则，遗嘱只能对法定继承权范围以外的那一部分财产进行处分，否则享有法定继承权者，如死者的生存配偶或子女，可对遗嘱效力提出异议。

在美国，遗嘱设立由州的法律规定。遗嘱生效还须符合生效地的州法律所规定的形式要件，否则遗嘱效力可因欺诈、错误或不当影响而受到异议。因为从做成遗嘱到遗嘱设立人死亡往往跨越多年,为使遗嘱具有法律效力,遗嘱检验(probate)是必须进行的,在法庭上进行遗嘱证明。

18. company, corporation

company 和 corporation 都有"公司"之意,但有人认为 company 是英式英语,而 corporation 是美式英语。而 *Cochran's Law Lexicon* 中的解释为"Company, a flexible term. ① A coporation;② an uncincorated association organized for commercial purposes"。由此可见,company 可被理解为"公司"和"商行"。

corporation 的意思是"公司",还可意为"法人"。作为"公司"理解时,company 和 corporation 可以互换使用。

19. duty of care

duty of care 的意思是"注意义务"或"谨慎义务",是英国上议院 1932 年在"Donoghue v. Stevenson"案中确立的。该案原告 Donoghue 夫人与朋友去酒吧喝酒,朋友为 Donoghue 夫人买了啤酒。啤酒瓶的玻璃不透明,因此 Donoghue 夫人根本不可能看到瓶中的情况。朋友将啤酒倒入杯中,Donoghue 夫人喝了杯中的啤酒。随后,朋友将剩下的啤酒倒入杯中时,惊讶地发现竟然倒出一只腐烂的蜗牛。由于已喝了被污染的啤酒,Donoghue 夫人感到十分恶心,随后患上了胃病。鉴于 Donoghue 夫人与酒吧老板及啤酒生产商均无合同关系(啤酒不是 Donoghue 夫人自己购买的),于是 Donoghue 夫人不得不以生产商侵权为由向法院提起诉讼。此案一直诉至英国最高的司法审理机构上议院。

duty of care 是过失侵权中的一个核心概念,只有行为人有注意义务,同时行为人的行为没有达到所需要的行为标准而违反该义务,才构成过失侵权,才可能向相对人承担责任。

20. negative act, forbearance, omission

negative act 是指"不履行法定义务",即不作为。严格来说,negative act 包括两种情况,即 forbearance 和 omission。forbearance 是指有意的不作为;omission 是指疏忽大意的不作为。

forbearance 在关于高利贷的立法中指债权人在约定的期限内不得要求债务人偿还到期的债务;推迟行使某项权利,不行使某项权利,不起诉;推迟债务人清偿债务的期限;延迟偿还债务的协议。

omission 是指忽视或未为一定行为,尤指未为法律、职责或特定环境要求从事的行为,一定条件下行为人须对此承担刑事责任。omission 多指一种非故意的不作为行为(an unintentional negative act)。

21. affiliate, subsidiary, branch, division, office

affiliate 和 subsidiary 都指具有法人地位的子公司。affiliate 的含义较广,可指与母公司联系松散,主要特征是参股,直接或间接拥有 5%或以上具有表决权的股份,不为母公司控股的公司,即所称的联姻公司或横向联合分公司;也可指与另一公司有联系的公司，即关联公司，此时其既可指 parent company，也可指 subsidiary、branch、division，甚至同为一母公司的子公司的姊妹公司（sister corporation）。

subsidiary（也称为 subsidiary corporation）与母公司的联系较紧密，多受母公司控股，是严格意义上的子公司。

branch 和 office 一般是指不具备法人地位的被称为分公司的一种分支机构。

division 多指公司的部门，常用于美国，可略为 div。

22. broker, intermediary, jobber, finder, middleman

broker 意为"经纪人"，是一种商业代理人。作为货物买卖的代理人，经济人的业务是撮合买卖双方当事人达成协议，或者受托于买主一方为其寻找卖主，或者受托于卖主一方为其寻找买主。因此，所得的报酬被称为佣金，一般按照所售货物价款的一定比例计算，但其并不占有这些货物或货物产权文书。经纪人对合同不承担个人责任，但保险经纪人例外，后者通常可以用自己的名义进行起诉，要求支付保险费。其与代销商不同：前者通常以委托人的名义签订合同，后者则既可以用委托人名义也可以用自己的名义签订合同；前者只是当事人之间的协调谈判者，不占有或控制合同项下的货物，后者则可以占有或控制货物。经纪人的业务范围可以是动产、不动产或服务，而且针对不同的对象可分成各种专业经纪人，如房地产经纪人（real estate broker）、股票经纪人（stockbroker）、保险经纪人（insurance broker）和海运经纪人（ship broker）。

intermediary 意为"仲裁人""调解人""经纪人"或"中介组织"。intermediary 还可指股票经纪人、证券商，包括代理他人从事股票买卖的经纪人与以自己的账户从事投机交易的证券商。在英国，intermediary 专指在伦敦证券交易所买卖股票的经纪人，亦作 stock jobber。

jobber 意为"中间商""批发商"，是指从制造商处进货再转卖给零售商的人，常与 wholesaler、middleman 等混用。

finder 意为"居间人""经纪人"或"中间人"。

middleman 意为"居间人"，是指为双方当事人提供缔约机会而不参与协商的人，如在卖方与买方、生产者与消费者、土地所有人与承租人之间履行经纪义务的人；还可意为"中间代理人"，指作为某人的代理人并依某人明示或默示授权委托复代理人的人；还可意为"转卖人"，指买受某物并将该物出卖的人，如将商品从生产者处买受后出卖给消费者的零售商。

23. transfer, assignment, conveyance, negotiation

这四个单词均有"转让"之意。

transfer 是指对财产或其利益进行处理和分割的任何方式，包括支付金钱、免除债务、租赁、设置负担等，也包括保留财产权，可以采用直接或间接、无条件或附条件、自愿或强制等各种类型的方法；还可指按照法律形式进行票据流通，包括通过背书、支付、转让、法律规定等方式；也有"转让"的意思，即财产、所有权等的让与。

assignment 是指财产、权利的转让、让与，指转让动产、属地动产（chattel real）或在不动产或动产上的一定权利。该词常被应用于土地、权利动产及无形动产（incorporeal chattel）、租赁产、定期地产和终身权益（life interests）的转移。

conveyance 意为"不动产（权）转让，不动产（权）转让契据"，是指通过书面文件及其他方式，使土地所有权由一人向他人进行自愿移转。在广义上，它包括土地的转让（assignment）、出租（lease）、抵押（mortgage）与财产负担（encumbrance）。有时，该词既指不动产转让契据本身，也指产（权）转移、财产（权）转移证书。在最广泛的意义上，该词亦可指包括动产在内的所有财产的转让。例如，美国《统一防止欺诈性转让法》（Uniform Fraudulent Conveyance Act）即把该词解释为包括对有体财产或无体财产的付款转让、转移、出租、抵押或质押，也包括创设任何留置或财产负担。

negotiation 也意为"转让"，由一人向另一人转移汇票或其他流通证券，从而使受让人成为票据持有人。

24. wind up, insolvency, bankruptcy

三者均有"破产"的含义。

wind up 意为"停业清理"。企业通过清算账目、清理资产将净资产分给股东或者合伙人的程序通常发生于企业解散或破产之时。

insolvency 意为"无力偿付债务"，是指一个人的全部财产和资产不足以偿付其债务。无力偿债可引起破产程序，也可引起债务和解（arrangement）。破产须经司法裁决。

bankruptcy 意为"破产"，既可指当事人无力偿还到期债务的状况，也可指已依破产法被宣告破产的事实或者已依破产法被宣告破产的当事人的地位，还可以指破产程序（bankruptcy proceeding）。

25. deposit, earnest money, down payment

deposit 意为"保证金""定金"，是指合同一方当事人向另一方当事人支付的用以保证合同履行的金钱，如其未能履行合同义务，则予以没收。它也可最终成为部分付款，从而使买受人成为合同标的物的真正所有权人。deposit 也可以被理解为"（无偿）寄托"，是指根据最初的信托目的而交付财物于受寄托人，由其无偿保管该财物。通常，某人将其动产移转给他人占有，后者负有为前者或第三人利益而保管、使用、收益或以种类物归还的义务。

大陆法将该种寄托分成三种：紧急寄托（necessary deposit），也称"灾害寄托"（miserable deposit），是指在突发灾害事故时未经充分和自由地选定受寄托人而仓促将其财物交由他人保管；任意寄托（voluntary deposit），是指根据当事人之间的合意或协议而产生的寄托；非任意寄托（involuntary deposit），是指未经寄托人同意而产生的寄托，如某人的林木被洪水冲至他人土地上。

earnest money 意为"定金，预付的部分货物"，是指合同一方当事人为担保合同的履行而预先向另一方交付的部分价款或货物，以表明其将履行合同的意图和能力。

down payment 意为"定金，履行保证金，（分期款的）首付款"，是指在订立买卖合同时以现金或其他等值物支付的部分款项，以作为履约担保或预付款项。

26. administrator，executor，personal representative

administrator 意为"遗产管理人"，是指由法院任命管理无遗嘱死亡者的资产及债务的人。遗产管理中所产生的费用（administration expenses）可依法从遗产总额中扣除。administrator ad colligendum 意为"（法院指定的）临时遗产管理人"，是指义务仅仅是收集并保存死者遗产的一种特殊的遗产管理人，其中 ad colligendum 在拉丁语中意为"收存"（collect and preserve）。

executor 是立遗嘱人指定的执行遗嘱条款的人。美国法律规定，遗嘱执行人在履行其职责过程中所付出的合理努力是可以自动获得补偿的，其补偿有时候在遗嘱中规定，遗嘱中无规定的则根据各州法律规定决定。而英国则无此种自动补偿规定，但立遗嘱人可在遗嘱中规定补偿，遗嘱执行人也可向法院申请获得补偿。

personal representative 即因一人无能力或死亡而代其管理其法律事务的人。严格来讲，若把遗嘱执行人定义为遗嘱中指定的遗产代理人，则遗产管理人就是遗嘱中未指定的遗产代理人。遗产代理人有时也写作 independent personal representative 或 legal representative。

一人立下遗嘱后死亡的或其遗嘱中指定的负责执行其遗嘱的（通常是遗产分配相关事宜）就是 executor，因为存在遗嘱，所以译为"遗嘱执行人"最为恰当；一人未立遗嘱即死亡（intestacy），处理此人遗产相关事宜的人即 administrator，因为不存在遗嘱，自然不可使用"遗嘱"一词，而应译为"遗产管理人"；而二者的统称即 personal representative。

除非另有说明，administrator 一词通常包括 executor 的含义。而苏格兰法律中无 administrator 的说法，任何一类的遗产代理人均被表述为 executor，遗嘱执行人被称为 executor nominate，遗产管理人被称为 dative executor。

遗嘱检验法院（probate court，美国有些州也称 surrogate court）负责认定是否存在遗嘱，当认定存在遗嘱且对遗嘱中指定的遗嘱执行人予以同意时，将出具一份遗嘱执行令（letters testamentary），在英国被称为遗嘱检验令（probate）；当认定不存在遗嘱或者认定遗嘱中未指定遗嘱执行人时，则出具一份遗产管理证书（letters of administration）以指定遗产管理人。死者若未立遗嘱，法院一般会将死者的最近亲（next of kin）指定为遗产管理人。

第三节　常见句型结构

1. … provide …

在普通英语文本中，provide 意为"提供"，而在法律英文文本中它与 stipulate 意思相同，译为"规定"，有时写作 unless otherwise provided that，与刑法英文文本中经常用到的 provided that 但书条款的意思截然不同。

如《民法典》第三十一条规定：

① 依照本条第一款规定指定监护人前，被监护人的人身权利、财产权利以及其他合法权益处于无人保护状态的，由被监护人住所地的居民委员会、村民委员会、<u>法律规定</u>的有关组织或者民政部门担任临时监护人。

Where the personal, proprietary, and other lawful rights and interests of the ward are not protected before a guardian is appointed in accordance with the first paragraph of this article, the neighborhood committee, the village committee, the relevant organization as <u>provided by law</u>, or the department of civil affairs in the place of the ward's domicile shall act as a temporary guardian.

再如《民法典》第一百一十七条规定：

② 为了公共利益的需要，依照<u>法律规定</u>的权限和程序征收、征用不动产或者动产的，应当给予公平、合理的补偿。

Where immovable or movable property is expropriated or requisitioned for a public purpose within the authority granted and in accordance with the procedure <u>provided by law</u>, fair and reasonable compensation shall be given.

2. … protection …

《民法典》中涉及"保护"的表达一般都译为 protection。

如《民法典》第一百二十八条规定：

③ 法律对未成年人、老年人、残疾人、妇女、消费者等的民事权利<u>保护</u>有特别规定的，依照其规定。

The laws that provide special <u>protection</u> to the civil law rights of minors, seniors, the people with disabilities, women, and consumers must be complied with.

再如《民法典》第一百八十三条规定：

④ 因保护他人民事权益使自己受到损害的，由侵权人承担民事责任，受益人可以给予适当补偿。

Where a person is injured in <u>protecting</u> the civil law rights and interests of another person, a tort feasor shall assume civil liability, and a beneficiary who has been rescued from the peril may give the injured person appropriate compensation.

3. in accordance with, according to

《民法典》中有不少条款用到"按照"（according to, in accordance with）。运用相关法条诠释或者定性某一行为、某一事件也离不开该表达。

如《民法典》第五条规定：

⑤ 民事主体从事民事活动，应当遵循自愿原则，<u>按照</u>自己的意思设立、变更、终止民事法律关系。

Civil persons when conducting civil activities shall act in accordance with the principle of voluntariness, creating, modifying, and terminating civil relationships according to their own will.

再如《民法典》第五十三条规定：

⑥ 被撤销死亡宣告的人有权请求依照本法第六编取得其财产的民事主体返还财产；无法返还的，应当给予适当补偿。

Where a declaration of death of a person is revoked, the person has the right to request the civil persons who have obtained his property according to Part VI of this Civil Code to return the property, or make appropriate compensation if the property cannot be returned.

《欧洲侵权行为法基本原则》中也有 according to 的类似用法。例如：

⑦ Damage must be proved according to normal procedural standards. The court may estimate the extent of damage where proof of the exact amount would be too difficult or too costly.

损害的证明必须依据通常的程序标准进行举证。在无法举证损害的确切数额或举证费用过高时，法院有权判定损害数额。

4. … compensate …, … compensation …

民法或民商事法律中，对"赔偿"结构使用较多。

如《民法典》第五十三条规定：

⑧ 利害关系人隐瞒真实情况，致使他人被宣告死亡而取得其财产的，除应当返还财产外，还应当对由此造成的损失承担赔偿责任。

If an interested person concealed the true information and caused the other person to be declared dead so as to obtain the latter's property, the interested person shall, in addition to returning the wrongfully obtained property, make compensation for any loss thus caused.

再如《民法典》第八十四条规定：

⑨ 营利法人的控股出资人、实际控制人、董事、监事、高级管理人员不得利用其关联关系损害法人的利益。利用关联关系造成法人损失的，应当承担赔偿责任。

A for-profit legal person's controlling capital contributors, actual controllers, directors, supervisors, and senior management officers shall not harm the legal person's interests by taking advantage of any affiliated relationship; otherwise, they shall compensate for any loss thus suffered by the legal person.

5. ... effective ...

民商事法律关系中有不少涉及某行为生效及某意思表示生效的表达,因此"... effetive ..."结构经常被用到。

如《民法典》第一百三十七条规定:

⑩ 以对话方式作出的意思表示,相对人知道其内容时生效。

以非对话方式做出的意思表示,到达相对人时生效。以非对话方式做出的采用数据电文形式的意思表示,相对人指定特定系统接收数据电文的,该数据电文进入该特定系统时生效;未指定特定系统的,相对人知道或者应当知道该数据电文进入其系统时生效。当事人对采用数据电文形式的意思表示的生效时间另有约定的,按照其约定。

An oral expression of intent is effective from the time the party to whom the intent is expressed knows its content.

An expression of intent made in a form other than oral is effective from the time it is received by the party to whom the intent is expressed. Where such an expression of intent is made through an electronic data massage and the party to whom the intent is expressed has identified a specific data-receiving system, it is effective from the time such data message enters that system; where a specific data-receiving system is not identified, it is effective from the time the party to whom the intent is expressed knows or should have known that the data message has entered the system. Where the parties otherwise agree upon the effective time of the expression of intent made in an electronic data message, such agreement shall prevail.

该条款中有 5 处提及生效,均用形容词 effective。effect 一般作"效力"来理解,如"与提起诉讼或者申请仲裁具有同等效力的其他情形"就译为 other circumstances with the similar effect as initiating a lawsuit or arbitration proceeding by the oblige。同样,"本法自 2021 年 1 月 1 日起施行"中的"施行"就是作"生效"理解,译为"This Law shall take effect since January 1, 2021"。

6. be deemed as ...

be deemed as 意为"视为",是对法律上的地位或效力的认可,在民商事法律文本中经常被用到。

如《民法典》第二十五条规定:

⑪ 自然人以户籍登记或者其他有效身份登记记载的居所为住所;经常居所与住所不一致的,经常居所视为住所。

The domicile of a natural person is the residence where the person registers his household, or the residence recorded in other valid identification registration system; if the place where a natural person usually resides is different from his domicile, such place is deemed as his domicile.

再如《民法典》第一百四十条规定：

⑫ 行为人可以明示或者默示作出意思表示。

沉默只有在有法律规定、当事人约定或者符合当事人之间的交易习惯时，才可以视为意思表示。

A person who makes an expression of intent may do so either expressly or implicitly.

Silence is deemed as an expression of intent only when it is provided by law, agreed upon by the parties, or in compliance with the course of dealing between the parties.

7. … ratify …

按照民法理论的理解，追认权（right of ratification）属于形成权，形成权是指依照权利人的单方意思表示就能使既存的法律关系发生变化的权利。

英文中常用ratify来对应翻译"追认"。ratify一般理解为"批准，同意"，在法律文本中有事后确认之前发生行为的效力之意，有溯及力。

如《民法典》第一百四十五条规定：

⑬ 相对人可以催告法定代理人自收到通知之日起三十日内予以追认。法定代理人未作表示的，视为拒绝追认。民事法律行为被追认前，善意相对人有撤销的权利。撤销应当以通知的方式作出。

A counterparty may demand such legal representative to ratify the act within thirty days after receipt of such notice. Inaction of the legal representative shall be deemed as refusal of ratification. A bona fide counterparty has the right to revoke the act before such act is ratified. Revocation shall be made by actual notice.

再如《民法典》第一百六十八条规定：

⑭ 代理人不得以被代理人的名义与自己实施民事法律行为，但是被代理人同意或者追认的除外。

An agent shall not, in the principal's name, conduct juridical acts with himself, unless it is consented to or ratified by the principal.

8. … assume …

"承担"多用在民法中表示承担义务、承担法律责任和承担连带责任，可以写成assume the obligation, assume legal liability 等。

如《民法典》第十三条规定：

⑮ 自然人从出生时起到死亡时止，具有民事权利能力，依法享有民事权利，承担民事义务。

A natural person acquires civil status from birth until death, and enjoys civil law rights and assumes civil law obligations in accordance with law.

再如《民法典》第六十七条规定：

⑯ 法人合并的，其权利和义务由合并后的法人享有和承担。

法人分立的，其权利和义务由分立后的法人享有连带债权，承担连带债务，但是债权人和债务人另有约定的除外。

Where two or more legal persons merge with each other or are otherwise consolidated, the rights and obligations of such legal persons shall be enjoyed and assumed by the surviving or otherwise designated legal person.

Where a legal person is separated into two or more legal persons, the rights and abligations of such legal person shall be enjoyed and assumed by the legal persons established after the seperation, unless otherwise a greed upon by the creditors and the debtors.

第四节　翻译实例分析

1. 授权委托书

授权委托书

如下签字人，×××，作为 AB 公司（一家在×××设立的公司，其注册地址为上海）的董事长及法人/授权代表，在此授予必要的权利与权限于：

×××先生/女士，_____（国籍）公民，居民身份证/护照号为：_____。

以 AB 公司的名义并代表其全权办理如下事宜：

与 CD 公司（卖方）签署与购买卖方在 EF 公司（目标公司）所持有的 30%的股权（"股买股权"）及组建合资公司有关的文件，包括但不限于股权转让协议、合资合同及经修订和重述之章程；

Power of Attorney

The undersigned, ×××, acting in my capacity as Chairman and Legal Representative of AB Company (a company incorporated in ××× with its registered address located at Shanghai), hereby delegate the necessary power and authority to:

Mr./Ms. ×××, _____ (nationality) citizen, ID/passport number: _____.

Acting in the name and on behalf of the AB Company, in the following matters:

To sign all necessary document, including but not limited to the Equity Transfer Agreement, Equity Joint Venture Contract, and the Amended and Restated Articles and association with CD Company (the Seller) for the purchase of 30% of the equity interest held by the Seller in EF Company (the Target Company) (the "Acquisition") and incorporation of the equity joint venture company;

办理所有与购买股权相关的所需行政审批和登记手续，签署相关部门所要求的行政文件；并于需要时加盖公司印章；	To carry out all the required administrative approval and registration formalities in connection with the Acquisition and to sign administrative documents required by the relevant authorities; and to affix the official seal of the company if necessary;
就上述目的，从事和进行该代理人认为必须或合适的所有行为。	To do and perform all acts and deeds that, in the opinion of the Delegate, he may consider necessary or desirable in connection with the foregoing.
本授权书于_____（年/月/日）签署，即时生效，有效期直至完成签署以上所提及的文件，或由公司书面通知的其他日期为止，以较早者为准。	This Power of Attorney is made on _____ MM/DD/YY, with immediate effect and is valid until the signing of afore said documents is completed or till such other date notified in writing by the Company, whichever is the earlier.

"授权委托书"一般译为 power of attorney。授权委托书的翻译难度不大，译者可对授权人、被授权人、委托事项、权利范围、授权时间等分别进行翻译。

第一段有几个术语，如"法人代表"（legal representative）、"注册成立"（incorporate）、"注册地址"（registered address）及"授予必要的权利和权限"（delegate the necessary power and authority to），按照逻辑顺序处理即可。

第四段中"包括但不限于"的译法，在有些译者看来显得生硬和不符合汉语表达习惯，但实践中不少文本还是习惯译为 including but not limited to。同段还有"股权转让协议"（Equity Transfer Agreement）、"合资合同"（Equity Joint Venture Contract），以及"修订和重述之章程"（Amended and Restated Articles）。

第五段有常用的"行政审批"和"登记手续"，分别译为 administrative approval 和 registration formalities，"相关部门"可译为 the relevant authorites。"加盖公司印章"可译为 affix the official seal of the company。此处涉及对 seal 的理解。seal 是一种书面身份证明（written identification），常替代手写签名用以证实一份文件的真实性。组织一般都有正式印章（official seal）。

2. 婚姻关系中的财产规定

Financial Agreements in Contemplation of Marriage Financial Agreements in contemplation of marriage are made pursuant to 90B of the Family Law Act 1975. This is essentially a contract where by each party agrees to divide their assets in a particular way, effectively deciding to	婚前财产协议 婚前财产协议根据1975年的《家庭法案》第90B条做出。它本质上是双方同意以特定方式分割其资产的合同，可以有

"contract out of the Act upon the breakdown of the marriage". Pursuant to 90G of the Act, a Financial Agreement in contemplation of marriage is binding where:

i. It has been signed by all parties to the Agreement;
ii. Before signing the Agreement, each person sought independent legal advice about the effect of the Agreement on their rights and the disadvantages of entering into the Agreement;
iii. Each party was provided with a signed statement from their legal practitioner;
iv. The signed statement has then been provided to the other party or their legal practitioner.

It then naturally follows the agreement can be set aside by a Court upon application by a party, such as where:
i. Either party has knowingly or recklessly made a false statement in relation to their circumstances, or has misrepresented them to the other person;
ii. The agreement has been entered into for the purpose of defeating a claim by third party creditors;
iii. The agreement is incomplete, uncertain or impracticable to carry out.

Financial Agreements during the Course of Marriage
For Financial Agreements made during the course of marriage, the legal requirements are similar to those made in contemplation of marriage.
Due to the complex nature of modern families, Financial Agreements signed during the course of marriage can promote marriage harmony.
A common scenario is when parties want to protect assets which are gifted or inherited from their respective parents. These assets are commonly accumulated through years of hard work and are often significantin amount. Given this, it is common for the parents to request for a financial

效地"在婚姻破裂时跳出法案"。根据该法第90G条,婚前财产协议在下列情况下具有约束力:
i. 协议各方已签字;
ii. 协议签署前,各方均就协议对其权利的影响以及签订本协议的不利之处寻求了独立的法律意见;
iii. 各方都获得了律师签署的声明;
iv. 该声明已提供给另一方或其律师。

在下列情况下,经一方当事人申请,法院可以撤销本协议:
i. 任何一方有意或不顾后果地就其情况做出虚假陈述;或向另一方做虚假陈述;
ii. 订立协议是为了逃避作为第三方的债务;
iii. 该协议不完整、不确定或无法实际执行。

婚姻期间的财产协议
婚姻期间财产协议的法律要求与婚前财产协议的法律要求类似。
由于现代生活的复杂性,婚姻期间的财产协议有助于促进婚姻的和谐。
由于财产是父母毕生劳动所得且一般数额巨大,婚姻双方希望保护其来自父母馈赠或从父母处继承的财产,而父母也通常要求双方当事人就在婚姻关

agreement to be signed prior to the gift or potential inheritance is made.

Property Settlement after Break Down of Marriage
There are two main methods for property settlement to be finalized in Australia:
i. By Financial Agreement between the Parties
This can be an agreement between the parties whether verbal or otherwise and is contractual in nature.

A more common and preferred method is for the parties to enter into a written agreement which is the approved by the court. A breach of the court order has legal consequences and the disadvantaged party will ordinarily seek enforcement through an application to Court.

ii. In the absence of agreement, the parties will ordinarily initiate litigation. This process is time-consuming and can be costly. It is commonly originated by the filing of an initiating application. Once proceedings are commenced the parties have a duty to make timely, full and frank disclosure of all information relevant to the issues in dispute including:

a. A schedule of assets, income and liabilities;
b. The party's three most recent taxation returns and assessments;
c. Superannuation records and details;
d. Corporation, trust and partnership documents.

系中所获赠予或潜在继承发生之前达成财产协议。

婚姻破裂后财产的处理
在澳大利亚，有两条主要的财产处理路径：
i. 由双方签订财产协议
当事人之间的协议，无论是口头协议还是其他协议，都具有契约性。

一种更为常见和受欢迎的方法是当事人双方签订经法院批准的书面协议。经法院批准的书面协议，被看作是法院命令。当事人一方违反法院命令，另一方可以请求法院强制执行。

ii. 没有协议的情况下，当事人可以通过诉讼解决财产分配问题。这个程序相当耗费时间，花费也高。诉讼过程由提交启动申请开始，一旦诉讼开始，双方有义务及时、全面和坦诚地披露与所涉争议问题有关的所有信息：

a. 资产、收入、负债明细表；
b. 最近三次纳税申报和纳税评估；
c. 退休金记录和细节；
d. 公司、信托及合伙关系文件。

本文本是澳大利亚有关婚姻财产问题的规定。英文文本中婚前、婚姻期间和婚姻破裂期间的表达值得借鉴，即 in contemplation of marriage, during the course of marriage 和 after break down of marriage。文中两次用到 legal practioner，有些译本译为"法律执业者"，但译为"律师"更佳。

"Either party has knowingly or recklessly made a false statement in relation to their circumstances" 中的 knowingly 译为"有意地"，而 recklessly 不可译为"鲁莽地"，而要

强调其"不顾后果"的含义。defeating a claim by third party creditors 译为"逃避作为第三方的债务"比较好。

"A common scenario is when parties want to protect assets which are gifted or inherited from their respective parents"段落的翻译调整幅度较大，按照汉语的逻辑结构先交代原因再介绍如何做比较容易理解，同时省略 a common scenario，这样既不缺失信息又减少读者的认知负载。

"... the disadvantaged party will ordinarily seek enforcement through an application to Court"句中，the disadvantaged party 并未被译成"弱势方"或"受害方"，而是译为"另一方当事人"；seek enforeecement through an application to Court 中的 Court 是"受理法院"的意思，剩余部分译为"请求强制执行"，其中"强制"是根据法律应有之意增加。

倒数第二句中的 superannuation 是澳大利亚的自有概念，也有人将其译为"超级年金""养老基金"。

3. 权利主张

我协会是经国家版权局正式批准成立的唯一音像著作权集体管理组织，依法对音像节目的著作权及与著作权有关的权利实施集体管理。2008年以来，我协会先后与权利人签署了《音像著作权授权合同》，以信托方式获得了权利人多首音乐电视作品的放映权、出租权、广播权、复制权，我协会有权以自己的名义对该音乐电视作品遭受侵权的行为提起诉讼。	Our association is the unique audio-video copyright administration established with the formal approval from National Copyright Administration and shall perform collective administration of the copyright of audio-video programs and the rights related to copyright law. Since 2008, our association has successively signed Audio-Video Copyright Authorization Contract with the right owner and obtained the right of playing, renting, broadcasting and reproducing many TV works of the right owner. Our association is entitled to lodge a complaint against the tort of the music TV works in the name of our own.
经查，ABC 公司未经权利人许可，也未支付费用，而在其营业场所的点唱机中完整地收录了我协会管理的 45 首音乐电视作品，侵犯了权利人的放映权、复制权。现我协会提起诉讼，要求 ABC 公司停止侵权，删除涉案音乐电视作品，赔偿经济损失及合理费用共计 20 万元。	In accordance with investigation, ABC Company has completely recorded 45 music TV works in its business places without approval of the right owner or paying any expenses, which infringes the right of playing and reproducing of the right owner. Hereby our association lodges a complaint to require that ABC Company to stop torting and delete the involved music TV works as well as compensate RMB 200,000 *yuan* in total for our economic loss and the reasonable expenses.

本文本的主题是知识产权纠纷，涉及一些知识产品方面的词汇，如"国家版权局"

(National Copyright Administration)、"放映权、出租权、广播权、复制权"（the right of playing, renting, broadcasting and reproducing）、"侵犯了权利人的放映权、复制权"（infringes the right of playing and reproducing of the right owner）等。第二段中的"经查"理解为"按照调查"，译为 according to 或 in accordance with。译文未译出"我协会管理的"也不影响理解，可以通过上下文推导出，译出反而显得啰唆。

4. 产品侵权

One engaged in the business of selling or otherwise distributing used products who sells or distributes a defective used product is subject to liability for harm to persons or property caused by the defect if the defect:	从事旧货销售或者以其他方式分发的经营者，销售或分发有缺陷的旧货，应对该缺陷所造成的人身或财产损害承担责任，如果该缺陷：
(a) arises from the seller, failure to exercise reasonable care; or	(a) 源于销售者未尽到合理注意义务；或
(b) is a manufacturing defect under 2 (a) or a defect that may be inferred under 3 and the seller, marketing of the product would cause a reasonable person in the position of the buyer to expect the used product to present no greater risk of defect than if the product were new; or	(b) 是第2条(a)款所规定的制造缺陷，或第3条规定的可以推断出的缺陷，并且销售者的产品营销会使处于与购买者相同环节的理性人期望该旧货不会比该产品全新时具有更大的风险；或者
(c) is a defect under 2 or 3 in a used product remanufactured by the seller or a predecessor in the commercial chain of distribution of the used product; or	(c) 是第2条和第3条规定的经过销售者或商业分发链条中的前手重制的旧货；或者
(d) arises from a used product, noncompliance under 4 with a product safety statute or regulation applicable to the used product.	(d) 源于根据第4条的规定，旧货违反了适用于旧货的产品安全法律或法规。
A used product is a product that, prior to the time of sale or other distribution referred to in this Section, is commercially sold or otherwise distributed to a buyer not in the commercial chain of distribution and used for some period of time.	旧货是指在本条中提到的销售或者以其他方式分发之前，被商业性地出售或者以其他方式分发给商业分发链条以外的购买者并被使用了一段时间的产品。

以上选自美国侵权法律文本，涉及二手商品经销中产生的问题，used product 译为"旧货"。其中一些短语表达在合同翻译中也被广泛使用，如 exercise reasonable care 意为"尽到合理注意义务"，而不是"行使合理注意义务"。

(b) 条款将购买者购买旧货的安全期待和购买新品的安全期待进行比较，译者需要理清 present no great risk of defect 的逻辑关系。最后一段是对旧货下定义。法律的每个概念不仅精密严谨，而且具体、有可操作性，译者要把握好每一个概念的界定，如commercially sold，distributed。

翻译练习

练习 1

因正当防卫造成损害的，防卫人不承担民事责任。正当范围超过必要限度，造成不应有的损害的，正当防卫人应承担适当的民事责任。

练习 2

因紧急避险造成损害的，由引起险情发生的人承担民事责任。危险由自然原因引起的，紧急避险人不承担民事责任，可以给予适当的补偿。紧急避险采取措施不当或者超过必要限度，造成不应有的损害的，紧急避险人应当承担民事责任。

练习 3

行为人没有代理权，超越代理权或代理权终止后，仍然实施代理行为，未经被代理人追认的，对被代理人不发生效力。

相对人可以催告被代理人自收到通知之日起一个月内予以追认。被代理人未做表示的，视为拒绝追认。行为人实施的行为被追认前，善意相对人有撤销的权利。撤销应当以通知的方式做出。

行为人实施的行为未被追认的，善意相对人有权请求行为人履行债务或者就其受到的损害请求行为人赔偿，但是赔偿的范围不得超过被代理人追认时相对人所能获得的利益。

相对人知道或者应当知道行为人无权代理的，相对人和行为人按照各自的过错承担责任。

练习 4

The most common type of property ownership today is the fee simple. Generally, the term "fee simple" is used to designate a fee simple absolute, in which the owner has the greatest possible aggregation of rights, priviliges, and power. The fee simple is limted absolutely to a person and his or her heirs and is assigned forever without limitation or condition. Furthermore, the owner has the rights of exclusive possession and use of property. A fee simple is potentially infinitely in duration and can be disposed of by deed or by will. When there is no will, the fee simple passes to the owner's legal heirs.

练习 5

Fixtures have been variously defined as objects which were originally personal property but which, by reason of their annexation to or use in association with real property, have become a part of the realty; as chattels so attached to realty that, for the time being, they become a part therof; and as chattels annexed to realty in such manner that they cannot be removed without injury to the freehold. However, there is no single statement defining such use which is capable of application in all situations. The principle significance of a determination that an object is a fixture is that it is thereafter treated as part and parcel of the land and may not generally be removed therefrom except by the owner of the realty.

第五章
民法的基本知识和翻译（下）

合同是双方或多方当事人（自然人或法人）关于建立、变更、消灭民事法律关系的协议。此类合同是产生债的一种最为普遍和重要的根据，故又称债权合同。合同有时也泛指产生一定权利、义务的协议，又称契约，如买卖合同、师徒合同、劳动合同、工厂与车间订立的承包合同等。

合同订立的原则有五点：合同当事人的法律地位平等，一方不得将自己的意志强加给另一方；当事人依法享有自愿订立合同的权利，任何单位和个人不得非法干预；当事人应当遵循公平原则确定各方的权利和义务；当事人行使权利、履行义务应当遵循诚实守信的原则；当事人订立、履行合同应当遵守法律、行政法规，尊重社会公德，不得干扰社会经济秩序、损害社会公共利益。

合同有效的一个重要要素是双方都需要付出对价。换句话说，如果只是单方做出承诺，如赐予某些物品给另一方，这类承诺不能成为有效合同。受益方也应做出对应的承诺或对价。

美国没有《合同法》，但有《统一商法典》（Uniform Commercial Code）。《统一商法典》共分9篇：总则（general provisions）；买卖（sales）；租赁（leases）；商业票据（negotiable instruments）；银行存款收款（bank deposits and collections）；大批转让（bulk transfer）；信用证（letters of credit），涉及提单和货栈收据（documents of title）；投资证券（investment securities）；有担保的交易（secured transactions）。其中以第2篇"买卖"的篇幅最长、最重要。这一法典代替了过去的一些单行商事法规，包括《统一流通票据法》《统一买卖法》《统一仓库收据法》《统一提单法》《统一股票转让法》《统一附条件销售法》《统一信托收据法》等。

英国合同法是英国规定合同的法律，其中包含《1979年的货物买卖法》（Sale of Goods Act 1979），英国合同法的基本原则几乎是法院制定的。它继承自中世纪商法，受司法能动主义影响，因此与澳大利亚、加拿大和印度等邦联国的合同法有共同之处。

澳大利亚合同法的根源是英国普通法。虽然大致是按照普通法起草的，但在某些方面，合同内容会受到条文法的影响，如《2010年联邦竞争和消费者权益法》（Competition and Consumer Act 2010）。

本章主要讲解《民法典》第三编"合同"部分中的常见术语，以及英美法系中有关合同订立、履行、违约、救济等重要部分的表达和理解。

第一节　常用术语

合同领域的常用术语见表 5-1。

表 5-1　合同领域的常用术语及其英文表达

术语	英译
适用法	applicable law
不动产	real estate
服务合同	service contract
货物买卖	sale of goods
标的物	subject matter
混合交易	mixed deals
货物租赁	lease of goods
可法律强制执行的，有法律效力的	legally enforceable
要约	offer
承诺	acceptance
要约人	offeror
受要约人	offeree
要约终止	termination of the offer
意思表示	manifestation
按需供应合同	requirement contract
产品包销合同，全部产出量合同	entire output contract
报价单	price quotation
无民事行为能力	incapacity
不可撤销要约	irrevocable offer
对价	consideration
经签署的书面承诺	signed/ written promise
反要约	counter offer
合理地可预见的	reasonably foreseeable
发出即生效主义	mailbox rule
未成年人	infant；minor
精神病人	mental incompetent

续表

术语	英译
准合同	quasi-contract
醉酒的人	intoxicated person
胁迫	duress
公众政策	public policy
误解	mistake
误述，不实陈述	misrepresentation
保证人	guarantor
保证	guarantee
部分履行	part performance
全部履行	full performance
合同修改	contract modification
签订合同	enter into contract
书面证据	written proof
汇票	bill of exchange
建筑承包商，营造商	building contractor
大买户	bulk buyer
大宗货物的交付	bulk delivery
业务状况	business status
另邮/函	by separate post/mail/cover
撤销订单/订货	cancel an order
标题所述订单	captioned order
运费保险费付至……	Carriage & Insurance Paid to...
运费付至……	Carriage Paid to (CPT)...
订货付款，随订单付现	Cash With Order (CWO)
限价	ceiling price
处理订单，备货	complete an order
连署签名	counter-signature
资信状况	credit status
现价	current/prevailing price
付款交单	documents against payment
预订金	down payment

续表

术语	英译
起草合同	draft a contract
未能履行某事	failure to do sth.
主要损害赔偿之诉	sue for damages
分期合同	installment contract
补救机会	cure opportunity
合理理由	reasonable ground
拒绝接收货物	rejection of the goods
尽合理注意义务	take reasonable care
不相符货物	nonconforming goods
合理信赖	reasonable reliance
第三方受益	third-party beneficiary
抗辩事由	defense
权利的转让	assignment
转让人	assignor
被转让人	assignee
义务人	obligor
禁止	prohibition
装运单据	shipping document
不可转让	not assignable
试销订单	trial order
业务/经营范围	line of business
标价，目录价格	list price
从订货到交货的间隔时间	lead time
毛价，总价	gross price
最大折扣	maximum discount
备货	meet an order
母公司	parent company
利润赚头/幅度	profit margin
即期装运	prompt shipment
临时订单	provisional order
数量折扣	quantity discount

续表

术语	英译
补充库存，进货	replenish stocks
最底价	rock-bottom price
禁令救济	injunctive relief
期待利益损失	expectation damages
结果性损失	consequential damages
附带支出	incidental costs
约定违约金	liquidated damages
根本违约	material breach
可分合同	divisible contract
预期违约	anticipatory repudiation
中止履行	suspend performance
明示条件	express condition
条件成就	satisfaction of a condition
合同解除	cancellation
替代履行	substituted performance
标的物毁损	damage of subject matter
履行不能	impossibility
补偿性损害赔偿金	compensatory damages
间接性损害赔偿金	consequential damages
惩罚性损害赔偿金	punitive damages

第二节 核心术语的表达和理解

1. outline of the contract

合同正文基本可以分为三部分：general provision（通用条款）、useful provision（常见条款）、operation provision（操作性条款）。

具体而言，合同结构（outline of the contract）如下所示：

一、标题

二、导言

（一）开场白

（二）鉴于条款

（三）过渡条款

三、正文

（一）通用条款

1. 定义条款（definition）

2. 陈述与保证（representations and warranties）

3. 补偿条款（indemnification/hold harmless）

4. 保密条款（confidentiality）

5. 期间与终止（term and termination）

6. 合同的转让与变更（assignment and modification）

7. 合同完整性（entire agreement）

8. 可分性条款（severability）

9. 不弃权（non-waiver）

10. 不可抗力（force majeure）

11. 竞业禁止（non-competition）

12. 知识产权（intellectual property rights）

13. 违约条款（breach of contract）

14. 纠纷解决条款（dispute resolution）

15. 其他条款（miscellaneous）

（二）常用条款

1. 先决条件（conditions precedent）

2. 保险条款（insurance）

3. 独立合同关系条款（independent contractor relationship）

4. 税收条款（taxation）

（三）操作性条款

四、结尾和附录

2. offer，acknowledgement

offer 意为"要约"，是一方当事人以缔结合同为目的向对方当事人提出合同条件，希望对方当事人接受的意思表示。发出要约的一方被称为要约人，接受要约的一方被称为受要约人。

acknowledgement 意为"承诺"，是受要约人同意要约的意思表示。承诺应当以通知的方式做出，但根据交易习惯或者要约表明可以通过行为做出承诺的除外。承诺的内容不得对要约做实质性的否定或更改，否则就是反要约，也就是一个新的要约。

3. consideration

consideration 一般译为"对价"，也有人将其译为"约因"。对价是作为换取承诺的代价，由作为或者不作为构成，而该作为或者不作为让允诺人受益或者受允诺人受损。在英美法系中，合同是一种允诺，对价对允诺人来说是损害，而对受允诺人是添益，它强调的是互为有偿、相互给付。对价必须是合法的，要具有某种价值，需要来自受允诺人。

executory consideration 意为"待履行对价"，是双方当事人达成协议时做出的一项承诺，即双方分别答应在未来某个时间做某事。

executed consideration 意为"已履行对价"，该对价的内容已经被合同当事人履行完毕。

past consideration 意为"过去的对价"。行动要么和承诺同时发生（已履行对价），要么在承诺之后发生（待履行对价），才算是有效的对价，如果行动在承诺之前发生了（过去的对价），那么这种对价是无效的。因此，过去的对价其实就是一种无效的对价。

4. power of attorney

授权委托书（power of attorney）是一种书面授权，有时简写为 POA，借此可以代表他人处理相关事务。

授权委托书主要涉及三类人员或组织：授予权利之人，被称为委托人；接收权利之人，被称为代理人或事实代理人（the attorney-in-fact）；代理人代表委托人与之互动的第三方（the agent interacts on the principal's behalf）。

5. privacy policy

隐私政策（privacy policy）是一种声明或法律文件，披露了一方收集、使用、披露和管理顾客或客户数据（个人信息）的部分或全部方式。

个人信息可以是任何可用于识别个人的信息，不限于个人的姓名、地址、出生日期（date of birth）、婚姻状况（marital status）、联系信息（contact information）、身份证签发和到期日期（ID issue and expiry date）、财务记录（financial records）、信用信息（credit information）、病史（medical history）等。

6. franchise agreement

特许经营协议（franchise agreemeet）是一项具有法律约束力的协议，概述了特许人对被特许人设定的条款和条件，以及特许人和被特许人应承担的义务。实施特许经营后，特许人将其专有技术、程序、知识产权、商业模式的使用、品牌以及出售其品牌产品和服务的权利授予被特许人。作为对价，被特许人须向特许人支付一定的费用，并同意履行通常在特许协议中载明的相关义务。

特许经营协议的基本要素：特许经营协议的期限（duration of the franchise agreement）；初始和持续费用（initial and continuing fees）；分配的许可区域（assigned territory）；选址和开发（site selection and development）；初始和持续的培训与支持（initial and ongoing training and support）；使用知识产权，包括商标、专利、说明书（use of the intellectual property including trademarks, patents, manuals）；保险要求（insurance requirements）；记录保存和审查被特许人记录的权利（record-keeping and the rights to audit the franchisee's records）。

7. non-waiver clause

non-waiver clause 意为"不弃权条款"，其制定目的是确保合同一方在另一方违反合同的情况下，不会意外或非正式地放弃（informally waive）其根据合同提起诉讼（bring proceedings）、追索损害赔偿（recover damages）等权利。此类条款可规定：合同权利（contractual rights）只能通过书面通知（a written notice）予以放弃。

8. breach of contract

breach of contract 意为"违约"。当一方或双方未能履行合同中规定的义务时（fail to perform its duties），即发生违约。民法旨在向受损害的一方提供损害赔偿，并使其恢复到违约发生前的状态（restore them to where they were before the breach occurred），或者恢复到如同合同已经执行时的状态（to a position as if the contract had been executed）。

对原告造成严重损害的案件的裁决可能包括金钱救济，如赔偿金（compensatory damages）、恢复原状（restitution）、违约赔偿金（liquidated damages）、象征性的损害赔偿（nominal damages）和惩罚性损害赔偿（punitive damages）。

9. assignment clause

assignment clause 意为"转让条款"，它决定协议项下的权利、义务和责任是否可以被全部或部分（in whole or in part）转让给另一方，以及在何种条件下可以进行转让。合同权利是可以自由转让或可委托（他人行使）的（freely assignable or delegable），除非协议另有规定或限制。

合同中的转让条款一般会写成"Neither party may assign this Agreement or any of their rights or obligations under this Agreement without the other party's written consent."，即未经另一方书面同意，双方均不得转让本协议或其在本协议项下的任何权利或义务。

10. force majeure

force majeure 意为"不可抗力"，是指为免除因自然灾害和不可避免灾害（该等自然灾害将中断事件的预期进程，并限制参与者履行其义务）产生的责任，而在合同中订立的条款。force majeure 是法语词，意思是"更强大的力量"。不可抗力与天灾的概念有关，在出现天灾的情况下，任何一方都无须为之负责。天灾包括地震、海啸、飓风等。不可抗力也包括人的行为，如武装冲突。一般来说，构成不可抗力的事件必须是不可预见的、合同双方以外的且不可避免的。这些概念在不同的司法管辖区有不同的定义和适用情况。

11. representations and warranties

绝大多数合同都有陈述和保证条款（representations and warranties），该陈述和保证基本上是根据合同条款提出的基本事项或事实。当出售诸如房产之类的东西时，卖方陈述其自身拥有出售该财产的合法权利，保证关于财产的事实如其所述。

合同的陈述和保证条款常见如下：

① Representations and Warranties of the Sellers. Except as set forth in the Seller Disclosure Schedule, each Seller hereby represents and warrants to the Companies as of the Closing Date as follows.

卖方的陈述和保证。除《卖方披露表》中所载情况外，截至交割日期，每一卖方特此向公司陈述并保证如下：

12. company，corporation，firm

company 是指数人为了共同目标，特别是为了营利而设立的一种联合组织，有独特的组织形式、经营管理方式和责任承担方式。其重要特征是具有法人地位，其存在不因公司成员的变化而受影响。

在英国有三种公司：一是股份有限公司（company limited by shares），即股东对公司承担提供资产的责任，但以其根据公司章程认购的股份中可能尚未缴清的股金为限，如果其已全部付足股金，则对公司债务不承担责任。这种公司以营利为目的，是最普通的公司形式。二是保证有限公司（company limited by guarantee），即股东的责任以其已在公司章程中做出的保证在公司清算时向公司承担提供资产的数额为限。三是无限公司（unlimited company），即股东对公司债务承担无限责任，该种公司形式并不常见。

company 在美国泛指任何企业，不论它是独资企业（sole proprietorship），还是合伙企业（partnership）或公司（corporation）。在普通法中，corporation 指一切具有法人资格的团体，而 company 既可表示合伙企业又可指非法人的人合团体。

corporation 最初是指法人。为了与自然人（natural person）相区别，法人有时又被称为拟制的人（artificial person）、法律上的人（juristic person）或团体人（corporate person）。在英国法中，法人分为集合法人（corporation aggregate）和独体法人（corporation sole）两类。corporation 还可以指公司。在美国，该词通常在此义项上被使用，即指根据法律授权而可以用独立于股东的人格实施行为并能够永续存在的实体（通常是商业实体）。在英国该词多被用于指市政法人（municipal corporation），即从事民用业务的市政当局。对应于"公司"义项，英国通常用 company。因此，公司法在英国是 company law，在美国则是 corporation law。

firm 可被理解为商行、非法人商务团体、两人或多人的合伙、（全体）合伙的成员。

13. indemnification

indemnification 是指赔偿条款，也被称为免责条款，是合同中用来将潜在成本从一方转移到另一方的条款。赔偿条款的主要利益着眼点是保护受偿方（the indemnified party）免受与合同有关的、因第三方索赔而引起的损失。一般赔偿条款可以写成：

② Each party agrees to indemnify, defend, and hold harmless the other party from and against any loss, cost, or damage of any kind (including reasonable outside attorneys' fees) to the extent arising out of its breach of this Agreement, and/or its negligence or willful misconduct.

每一方同意赔偿、辩护并使另一方免受因其违反本协议和/或其疏忽或故意不当行为导致的任何损失、成本或损害（包括合理的外部律师费）。

14. waiver

waiver 通常是指对合法权利或要求的放弃。相应地，non-waiver 就是"不弃权"的意思。waiver 通常是指对某一法律文件内规定的所有相关权利的放弃，不过对其具体含义要根据条款的上下文语境进行理解，如下例中就是放弃追索违约行为的权利。

③ No waiver by either party of the breach of any term or covenant contained in this agreement, whether by conduct or otherwise, in one or more instances, shall be deemed to be, or construed as, a further or continuing waiver of any breach, or a waiver of the breach of any terms or covenants contained in this agreement.

任意一方放弃追索任何违反本主服务协议任何条款或协约的行为，无论是否通过行为暗示弃权，也无论存在一次还是多次弃权，均不得视为或理解为对任何违约行为的进一步或持续弃权，或对违反本主服务协议任何条款或协约的弃权。

15. remedial measure

remedial measure 意为"补救措施"，是指在当事人发生违约的事实后，为防止损失的发生或者扩大，而由违约方按照法律的规定或者合同的约定采取的修理（repairing）、更换（substituting）、重做（reworking）、退货（returning the goods）、减少价款（reducing the price）或者付报酬（remuneration）、补充数量（supplementing quantities）等措施，以使另一方弥补或者减少损失的违约责任形式。

补救措施主要是针对标的物质量不符合合同约定而采取的一种违约责任形式，这种违约行为的构成要件有：债务人做出了履行，只是履行不当，这种不当是指质量上不符合规定；不当履行合同无正当理由。在采取补救措施后，买方还有其他损失的，卖方应当赔偿损失。如约定为：

④ 货物到达目的地时，如发现与合同规定的样品不符，买方有权要求卖方承担更换或退货的违约责任。在卖方采取上述措施后，买方还有其他损失的，卖方仍应赔偿损失。

Should the goods be found, on their arrival at destination, to be different from the sample specified in the Contract, the Buyer shall request the Seller to bear the liabilities for substituting or returning the Goods. The Seller shall, after taking the remedial measures hereinabove, compensate for the losses, if the Buyer suffers from other losses.

16. penalty

违约金（penalty）可以分为法定违约金（legal penalty）和约定违约金（contractual penalty）。《民法典》第五百八十五条规定：

⑤ 当事人可以约定一方违约时应当根据违约情况向对方支付一定数额的违约金，也可以约定因违约产生的损失赔偿额的计算方法。

The parties may stipulate in a contract that if either party breaches the contract it shall pay a certain amount of damages for breach of the contract to the other party, depending on the situation of the breach of the contract. They may also stipulate a method for calculating the damages resulting from such a breach.

17. severance

severance 意为"可分割性"，指的是若合同的某项规定被判为无效、违法或无法强制实施，则该规定不被视为本合同的组成部分，其他规定的有效性与可实施性不受影响。具有代表性的可分割性条款如下文：

⑥ If any provision of this Agreement (or part of any provision) is found by any court or other authority of competent jurisdiction to be invalid, illegal or unenforceable, that provision or part-provision shall, to the extent required, be deemed not to form part of this Agreement, and the validity and enforceability of the other provision of the Agreement shall not be affected.

若本合同的任何规定（或任何规定的其中一部分）被任何法庭或其他司法机构判为无效、违法或无法强制实施，按照法律要求，该规定或部分规定则不被视为本合同的组成部分，本合同其他规定的有效性与可实施性不受影响。

⑦ If a provision of this Agreement (or part of anyprovision) is found illegal, invalid or unenforceable, that provision shall in good faith with a view to realizing the purpose of this Agreement, apply with the minimum modification necessary to make it legal, valid and enforceable.

若本合同的任何规定（或任何规定的其中一部分）被发现无效、违法或无法强制实施，合同各方应本着善意真诚的态度进行协商，尽量修改该规定，使其合法、有效且可执行。

18. govern, apply, prevail

三个单词都有"适用"和"管辖"的意思。

普通英语中，govern 可理解为"统治""治理"等，跟"管辖"在本质上是一致的。

apply 的含义很多，但在特定语境中，用法等同于 govern，特别是在合同中的法律适用条款。如"Does the same copyright law apply to electronic materials as printed materials?"（用于印刷物的著作权法是否同样适用于电子图书?）。有些法律文本将

govern 和 apply 并用，如"These general Terms and Conditions of Purchase shall govern and apply to all orders placed by companies of the SICK group within …"（这些通用的采购合同条款应适用于 SICK 集团旗下公司的所有订单……）。

prevail 在普通英语中可理解为"占优势"和"普遍接受"，但译成汉语往往是"以……为准"，常用在有比较的情境中，如"When a law of State is inconsistent with a law of the Common Wealth, the latter shall prevail."（如果州的法律和国家法律相冲突，适用国家法律）。

19. abide by, comply with

abide by 与 comply with 都有"遵守"的意思。主语是人时，"遵守"的英译须用 abide by；主语是非人称时，则用 comply with，如"Both parties shall abide by the contractual stipulations."（双方都应遵守合同规定），"All the activities of both parties shall comply with the contractual stipulations."（双方的一切活动都应遵守合同规定）。

20. shipping advice, shipping instructions

shipping advice 意为"装运通知"，是由出口商（卖主）发给进口商（买主）的。shipping instructions 意为"装运须知"，是进口商（买主）发给出口商（卖主）的。另外要注意区分 delivery note（送货回执）与 delivery order（交货单）、vendor（卖主）与 vendee（买主）、consignor（发货人）与 consignee（收货人）。英译上述四对词语时极易产生笔误。

21. ex, per, by

源自拉丁语的介词 ex 与 per 有各自不同的含义。翻译由某轮船"运来"的货物用 ex，翻译由某轮船"运走"的货物用 per，而翻译由某轮船"承运"的货物用 by。例如：

⑧ 由"维多利亚"轮运走/运来/承运的最后一批货将于 8 月 10 日抵达伦敦。

The last batch per/ex/by S. S. "Victoria" will arrive at London on 10th August. (S. S. = Steamship)

22. in, after

多少天之后的时间往往是指多少天之后的具体某一天，英译必须用介词 in，而不能用 after，因为 after 指的是多少天之后的不确切的任何一天。例如：

⑨ 该货于 8 月 10 日由"巨浪"轮运出，41 天后抵达纽约港。

The goods shall be shipped per M. V. "JuLang" on 10th August and are due to arrive at New York Port in 41 days. (M. V. = motor vessel)

如果用 after 代替 in，就是指在 41 天之后的某一天抵达，而不是确切的 41 天后。

第三节　常见句型结构

合同文件是合同双方签订并必须遵守的法律文件，而合同本身也不能违背相关法律法规，因此合同中的语言应体现其权威性。英文合同用语的特点之一就表现在特定结构上，即选择特定用词结构及正式用词，使合同表达的意思准确无误，达到双方对合同中使用的词无可争议的程度，从而减少隐患和不必要的诉讼纠纷。

1. … subject to …

在法律文本中，subject to 是"遵照，依从"的意思，可以理解为 dependent upon，如"The proposed merger with Abliba is subject to the approval of all the shareholder."。subject to 还可以理解为 under the authority of。它的强制性遵守程度接近 abide by，有时与 shall 或 must 连用。

即使在合同翻译中不与 must 或 shall 连用，subject to 的强制意味也不弱。例如：

⑩ Employee shall perform the duties consistent with his role as President and Chief Executive Officer, <u>subject to</u> direction from THE COMPANY's Board of Directors.

雇员应履行他作为主席和首席执行官的义务，并<u>遵守</u>公司董事会的指示。

2. … hereby …

hereby 是"特此，因此，兹"的意思，常用于法律文件、合同、协议书等正式文件的开头语；也可用于条款中需要强调时，常被置于主语后，紧邻主语。例如：

⑪ The Employer <u>hereby</u> covenants to pay the Contracting consideration of the execution and completion of the Works and the remedying of defects therein the Contract Price or such other sum as may become payable under the provisions of the Contract at the time and in the manner prescribed by the Contract.

业主特此立约保证在合同规定的期限内，按合同规定的方式向承包人支付合同对价，或合同规定的其他应支付的款项，以作为本工程施工、竣工及修补工程中缺陷的报酬。

⑫ We <u>hereby</u> certify to the best of our knowledge that the foregoing statement is true and correct and all available information and data have been supplied herein, and that we agree to provide documentary proof upon your request.

<u>特此证明</u>，据我们所知，上述声明内容真实、正确无误，并提供了全部现有的资料和数据，我们同意应贵方要求出具证明文件。

hereby 还常见于合同的开始部分，用在 contract 之后。例如：

⑬ This Contract is <u>hereby</u> made and concluded by and between ABC Co. (hereinafter referred to as Party A) and DEF Co. (hereinafter referred to as Party B) on

_____（Date）, in Nantong, China, on the principle of equality and mutual benefit and through amicable consultation.

本合同双方，ABC公司（以下称"甲方"）与DEF公司（以下称"乙方"），在平等互利的基础上，通过友好协商，于_____年____月____日在中国南通，特签订本合同。

3. … hereof …

hereof 可理解为"本合同的/本文件的……"，如表示本合同条件、条款时，可以说 the terms, conditions and provisions hereof, hereof 表示 of this Contract；又如表示本工程的任何部分，可以用 any parts hereof, hereof 表示 of this Works。hereof 一般被置于要修饰的名词后面，与之紧邻。

hereof 强调 of this, thereof 表示 of the Contract。例如：

⑭ Whether the custom of the Port is contrary to this Clause or not, the owner of the goods shall, without interruption, by day and night, including Sundays and holidays (if required by the carrier), supply and take delivery of the goods. The owner of the goods shall be liable for all losses or damages including demurrage incurred in default on the provisions hereof.

不论港口习惯是否与本款规定相反，货方都应昼夜地，包括星期日和假日（如承运人需要），无间断地提供和提取货物。货方对违反本款规定所引起的所有损失或损坏，包括滞期应负担赔偿责任。

⑮ 本法所称对外贸易经营者，是指依照本法规定从事对外贸易经营活动的法人和其他组织。

Foreign trade dealers as mentioned in this Law shall, in accordance with the provisions hereof, cover such legal entities and other organizations as are engaged in foreign trade dealings.

4. … hereto …

hereto 意为"至此，在此上"，表示上文已提及的"本合同的……, 本文件的……"。表示"本合同双方"，用 the Parties hereto, hereto 表示 to this Contract；表示"本协议附件1"，可用 Appendix 1 hereto, hereto to this Agreement。同 hereof 和 thereof 的区别类似，hereto 强调的是 to this。例如：

⑯ All disputes arising from the performance of this Contract shall, through amicable negotiations, be settled by the Parties hereto. Should, through negotiations, no settlement be reached, the case in question shall then be submitted for arbitration to the China International Economic and Trade Arbitration Commission, Beijing and the arbitration rules of this Commission shall be applied. The award of the arbitration shall be final and binding upon the Parties hereto. The Arbitration fee shall be borne by the losing party unless otherwise awarded by the Arbitration Commission.

对于因履行本合同所发生的一切争议，本合同双方应通过友好协商解决，如协商无法解决争议，则应将争议提交中国国际经济贸易仲裁委员会（北京），依据其仲裁规则进行仲裁。仲裁裁决是终局性的，对双方都有约束力。仲裁费用应由败诉方承担，但仲裁委员会另有裁定的除外。

例⑯的条款是仲裁条款。the performance of this Contract 译为"履行本合同"；amicable negotiations 译为"友好协商"；the Parties hereto 可以理解为 the Parties to this Contract，即"本合同双方"；shall then be submitted for arbitration 译为"提交进行仲裁"；the China International Economic and Trade Arbitration Commission, Beijing 是仲裁机构，即中国国际经济贸易仲裁委员会（北京）；the arbitration rules of this Commission 译为"其仲裁规则"；the award of the arbitration 译为"仲裁裁决"；unless otherwise awarded by the Arbitration Commission 译为"仲裁委员会另有裁定的除外"，其中 award 并非普通英语中的"奖励"，而是"裁定"。再如：

⑰ The parties to this Agreement agree that either Party hereto shall, immediately and fully, notify the other Party hereto of any such matters comprising an improvement, modification, further invention or design.

本协议各方同意，一方所做的改进、修正、更新发明或设计均应立即全部通知另一方。

该句中有两处 hereto，分别位于合同主体之后，可理解为 to this agreement，表示是本合同的主体。请再看一例：

⑱ The Parties to this Agreement agree that the Board of Directors authorized by the Parties hereto to administrate or manage FCAM shall be responsible for approving the overall business management plan of the company, and monitoring the execution of the plan in question. Provided that the business management plan in question shall be submitted to the Parties hereto for review and approval.

本协议双方同意授权管理 FCAM 的董事会对公司整体经营计划的报批和监督执行负责。该经营计划需要提交协议双方审阅和批准。

例⑱的表述中有一些固定表达，如 Board of Directors authorized by the Parties hereto（本协议双方授权的董事会）、to administrate or manage FCAM（管理 FCAM）。administrate 一般理解为"行政管理"，而 manage 译为"业务管理"。the overall business management plan of the company 译为"公司整体经营计划"，monitoring the execution of the plan in question 译为"监督该计划执行"，review and approval 常译为"审阅和批准"。两处 hereto 都位于 the Parties 之后，可理解为 Parties to this Agreement。

5. … herein …

herein 是"此中,于此"的意思,如"本法(中)所称的不正当竞争"可译为 unfair competition mentioned herein,herein 表示 in this Law;"本协议(中)内容"可译为 the Contents herein,herein 表示 in this Agreement。herein 常被置于所修饰词之后,紧邻所修饰词。例如:

⑲ Unfair competition mentioned in this Law refers to such acts of business operators as contravene the provisions hereof, with a result of damaging the lawful rights and interests of other business operators, and disturbing the socio-economic order.

Business operators mentioned herein refer to such legal persons, other economic organizations and individuals as engage in the trading of goods or profit-making services (hereafter called Goods including services).

本法所称的不正当竞争,是指经营者违反本法规定,损害其他经营者的合法权益,扰乱社会经济秩序的行为。

本法所称的经营者,是指从事商品经营或营利性服务(以下所称商品包括服务)的法人、其他经济组织和个人。

⑳ This Law is hereby formulated and prepared in order to develop the foreign trade, maintain the foreign trade order and promote the healthy development of the socialist market economy.

Foreign trade mentioned herein shall cover the import and export of goods, technology and the international trade in services.

为了发展对外贸易,维护对外贸易秩序,促进社会主义市场经济的健康发展,兹制定本法。

本法所称对外贸易,是指货物进出口、技术进出口和国际服务贸易。

6. … whereby …

whereby 的英文解释为 by the agreement/by the following terms and conditions 等,一般译为"凭此协议,凭此条款"等。例如:

㉑ This Agreement is made and concluded by and between Dump Corporation (hereinafter referred to as Party A) and Tump Company (hereinafter referred to as Party B) whereby the Parties hereto agree to enter into the compensation trade under the terms and conditions set forth below…

本协议由 Dump 公司(以下简称"甲方")和 Tump 公司(以下简称"乙方")签订。双方同意按下列条款进行补偿贸易……

7. ... as ...

合同中 as 出现的频率极高，用法灵活多变。因此，在法律翻译界，有人甚至认为对 as 使用的熟练程度可以衡量合同拟订人的英语造诣。

as 位于意为"规定"的 provide, stipulate, set forth, prescribe 等词的过去分词前，译为"依照某规定"。例如：

㉒ For purpose of this, Capital Account shall be adjusted hypothetically as provided for in Section 4.6 herein.

基于此，应依照本合同第四条第六款调整资金账户。

㉓ based on their respective Venture interests as set forth in Section 5.2 hereof

基于本合同第五条第二款规定的各方在合资公司中的权益

另有 except as otherwise provided 结构，表示"除非本文/某条款另有规定"。例如：

㉔ Except as otherwise provided herein, all notices or demands sent by registered airmail shall be deemed received 8 days after they have been sent and notices or demands sent by telex shall be deemed received at the time of the dispatch thereof.

除非本合同另有规定，所有通知和请求以航空挂号信寄出则发出后 8 日应视为送达收悉，以电传方式发出则在发送时视为收悉。

as 构成 as the case may be（视具体情况而定）、as the case may require（视具体要求而定）、as the Venturers may determine（视投资者决策而定）等短语。例如：

㉕ The Venture may relocate its office from time to time or have additional offices as the Venturers may determine.

该合资公司视投资者决策，可随时迁址或增添营业场所。

as 构成 as of 短语，是"自某年某月某日起"的意思，为最正式的表达方式。例如：

㉖ In witness whereof, the parties have caused this instrument to be duly executed as of the day and year first above written.

合同双方签订本文件，该文件自以上书就日期即时生效，特此为证。

as 还被用在 as soon as practical 短语中，意义和用法相当于 as soon as possible。例如：

㉗ During the Employment Period, the Company agrees that it shall recommend to the Board the election of the Employee as a Director of the Company on the Commencement Date or as soon as practical thereafter.

本公司同意在聘用期间，应自本协议开始或其后尽早的时间向董事会推选受聘方为本公司董事。

8. remain the property of sb., be vested in sb.

表示某物的所有权属于某人，如果用 the ownership of sth. belongs to sb. 或 sb. owns/

possesses sth. 不够正式，而且 possess 指目前属于某人，并不能说明来源，而 own 只表示"对……的合法占有"，显然不适合用在字斟句酌的法律文本中。我们建议使用 sth. be／remain the property of sb.，be vested in sb. 等结构。例如：

㉘ Any drawings or technical documents interested for use in the Construction of the Plant or of part thereof and submitted to the Seller by the Buyer prior or subsequent to formation of the Contract <u>remain the exclusive property of the Buyer</u>.

本合同订立前后由买方送交卖方用于建筑设备或其部分设备的图纸或技术资料<u>仍为买方的专有财产</u>。

㉙ Licensee hereby agrees that at the termination or expiration of this agreement Licensee will be deemed to have assigned, transferred and conveyed to Licensor any rights, equities, good will, titles or other rights in and to the Name which may have been obtained by Licensee or which may have <u>been vested in Licensee</u> in pursuance of any endeavors covered hereby, and that Licensee will execute any instruments requested by Licensor to accomplish or confirm the foregoing.

被许可方特此同意本协议终止或届满时，被许可方视为以和对该名义可能已获得或经努力已所有的任何权利、权益、商誉、所有权或其他权利转让给许可方，并且被许可方应在许可方的要求下签署完成或确认上述内容的任何文件。

9. saving clause

在英文合同中，saving clause（除外条款，但书条款）通常有 save that 句型和 save as 句型，表示"……者例外"。例如：

㉚ The provisions of Paragraph 5 and Paragraph 11 of the US Plan apply mutatis mutandis to the UK Scheme, <u>save that</u> if an amendment is made to the UK Scheme or to the terms of an Approved Stock Option at a time when the UK Scheme is approved by the Inland Revenue under Schedule 8, the approval will not thereafter have effect unless the Inland Revenue have approved the alteration or addition.

对应用于英方方案的美方规划的第 5 节和第 11 节的规定已做必要的修正，<u>除非对英方方案或已批准股票期权条款的修改时值根据附件 8 英方方案已获批准，此后该批准不得生效，除非内税局已批准该改变或增补</u>。

㉛ <u>Save as</u> expressly provided herein, this Agreement may be amended or terminated, and any of the terms hereof waived, only by a document in writing specifically referring to this Agreement and executed by the parties hereto or, in the case of a waiver, by the party waiving compliance.

<u>除非本协议明确规定</u>，本协议可被修改或终止，本协议任一条款可被放弃，当且仅当通过书面文件特别提及本协议并由本协议双方执行或一方通过弃权声明放弃遵守。

此外，proviso 表示限制条款或但书。例如：

㉜ Legal Proceedings; Injunctions. (a) The Seller, the Buyer and the Company shall use commercially reasonable efforts [subject to the proviso in Section 5.6 (b)] to cooperate with each other in connection with any claim, action, suit, proceeding, inquiry or investigation with any other person which relates to the execution and delivery of this Agreement or the consummation of the transactions contemplated hereunder.

法律诉讼；禁止令 (a) 卖方、买方和本公司应竭尽全力[除第5.6 (b) 款的但书规定外]互相配合处理涉及本合同履行与交付及本合同项下预期交易完成的与他方有关的索赔、诉讼、案件、诉讼程序、质询或调查。

㉝ Tenant shall not be required to join in any proceedings referred to in the proviso at the end of 4.6 hereof unless the provisions of any law, rule or regulation at the time in effect shall require that such proceedings be brought by or in the name of Tenant, in which event Tenant shall join and cooperate in such proceedings or permit the same to be brought in its name, but shall not be liable for the payment of any costs or expenses in connection with any such proceedings, and Landlord shall reimburse Tenant for, and indemnify and hold Tenant harmless from and against, any and all costs or expenses which Tenant may reasonably pay, sustain or incur in connection with any such proceedings.

承租人不得被应要求参加本合同第四条第六款最后但书/限制性条款提及的任何诉讼，除非当时生效的法律法规要求该诉讼应由承租人或以承租人名义提起，此种情况下，承租人应参加配合该诉讼或允许该诉讼以其名义提起，但概不承担任何与该诉讼有关的费用和花费，业主应偿还并保证赔偿承租人合理支付的因该诉讼产生的或承受的全部费用和花费，且确保承租人免于以上责任。

10. in respect of, in respect thereof, with respect to, as regards

四个短语的意思大致相同，都可译为"涉及，至于"。英文合同中常用 in respect of, in respect thereof, with respect to 表示"与本合同/协议/条款有关的问题"，比普通文本中的 about, concerning as regards 等表达更正式。例如：

㉞ Notwithstanding Clause 16.1, Party B shall not be entitled to claim for itself in respect of any Force Majeure in Clause 16.1.

不管16条第一款的规定，乙方无权根据16条第一款为其自身提出有关不可抗力的索赔。

㉟ Upon the termination of the Existing Letter of Credit and the payment of all amounts (if any) owing in respect thereof, Bank Boston, N.A. shall cease to be an Issuing Bank hereunder.

现有信用证一经期满，所有相关应付款项支付（如果有的话）即告终止，北美波士顿银行不再是该信用证项下的开证行。

㊱ Party C or New Company shall retain all rights with respect to the specifications, plans, drawings and other documents and Party B undertakes not to disclose the same or divulge any information contained therein to any third country without the prior written consent of Party C or New Company.

丙方或新公司应保留有关说明书、计划书、图纸和其他文件的所有权利，且乙方应承诺未经丙方或新公司事先书面同意不披露上述文件或泄露上述文件所包含的任何信息给第三国。

另外，pertaining to 和 pertaining thereto 也表示"涉及，与……有关"。例如：

㊲ Broker is in the business of brokering real estate loans and engages sales representative to perform services pertaining to such business.

经纪人在房地产贷款经纪业务中聘用销售代表提供有关该业务的服务。

11. in favor of, in one's favor

in favor of, in one's favor 一般译为"以……为受益人"，是贸易合同中较为常见的表达。例如：

㊳ One original and one copy of the irrevocable letter of guarantee issued by the Licensor's Bank for a sum of 10% of the total price for the technical know-how in favor of the Licensee.

由许可方银行开具，以被许可方为受益人，金额为专有技术总价10%的不可撤销保函正本和副本各一件。

㊴ We hereby establish this irrevocable letter of credit in your favor for account of Johnson Company in the amount of U.S. $_____（amount in words），available against your draft(s) drawn at sight on Credit Bank, N. A. , Letter of Credit Department, Los Angeles, California, accompanied by your signed and dated statement as follows …

我行特此开立在Johnson公司账上以贵方为受益人，总额为美元_____（大写金额），凭加州洛杉矶北美信贷银行信用证部开出的即期汇票付款的不可撤销的信用证，附有贵方签字和具名日期声明如下……

但是 in favor 并不都是此意，不可生搬硬套。例如：

㊵ Our goods that we offer you are much in favor in the European Continent.

我方向你方报盘的货物，在欧洲大陆颇受好评。

12. … in lieu of …

in lieu of 一般出现在英文合同中，意为"替代"，相当于普通英语中的 in place of, instead of 的正式表达。例如：

㊶ In circumstance provided above in Clause 18.1, Party C or New Company shall, at its sole option and discretion, be entitled to transfer to Party B all or part of Party C or New Company's proprietary rights and ownership of the infrastructure project, under construction or after Completion Date, as liquidated damages, <u>in lieu of</u> computing and compensating the actual damages provided that such transfer shall be conducted of Party C's own free will or rendered in the arbitration award as stipulated in clause 23.

在上述第十八条第一款规定的情形下，丙方或新公司自行选择，有权向乙方转让丙方或新公司的所有权及在建或竣工后基础设施的所有权的全部或部分作为约定的固定数额的违约金来<u>替代</u>计算赔偿实际损害，但该转让应为丙方自己自愿实施的行为或根据二十三条的规定基于仲裁裁决的处分。

信用证条款常涉及一种表述，即"payment shall be effected in the currency of this credit, commission in lieu of exchange of 1/4 pct（min hkd 350 or equivalent）will be deducted and proceeds will be remitted according to presenting bank's instructions."。外贸行业新手或者合同翻译的初学者对 CILE 比较陌生，CILE 的全称为 commission in lieu of exchange，可理解为"兑换手续费"，就是外币转账时银行之间的收费。

信用证业务中的 CILE 相对于其他显性费用，如通知费、议付费、电传费、邮寄费等来说，属于隐性费用。

13. WITNESSETH, Whereas, Now Therefore, NOW THESE PRESENTS WITNESS, KNOW ALL MEN by these presents, In Witness Whereof, In Testimony Whereof, undersigned

WITHNESSETH, Whereas, Now Therefore 用于英文合同前言部分，而 In Witness Whereof 用于合同结尾证明部分。In Testimony Whereof, in Witness Whereof 译为"以此为证，特立此证"。例如：

㊷ <u>In Testimony Whereof</u> we have hereto signed this Document on _____ (DD/MM/YY) accepted on _____ (DD/MM/YY).

我方于____年____月____日签署本文件，并于____年____月____日接受该文件，<u>特此为证</u>。

NOW THESE PRESENTS WITNESS 译为"兹特立约为据"，用于 WHEREAS 条款之后引出具体协议事项。例如：

㊸ <u>NOW THESE PRESENTS WITNESS</u> that it is hereby agreed between the parties hereto as follows …

<u>兹特立约为据</u>，并由订约双方协议如下……

KNOW ALL MEN by these presents 可译为"根据本文件，特此宣布"，通常用于前言部分。例如：

㊹ KNOW ALL MEN by these presents that we _____ (bank's name) having our registered office at _____ (herein after called "the Bank") will be bound unto _____ (the Owner's name) (herein after called "the Owner") in the sum of _____ for payment well and truly to be made to the said Owner, the Bank will bind itself, its successors and better assignee by these presents.

根据本文件，兹宣布，我行_____（银行名称），其注册地点在_____（以下简称"本银行"）向_____（业主名称）（以下简称"本业主"）立约担保支付_____（金额数）的保证金。本保证书对本银行及其继受人和受让人均具有约束力。

undersigned 是文件末尾的签名者，前面加定冠词 the，是文件签署者的自称。例如：

㊺ The undersigned Seller and Buyer have agreed to close the following transaction in accordance with the terms and conditions stipulated as follows …

兹经签约的买卖双方同意，按下列条款达成这笔交易……

14. unless otherwise, except (as) otherwise

unless otherwise 和 except (as) otherwise 在合同中理解为"除非……另有规定"，常常被用到，在句中的位置非常灵活，可在句首、句末或句中，后接 stipulate, provide, require, state, specify 等动词或其过去分词。例如：

㊻ On the Transfer Date New Company shall transfer to B, free from any lien or encumbrance created by New Company and without the payment of any compensation, all its right, title to and interest in the infrastructure project, unless otherwise specified in the Agreement or any supplementary agreement.

新公司应在转让日转让给乙方，概不承担新公司设定的质押或担保并概不支付基础设施工程中的赔偿、全部权利、所有权和权益，除非本协议或补充协议另有规定。

㊼ Except as otherwise provided herein, all import permits and licenses and the import duties, customs fees and all taxes levied by any government authority other than the Seller's country shall be the sole responsibility of the Buyer.

除非本协议另有规定，所有进口许可证照和政府机关（不是卖方国家）征收的进口关税和所有税费均应由买方独自承担。

15. use all reasonable endeavors (efforts) to do sth., make full endeavors (efforts) to do sth., exert one's effort (s) to do sth. / exert oneself to do sth.

英文合同中有"尽力做某事"的表达时，常常用到这几个句型结构，而不用普通英语文本中的 try one's best to do sth. 等句型。例如：

㊽ Except as contemplated by this Agreement, from the date hereof through the

Closing Date, Matt shall cause each Oracle Subsidiary to <u>use commercially reasonable efforts to</u> conduct its business in the ordinary course in all material respects, and shall <u>use commercially reasonable endeavors to</u> preserve its business relationships intact, keep available the service of its employees and maintain satisfactory relationships with its suppliers and customers.

除非本协议预期，从本协议签订日期到成交日，Matt公司应促使Oracle子公司<u>竭尽全力</u>在所有实质方面按通常程序进行交易，<u>应尽力</u>来保持其商业关系完整，获得其员工的服务并与供应商和客户维持良好的关系。

16. foregoing, aforesaid, the said, aforementioned, abovementioned, in question

这一组词通常在名词前作限定语，理解为"上述的、为避免重复已经提到的姓名或名称"。例如：

㊾ The Bank shall give prompt written or telex notice to the Borrower of the Interest Rate in effect from time to time in accordance with the <u>foregoing</u> sentence.

本银行将根据<u>上述句子</u>以书面或电传形式随时及时通知借款方生效的利率。

㊿ The contract shall be written in Chinese and in English. Both language versions are equally authentic. In the event of any discrepancy between the two <u>aforementioned</u> versions, the Chinese version shall prevail.

本合同应以中文和英文起草，两个语言版本具有同等法律效力。<u>前述</u>两种文本如有歧义，以中文文本为准。

in question 通常表示在考虑或讨论中的某件事或问题，可译为"这问题或该问题"。例如：

㉛ All prices to be paid by the Buyer under its obligations of the buyback/counter-purchase Contract shall be the world market prices taking into account the other delivery terms for the goods <u>in question</u>.

买方根据返销或回购货物合同的义务所支付的价格应为世界市场价格，结合考虑<u>该货物</u>的其他交货条件。

17. notwithstanding

notwithstanding 一般理解为"即使，尽管"。例如：

㉜ <u>Notwithstanding</u> any other provisions to the contrary herein, insurance coverage and limits shall be subject to approval of all the parties.

<u>即使</u>有与本合同相悖的规定，保险范围和责任限制应以合同各方同意为准。

㉝ <u>Notwithstanding</u> Article 2.2, the parties may agree to extend the Expiration date to such date as is reasonable in the circumstances if any of the conditions precedent referred to in Article 2.1 is not satisfied or waived on or before the Expiration Date, any such agreement or waiver to be in writing.

尽管有本合同第二条第二款规定，如上述第二条第一款规定的先决条件在合同期满日之前既未实现又未放弃，合同各方亦可根据具体情况，约定合理延长合同的期满日。

18. 时间、期间的表达中虚词的使用

on 表示确定的某日期。例如：

(54) Party A shall deliver the goods to Party B on July 30, 2020.

甲方应在 2020 年 7 月 30 日将货物送给乙方。

by 表示终了时间，其间的终止日期包括表示日期。例如：

(55) Party A shall deliver the goods to Party B by July 30, 2020.

甲方应于 2020 年 7 月 30 日之前将货物送给乙方。(包括 7 月 30 日)

before 用于说明其间的终止日期在表示日期的前一天。例如：

(56) Party A shall deliver the goods to Party B before July 31, 2020.

甲方应于 2020 年 7 月 31 日前将货物送给乙方。(不包括 7 月 31 日)

on and after 表示从某日起。例如：

(57) Party A shall be unauthorized to accept any order sort to collect any account on and after September 20.

从 9 月 20 日起，甲方无权接受订单收款。

on or before 表示"不迟于，不晚于"。例如：

(58) Our terms are cash within three months, i. e. on or before May 1.

我公司的条件是：3 个月内，即不得晚于 5 月 1 日，支付现金。

no later than 表示"不迟于"。例如：

(59) Party B shall ship the goods within one month of the date of signing this Contract, i. e. not later than December 15.

自本合同签字之日一个月内，即不迟于 12 月 15 日，你方须将货物装船。

19. and/or, by and between

合同必须明确规定双方的责任。为译出双方责任的权限与范围，常常使用连词和介词的固定结构，如常用 and/or 对应合同中的"甲和/或乙"，以避免漏译其中的一部分。例如：

(60) 如果上述货物对船舶和/或船上其他货物造成任何损害，托运人应负全责。

The shipper shall be liable for all damage caused by such goods to the ship and/or cargo on board.

by and between 强调合同是由双方签订的,因此双方必须严格履行合同所赋予的责任。例如:

㉖ 买卖双方同意按下述条款购买、出售下列商品并签订本合同。

This Contract is made <u>by and between</u> the Buyer and the Seller, whereby the Buyer agrees to buy and the Seller agrees to sell the undermentioned commodity subject to the terms and conditions stipulated below.

20. SAY, ONLY

为避免合同中金额数量的差漏、伪造或涂改,英译时常用以下方法:把英译金额放在阿拉伯数字所代表的小写金额之后,在括号内用大写文字重复写出该金额,即使原文合同中没有大写金额,英译时也有必要加上大写金额。

在大写文字前加上 SAY,意为大写;在最后加上 ONLY,理解为"整"。小写与大写的金额数量要一致。例如:

㉗ 聘方须每月付给受聘方美元 500 元整。

Party A shall pay Party B a monthly salary of US \$800 (<u>SAY</u> EIGHT HUNDRED US DOLLARS <u>ONLY</u>).

英译金额必须注意区分和正确使用各种不同货币符号,如"\$"既可代表美元又可代表其他某些地方的货币,而"￡"不仅代表英镑也可代表其他某些地方的货币。

用阿拉伯数字书写金额时,金额数字必须紧靠货币符号,如"Can \$891,123",不能写成"Can \$ 891,123"。另外,还要特别注意金额中是小数点还是分节号。

21. promissory estoppel

promissory estoppel 意为"允诺禁反言",又称"允诺后不得翻供"或"不得自食其言",是指根据诚信原则,允诺人所做的赠予的允诺或无偿的允诺具有拘束力,须加以强制执行。允诺禁反言制度的存在使得允诺人在不存在对价的情形下也必须履行承诺。

22. chapter, article/section/clause, paragraph, subparagraph

chapter, article/section/clause, paragraph, subparagraph 分别表示英文合同中的章、条、款、项。例如:

㉘ The Borrower further irrevocably consents to service of process upon it out of said courts in any such action or proceeding by mailing copies thereof by United Stated registered air mail, postage prepaid, to the Borrower at the address specified in <u>Section 10.5</u> hereof.

借款人进一步不可撤销同意上述法院就该事宜诉讼或程序的送达,接受按照本合同第十条第五款指定的借款人地址寄来的美国航空挂号信,邮资已付邮件中的副本。

23. perform, fulfill, execute, implement

表示"履行"时经常用到这几个词。perform 表示 to do what one party is obliged to do by a contract，泛指双方履行合同的各项责任和义务。fulfill 表示 to do everything which is promised in a contract，强调合同一方具体履行合同的义务。execute 和 implement 则强调具体实施，execute 也有表示"签约，生效"的用法。例如：

⑭ With respect to the outstanding 180 M/T of low-density polyethylene NY2-11 under Contract No.79hp-106, we insist that you must open the covering letter of credit the soonest possible to secure the performance of the contract. We hereby would like to call your attention to the fact that the Adviser Inc., who purchased LDPE NY2-11 from us at the same time as you did have <u>fulfilled</u> their commitment under the previous Contract not long after we offered our regulated price and signed a new contract covering substantial quality.

有关第 79hp-106 号合同项下 180 公吨的低密度聚乙烯（NY2-11）未付款项，我方坚持要求贵方尽快开立信用证以保证合同的履行。我方在此提请贵方注意该事实，同时从我公司购买低密度聚乙烯（NY2-11）的 Adviser 公司已经按先前的合同<u>履行完义务</u>，不久后，我方就提供了调整的价格并签订了一份产品品质优良的新合同。

⑮ Each of the parties to this Agreement shall use its reasonable best efforts to effect the transactions contemplated hereby and to fulfill and cause to <u>be fulfilled</u> the conditions to Closing under this Agreement including, without limitation, Parent using reasonable best efforts to obtain the Parent Stockholder Approval at the meeting of Parent's stockholders scheduled to be held on June 25, 1999 or at any adjournment or postponement thereof (the "June 25 Meeting"). Each party hereto, at the reasonable request of another party hereto, shall <u>execute</u> and deliver such other instruments and do and perform such other acts and things as may be necessary or desirable for effecting completely the consummation of this Agreement and the transactions contemplated hereby.

合同任一方应竭尽全力来完成在此预期的交易并按本协议<u>履行</u>或促使交易的成交条件的履行，包括但不限于母公司尽力按日程在 1999 年 6 月 25 日召开的母公司股东会或该日期延后或休会期间通过母公司股东批准。本合同一方在他方合理的要求下，应签署并交付其他文件并切实<u>履行</u>本协议和预期交易完全达成所必需或需要的行为和事宜。

⑯ All disputes arising in connection with this contract or in the <u>execution</u> thereof, should be settled amicably through negotiations.

所有与合同或合同<u>履行</u>有关的争议，应通过友好协商解决。

24. effect, come into effect, in effect

在普通英语文本中，effect 一般作名词，指效果或影响。come into effect 意为"生效"，in effect 意为"生效的"。除了这些基本用法外，effect 还常用作动词，意为"实现，完成"。例如：

⑥⑦ This contract shall come into effect on the date when it is signed by both parties.

本合同从双方签字之日起生效。

⑥⑧ Buyer shall accept the bill of exchange immediately upon the first presentation of the bill of exchange and the required documents and shall effect the payment on the maturity date of the bill of exchange.

汇票一经承兑交单，买方应在汇票到期时完成支付。

此外，表达"实际上的，事实上的"常用 in effect，而不是 in fact。

25. represent, warrant, undertake, guarantee

这几个词都可意为"保证"。represent 和 warrant 往往被连用，出现在合同的声明保证部分。例如：

⑥⑨ Both the Seller and the Purchaser warrant and represent that no broker was involved in negotiating this purchase and sale, and both the Seller and the Purchaser agree to indemnify and hold each other harmless against any and all claims for brokerage.

买卖双方保证并声明没有中介介入交易磋商，且保证赔偿对方因中介引起的索赔并使其免受损害。

⑦⑩ Under FOB terms, the Seller shall undertake to load the contracted goods on board the vessel nominated by the Buyer on any date notified by the Buyer, within the time of shipment as stipulated in Clause 8 of this Contract.

根据离岸价格术语，卖方应保证在本合同第八条规定的时限内，按买方通知的日期，装运货物至买方指定船只。

⑦① Party B guarantees that the machines and equipment are unused, sophisticated and of best quality, and that the machines and equipment are capable of manufacturing the steel wire rope.

乙方保证机器设备未经使用、性能良好、品质卓越且该设备能生产出钢丝绳。

26. principal place of business (principal office), domicile, business premise, registered office

这四组词分别表示"主营业地""住所地""营业场所""注册地"，往往出现在前言的 parties 部分。例如：

⑦② This Contract made on April 1, 2020, at Nantong, China, between ABC Co. with its principal office at Shanghai, China (hereinafter called Party A), and XYZ Co. with its principal office at New York, USA (hereinafter called Party B).

本合同于2020年4月1日于中国南通签订，合同双方为ABC公司（以下简称"甲方"），其主营业地位于中国上海，和XYZ公司（以下简称乙方），其主营业地为美国纽约。

⑦③ If franchisee is declared in default of the agreement, the franchiser has the right to conclude the terms of the agreement and also has the right, without notice to execute any dutiful and authorized acts, on the business premise necessary.

如被特许方承认违约，许可方则有权终止该协议且有权未经通知在必要的营业场所采取任何尽责和授权行为。

27. have the right to do, be entitled to do, reserve the right to do, be (duly) authorized to do, have the authority to do, do sth. at one's option or/and discretion

have the right to do 意为"有权利做某事"。

be entitled to do 表示 give sb. the right to do sth.，体现该权利在法律上的强制性。reserve the right to do 表示 to have a specified power of right in law，体现法律规定的权利。

be (duly) authorized to do 和 have the authority to do 指经授权而有的权利，do sth. at one's option or/and discretion 则指行为人自主决定的权利。例如：

㉔ The Buyer shall nevertheless have the right to cancel in part or in whole of the contract without prejudice to the Buyer's right to claim compensations.

尽管如此，买方有权撤销合同的全部或部分，概不妨碍买方索赔权之行使。

㉕ In circumstance provided above in Clause 14.1, C or New Company shall, at its sole option and discretion, be entitled to transfer to B all or part of C or New Company's proprietary rights and ownership of the infrastructure project, under construction or after Completion Date, as liquidated damages, in lieu of computing and compensating the actual damages provided that such transfer shall be conducted of C's own free will or rendered in the arbitration award as stipulated in clause 23.

在上述第十四条第一款规定的情形下，丙方或新公司自行选择决断有权向乙方转让丙方或新公司的所有权及在建或竣工后基础设施的所有权的全部或部分作为约定的固定数额的违约金来替代计算赔偿实际损害，但该转让应为丙方自己自愿实施的行为或根据二十三条的规定基于仲裁裁决的处分。

第四节　翻译实例分析

1. 房屋租赁

TENANT shall not change or install locks, paint, or wallpaper said premises without LANDLORD's prior written consent, TENANT shall not place placard, signs, or other exhibits in a window or any other place where they can be viewed by other residents or by the general public.	如事先未经出租人/房东/业主书面同意，承租人不得更换或者安装上述房屋的门锁、粉刷住所或者贴墙纸；也不得将招牌、告示牌或者其他展示牌放置在窗户上，或者其他住户或公众看得见的任何地方。

If the premises cannot be delivered to TENANT on the agreed date due to loss, total or partial destruction of the premises, or failure of previsous TENANT to vacate, either party may terminate this agreement upon written notice to the other party at their last known address.

如本住所因为损毁、全部或者部分毁坏，或者由于上一任承租人未能搬走清空而不能按照约定的日期提供给承租人，双方可以按照最新地址书面通知对方以终止本租赁合同。

英文中情态动词的用法值得关注。租赁合同中会有不少禁止承租人某些行为的条款，所以 shall not do 或 No ... shall do 都可以表示一般性禁令。

按照李克兴（2007）的统计，禁令性表达中 shall not 的使用最为普遍，may not 的使用次数排第二，must not 的使用反而最少，因此他提出应将所有情态动词的否定句都译为"不得"。因此，译者在翻译时需要准确把握语感，分辨出各种禁令中所包含的强制程度，区别并选用不同的情态动词或表达方式。

第二段的 cannot be 可理解为"有能力做到但是没有做到"，而表示"可以做到"或"不可以做到"用 may 或 may not。前者译为"不能"，后者译为"不可，不得"。

2. 不可抗力条款

a. Acts of God, including but not limited to fire, flood, earthquake, windstorm or other natural disaster;
b. War, armed conflict, imposition of sanctions, embargo, breaking off of diplomatic relations or similar actions;
c. Terrorist attack, civil war, civil commotion or riots;
d. Nuclear, chemical or biological contamination or sonic boom;
e. Voluntary or mandatory compliance with any law (including a failure to grant any licence or consent needed or any change in the law or interpretation of the law);
f. Fire, explosion or accidental damage;
g. Collapse of building structures, failure of plant machinery, machinery, computers or vehicles;
h. Interruption or failure of utility service, including but not limited to electric power, gas or water.

a. 自然灾害，包括但不仅限于火灾、洪水、地震、暴风或其他自然灾害；
b. 战争、武装斗争、制裁征收、贸易禁令、外交突然中断或类似事件；
c. 恐怖袭击、内战、民众骚乱或暴乱；
d. 核污染、化学污染或生物污染，或超音波爆声；
e. 自愿或强制遵守任何法律（包括任何许可或批准的无法授权，法律或法律释义的任何变更）；
f. 火灾、爆炸或意外损失；
g. 建筑物倒塌，工厂机器、器械装置、计算机或交通工具故障；
h. 公用服务的中断或故障，包括但不仅限于电力、燃气或自来水。

本段文字常见于合同的不可抗力条款，描述8种被视为不可抗力的情形，合同双方无需对这些原因造成的损失或者合同的无法履行承担责任。"自然灾害"在合同中一般译为 acts of God，而不是普通文本中的 natural disasters。对于 including but not limited to，不少文本都是按照英文结构，直接翻译为"包括但不限于……等"，但也有人提出反对意见，认为这是食洋不化的表现，完全按照英文结构翻译并不符合汉语表达规范，因为在汉语的语法中表示转折一般是从谓语开始，所以建议翻译为"包括……等"。b—g 条款在汉语中基本都能找到直接对应的表达，无理解障碍。

最后的 h 条款中，utility 一般指公共设施及水、电、天然气等，有时也包含污水处理费等费用，具体范围须在合同中被明确约定，此处将其译为"公用"。

3. 保密条款

本协议所称"保密信息"，系指与贵宾楼项目提供方有关、不为公众所知悉、能为权利人带来现时或潜在经济利益且经权利人采取合理保密措施的任何信息，其包括但不限于：

The term "confidential information" as used in this Agreement refers to any information which is related to the project provider of VIP Building, is not known to the public, can bring current or potential economic benefits to the obligee and is subject to reasonable confidentiality measures by the obligee, including but not limited to:

a. 无论依附于何种载体的有关提供方的业主本人及家人成员信息、文件资料、报表、凭证、电子记录、客户名单、商业情报内容及其获取途径、提供服务的方式及内容。

a. Information of the owner himself and his family members, documents, reports, vouchers, electronic records, customer lists, business information contents and their acquisition channels, service providing methods and contents of the relevant provider, regardless of the carrier attached.

b. 提供方的经营状况、财务状况、人员状况、与任何第三方的合作和涉及争议的情况。

b. The provider's operating status, financial status, personnel status, cooperation and dispute status with any third party.

c. 相关上级或行业主管机关的意见、批件或批示内容的部分或全部。

c. Some or all of the opinions, approval documents or instructions of the relevant superiors or industry competent authorities.

d. 双方就合作相关事宜签署的文件内容及进行磋商的进展，包括但不限于各方口头或书面开出的条件、双方已经达成的协议和目前尚存的分歧等。

d. The contents of the documents signed by the two sides on cooperation-related matters and the progress of the negotiation, including but not limited to the conditions offered orally or in writing by the parties, the agreements already reached by the two sides and the existing differences, etc.

"保密信息"多译为 confidential information。第一段是保密信息的定义，明确界定它的内涵和外延。其中"现时和潜在"译为 current or potentia。对"经权利人采取合理保密措施的任何信息"的翻译需要使用 be subject to，这里的 be subject to 不能理解为

"受……支配"。"文件资料""报表""凭证"三个词在公司运营中经常可以见到,分别译为 documents, report, voucher。"经营状况"译为 operating status,"财务状况"译为 financial status,"人员状况"译为 personnel status。

"与任何第三方的合作情况和涉及争议情况"译为 cooperation and dispute status with any third party。"意见、批件或批示内容"的译法为 opinions, approval documents or instructions,"上级或行业主管机关"译为 superiors or industry competent authorities。

4. 房屋租赁条款

Condition of premises:TENANT acknowledges that the premises have been inspected. TENANT acknowledges that said premises have been cleaned and all items, fixtures, appliances, and appurtenances are in complete working order. TENANT promises to keep the premises in a neat and sanitary condition and to immediately reimburse landlord for any sums necessary to repair any item, fixture or appurtenance that need service due to TENANT'S, or TENANT's invitee, misuse or negligence.

TENANT shall be responsible for the cleaning or repair to any plumbing fixture where a stoppage has occurred. TENANT shall also be responsible for repair or replacement of the garbage disposal where the cause has been a result of bones, grease, pits, or any other item which normally causes blockage of the mechanism.

住所状况:承租人确认他已经检查过该住所。承租人确认该住所已经打扫干净,所有的物品、附属设施、电器和其他配置状况良好。承租人承诺保持住所的干净卫生;如因为承租人或承租人的客人因不当使用或疏忽而造成住所的任何物品、附属装置或配置损坏需要维修的,承租人同意及时向业主支付必要的维修费用。

如任何水管装置发生堵塞,承租人须负责清理或者维修。厨房垃圾处理器如因骨头、油脂、果核或者其他通常会将垃圾处理器堵塞的物品而损坏,需要维修或更换的,承租人需要承担相应费用。

在房屋租赁合同中,表示"房屋"或"住所"一般用 premises, tenant 可译为"租客"或"承租人",而 landlord 则可译为"出租人""房东""业主"等。

garbage disposal 是指厨房水槽下方用来粉碎食物残渣的小型装置,美国不少公寓的厨房内都装有此类装置。另外需要区分的是,apartment 是专门用来出租的公寓但不能独立出售,而可以独立销售的公寓应该对应为 condo,两者之间存在差异,译者在翻译时要注意选择使用。

5. 租赁合同

Premises Lease Contract
Lessor (hereinafter referred to as Party A)
Lessee (hereinafter referred to as Party B)
Party A and B have, in respect of leasing the legitimate premises owned by Party A to Party B, reached an

租赁合同
出租方(甲方):
承租方(乙方):
根据国家有关法律、法规和本市有关规定,甲、乙双方在平等自

agreement through friendly consultation to conclude the following contract under the relevant national laws and regulations, as well as the relevant stipulations of the city.

(1) Location of the premises

Party A will lease to Party B the premises and attached facilities owned by itself which is located at _____ (Location) and in good condition.

(2) Size of the premises

____ square meters (Gross size).

The registered size of the leased premises is ____.

(3) Lease term

The lease term will be from _____ (MM/DD/YY) to _____ (MM/DD/YY), Lease _____ Term year(s). Party A will clear the premises and provide it to Party B for use before _____ (MM/DD/YY).

(4) Rental

a. Amount: The rental will be _____ RMB per month (including management fees). Party B will pay the rental to Party A in the form of cash.

b. Payment of rental will be one installment every month(s). The first installment will be paid before _____ (MM/DD/YY). Each successive installment will be paid by _____ (date) of each month. Party B will pay the rental before using the premises and attached facilities (In case Party B pays the rental in the form of remittance, the date of remitting will be the day of payment and the remittance fee will be borne by the remitter). Party A will issue a written receipt after receiving the payment.

c. Where the rental is more than 7 working days overdue, Party B will pay 0.3 percent of monthly rental as overdue fine every day, if the rental be paid 10 days overdue, Party B will be deemed to have withdrawn

愿的基础上，经友好协商一致，就甲方将其合法拥有的房屋出租给乙方、乙方承租使用甲方房屋事宜，订立本合同。

(1) 房屋地址

甲方将其所有的位于____市____区____的房屋及其附属设施在良好状态下出租给乙方使用。

(2) 房屋面积

_____平方米（建筑面积）。

出租房屋的登记面积为_____。

(3) 租赁期限

租赁期限自____年____月____日起至____年____月____日止，租期为____年。甲方应于____年____月____日前将房屋腾空并交付乙方使用。

(4) 租金

a. 数额：双方商定租金为每月____元（含管理费）。乙方以现金形式支付给甲方。

b. 租金按月为壹期支付；第一期租金于____年____月____日以前付清；以后每期租金于每月的____日前缴纳。乙方先付后住（若乙方以汇款形式支付租金，则以汇出日为支付日，汇费由汇出方承担）；甲方收到租金后予以书面签收。

c. 如乙方逾期支付租金超过七天，则每天以月租金的0.3%支付滞纳金；如乙方逾期支付租金超过十天，则视为乙方自动退

from the premises and breach the contract. In this situation, Party A has the right to take back the premises and take actions against Party B's breach.

(5) Deposit

a. Guarantying the safety and good conditions of the premises and attached facilities and account of relevant fees are settled on schedule during the lease term, Party B shall pay ____ RMB to Party A as a deposit before ____ (MM/DD/YY). Party A shall issue a written receipt after receiving the deposit.

b. Unless otherwise provided for by this contract, Party A will return full amount of the deposit without interest on the day when this contract expires and Party B clears the premises and has paid all due rental and other expenses.

c. In case Party B breaches this contract, Party A has right to deduct the default fine, compensation for damage or any other expenses from the deposit. In case the deposit is not sufficient to cover such items, Party B should pay the insufficiency within ten days after receiving the written notice of payment from Party A.

d. If Party B can't normally use the apartment because of Party A, Party A should return the deposit to Party B at once. And Party B has the right to ask for the compensation from Party A.

(6) Obligations of Party A

a. Party A will provide the premises and attached facilities (see the appendix of furniture list for detail) on schedule to Party B for using.

b. In case the premises and attached facilities are damaged by quality problems, natural damages or accidents, Party A will be responsible to repair and pay the relevant expenses. If Party A can't repair the damaged facilities in two weeks so that Party B can't use the facilities normally, Party B has the right to terminate the contract and Party A must return the deposit.

租，构成违约，甲方有权收回房屋，并追究乙方的违约责任。

（5）押金

a. 为确保房屋及其附属设施之安全与完好，及租赁期内相关费用之如期结算，乙方同意于____年____月____日前支付给甲方押金_____元，甲方在收到押金后予以书面签收。

b. 除合同另有约定外，甲方应于租赁关系消除且乙方清空、点清并付清所有应付费用后当天将押金全额无息退还乙方。

c. 因乙方违反本合同的规定而产生的违约金、损坏赔偿金和其他相关费用，甲方可在押金中抵扣，不足部分乙方必须在接到甲方付款通知后十日内补足。

d. 因甲方原因导致乙方无法在租赁期内正常租用该物业，甲方应立即全额无息退还押金于乙方，且乙方有权追究甲方的违约责任。

（6）甲方义务

a. 甲方须按时将房屋及附属设施（详见附件）交付乙方使用。

b. 房屋设施如因质量原因、自然损耗、不可抗力或意外事件而受到损坏，甲方有修缮并承担相关费用的责任。如甲方未在两周内修复该损坏物，以致乙方无法正常使用房屋设施，乙方有权终止该合约，并要求退还押金。

c. Party A will guarantee the lease right of the premises. In case of occurrence of ownership transfer in whole or in part and other accidents affecting the right of lease by Party B, Party A shall guarantee that the new owner, and other associated, third parties shall be bound by the terms of this contract. Otherwise, Party A will be responsible to compensate Party B's losses.

d. Party A must register this contract with the relevant government authority. If not doing so resulting that this contract is invalid or Party B's right of leasing may be damaged, Party A should take the all responsibilities. Party A should also bear the all the relevant taxes.

(7) Obligations of Party B

a. Party B will pay the rental and the deposit on time.

b. Party B may add new facilities with Party A's approval. When this contract expires, Party B may take away the added facilities without changing the good conditions of the premises for normal use.

c. Party B will not transfer the lease of the premises or sublet it without Party A's approval and should take good care of the premises. Otherwise, Party B will be responsible to compensate any damages of the premises and attached facilities caused by its fault and negligence.

d. Party B will use the premises lawfully according to this contract without changing the nature of the premises and storing hazardous materials in it. Otherwise, Party B will be responsible for the damages caused by it.

e. Party B will bear the cost of utilities such as water, electricity, gas, telephone and Internet service on time during the lease term.

c. 甲方应确保享有出租房屋的权利，如租赁期内该房屋发生所有权全部或部分转移、设定他项物权或其他影响乙方权益的事件，甲方应保证所有权人、他项权利人或其他影响乙方权益的第三者能继续遵守本合同所有条款，反之如乙方权益因此遭受损害，甲方应负赔偿责任。

d. 甲方应为本合同办理登记备案手续，如因未办理相关登记手续致该合同无效或损害乙方租赁权利，应由甲方负责赔偿，且甲方应承担所有税费。

(7) 乙方义务

a. 乙方应按合同的规定按时支付租金及押金。

b. 乙方经甲方同意，可在房屋内添置设备。租赁期满后，乙方将添置设备搬走，并保证不影响房屋的完好及正常使用。

c. 未经甲方同意，乙方不得将承租的房屋转租或分租，并应爱护该房屋，如因乙方过失或过错致使房屋及设施受损，乙方应承担赔偿责任。

d. 乙方应按本合同规定合法使用该房屋，不得擅自改变使用性质。乙方不得在该房屋内存放危险物品。否则，如该房屋及附属设施因此受损，乙方应承担全部责任。

e. 乙方应承担租赁期内的水费、电费、煤气费、电话费、因特网费等一切因实际使用而产生的费用，并按单如期缴纳。

(8) Termination and dissolution of the contract

a. Within one month before the contract expires, Party B will notify Party A if it intends to extend the lease. In this situation, two parties will discuss matters over the renewal. Under the same terms Party B has the priority to lease the premises. 7

b. When the lease term expires, Party B will return the premises and attached facilities to Party A within days. Any belongings left in it without Party A's previous understanding will be deemed to be abandoned by Party B. In this situation, Party A has the right to dispose of it and Party B will raise no objection.

c. This contract will be effective after being signed by both parties. Any party has no right to terminate this contract without another party's agreement. Anything not covered in this contract will be discussed separately by both parties.

(9) Breach of the contract

a. During the lease term, any party who fails to fulfill any article of this contract without the other party's agreement will be deemed to breach the contract. Both parties agree that the penalty will be _____ RMB. In case the penalty is not sufficient to cover the loss suffered by the faultless party, the party in breach should pay additional compensation to the other party.

b. Both parties will settle the disputes arising from execution of the contract or in connection with the contract through friendly consultation. In case the agreement cannot be reached, any party may summit the dispute to the court that has the jurisdiction over the matter.

(10) Miscellaneous

a. Any annex is the integral part of this contract. The annex and this contract are equally valid.

b. There are 2 originals of this contract. Each party will hold 1 original.

(8) 合同的终止及解除

a. 乙方在租赁期满后如需续租，应提前一个月通知甲方，由双方另行协商续租事宜。在同等条件下，乙方享有优先续租权。

b. 租赁期满后，乙方应在日内将房屋交还甲方；对于任何滞留物，如未取得甲方谅解，均视为乙方放弃，任凭甲方处置，乙方决无异议。

c. 本合同一经双方签字后立即生效；未经双方同意，任何一方不得任意终止，如有未尽事宜，甲、乙双方可另行协商。

(9) 违约及处理

a. 甲、乙双方任何一方在未征得对方谅解的情况下，不履行本合同规定条款，导致本合同中途终止，则视为该方违约，双方同意违约金为_____元，若违约金不足以弥补无过错方之损失，则违约方还须就不足部分支付赔偿金。

b. 若双方在执行本合同或与本合同有关的事情时发生争议，应首先友好协商；协商不成，任何一方可向有管辖权的人民法院提起诉讼。

(10) 其他

a. 本合同附件是本合同的有效组成部分，与本合同具有同等法律效力。

b. 本合同壹式贰份，甲、乙双方各执一份。

该文本为租赁协议，涵盖了房屋租赁主要条款，如租金（rental）、押金（deposit）、甲方义务（obligations of Party A）、乙方义务（obligations of Party B）、合同的终止和解除（termination and dissolution of the contract）等，特别是对甲乙双方的主要义务有详细的描述，对翻译和起草中英文房屋租赁合同具有借鉴意义。

在美国租房子大致有两种情形：一种是与个人签订租赁合同；另外一种是与中介公司或运营apartment的物业公司签订租赁合同。与公司签订租赁合同，很多时候需要承租人提供信用报告，如experia，trans union，equifax等，还需要个人的社会保障号（social security number），以及银行的收入证明。合同中的条款规定比较详细，比如支付用现金等。

翻译练习

练习1

Unless otherwise expressly provided for herein, if all disputes, controversies or differences arising out of or in relation to the execution of this Agreement between the Parties hereto, or any breach or default of the provisions hereof (including but not limited to, a dispute concerning the existence or continued existence of this Agreement, and the validity of the Arbitration Clause) fail to be settled amicably, the dispute, controversies or differences in question shall be submitted for arbitration.

练习2

The Borrower shall, under this Agreement and the Note, fulfill the obligations of making all payments. All the reimbursements to the Bank shall be free and clear of any other charges and exempt from all taxes and such reimbursements as are received by the Bank will not be subject to taxes. The Borrower shall, under this Agreement, pay all taxes as provided for herein.

练习3

本工程由乙方进行设计，提供施工图纸一式两份，双方签字确认。

因甲方提供的材料、设备质量不合格而影响工程质量，其返工费用由甲方承担，工期相应顺延；

由乙方原因而造成质量事故，其返工费用由乙方承担。

在施工过程中，甲方提出设计修改意见及增减工程项目，须提前与乙方联系，在双方签订《工程项目变更单》后，方能进行该项目的施工，因此影响工程竣工日期的，责任由甲方承担。凡甲方私自与施工人员商定更改施工内容、增加施工项目所引起的一切后果，甲方自负，给乙方造成损失的，甲方应予以赔偿；

工程验收：乙方负责隐蔽工程和中间工程的检查与验收手续。乙方组织专门人员进行验收。一切隐蔽工程和中间工程的质量由乙方负责；

工程竣工：乙方完工后应立即通知甲方验收，甲方应在竣工当日组织验收，并办理验收移交手续，双方签订《工程质量验收单》。如果甲方在规定时间内不能组织验收，须及时通知乙方，另行商定验收日期。如通过竣工验收，甲方应承认原竣工日期，并承担因此造成的乙方的看管费用和其他相关费用；

工程保修期为一年。工程竣工验收后，甲、乙双方签署《工程保修单》，凭保修单实行保修，保修期为一年，从竣工验收签章之日起算。

练习 4

（1）甲方的权利与义务

a. 甲方有权对冷柜的使用进行监督和管理。且甲方有义务在每次检查后将相应结果告知乙方。

b. 如乙方冰柜未投放在指定市场或未投放至终端，甲方有权不予支付全部剩余补贴，同时甲方有权终止本合同。

c. 合同有效期限内，乙方违反合同约定而展示甲方产品以外其他产品，张贴其他厂家的宣传画，累计达两次的，甲方有权不予支付第二次当季度的所有冰柜租赁费用；累计达三次以上（包括三次），甲方有权不予支付剩余所有租赁费用。

（2）乙方的权利与义务

a. 乙方购买的冰柜（为甲方的冷饮产品所使用），其所有权归乙方所有，基于冰柜所产生的一切直接或间接的费用或损失均由乙方单独承担。

b. 乙方应当确保乙方冰柜不得展示其他产品，不得张贴其他厂家的宣传画，不得出租、出售、转借他人。冰柜使用期间应保持冰柜清洁、外观良好，不得损害甲方形象。

c. 乙方负责冰柜的投放、日常管理、服务及产品供应。乙方将冰柜投放市场后须建立冰柜管理台账，并使用资产管理系统建立终端信息并及时更新，每周须将冰柜管理台账提供给甲方业务人员，以便于甲方检查和管理。

d. 主合同期限届满后，乙方若继续经营甲方冷饮，有权经甲方同意后继续使用甲方的统一形象；若不再经营甲方冷饮业务，不得继续使用甲方的统一形象。

第六章
民事诉讼法的基本知识和翻译

民事诉讼是指法院在当事人和其他诉讼参与人的参加下审理解决民事案件的活动以及由这种活动所产生的诉讼关系的总和。具体而言,民事诉讼是指公民之间、法人之间、其他组织之间以及它们相互之间因财产关系和人身关系提起的诉讼。也可以这样理解,民事诉讼是指人民法院、当事人和其他诉讼参与人,在审理民事案件过程中所进行的各种诉讼活动,以及由这些活动所产生的各种关系的总和。诉讼参与人包括原告、被告、第三人、证人、鉴定人、勘验人等。

《中华人民共和国民事诉讼法》(以下简称《民事诉讼法》)是以宪法为根据,结合中国民事审判工作的经验和实际情况制定的,于1991年4月9日在第七届全国人民代表大会第四次会议上通过,自公布之日起施行。随后在2014年和2017年得到修正,现行《民事诉讼法》为2017修正版,一共分为四编(总则、审判程序、执行程序和涉外民事诉讼程序)、二十七章,共有二百八十四条。

1938年以前,美国联邦法院在诉讼程序法的适用上较为混乱,并引发了诸多问题。为统一联邦法院适用的程序法,美国国会于1934年通过了《授权法案》(Enabling Act),授权联邦高院颁布适用于联邦地区法院普通法案件的民事诉讼规则,只要求这些规则不改变当事人的实体法权利。历经多次讨论和修改,《美国联邦民事诉讼规则》(Federal Rules of Civil Procedure)于1938年获得通过并正式生效,尽管自生效时起已被修订多次,但至今仍然是调整联邦法院审判民事案件的诉讼规则。美国约有26个州的民事诉讼在很大程度上采纳了联邦规则模式,其对所有州的影响都极大。

英国在1998年12月签署了《民事诉讼规则》(Civil Procedure Rules),成功统一了英国所有民事法院的民事诉讼规则,结束了不同层级法院适用不同诉讼规则的历史。

第一节 常用术语

民事诉讼法的常用术语见表6-1。

表 6-1 民事诉讼法的常用术语及其英文表达

术语	英译
诉讼权利	litigation right
自愿和合法原则	the principles of voluntariness and lawfulness
审理民事案件	adjudicate civil cases
人民调解委员会	the people's conciliation committees
级别管辖	jurisdiction by levels of courts
答辩状	answer
口头答辩	answer by word of mouth
书面答辩	answer in writing
证据保全	measures of evidence preservation
最终的审前会议	the final pretrial conference
属人管辖权	personal jurisdiction
起诉书副本	copy of complaint
宣誓声明	affidavit
对立占有	adverse possession
证词	deposition
集体诉讼，集团诉讼	class action
共同诉讼	joint action
代表人诉讼	representative action; joint action brought by representatives
公益诉讼	public interest action
常任裁判官	permanent magistrate
婚姻无效或解除	the dissolution or nullity of marriage
暂准判令	the decree nisi
由法院或者法庭酌情解决	left to the discretion of the court or tribunal
质疑仲裁裁决	a challenge against an arbitral award
上诉许可	leave to appeal
债务人的个人情况	the personal circumstances of the debtor
仲裁员	umpire
法警，执行官	bailiff
高等法院首席法官	the chief judge of the high court
上诉法院副庭长	the vice-president of the court of appeal
上诉法院法官	the justice of the court of appeal

续表

术语	英译
司法常务官	registrar
审判长	the presiding judge
合议庭	the collegial bench
执行令	writ of execution
义务令、禁止令及移审令	orders of mandamus, prohibition and certiorari
政府债券	government stock
扣押债务人财产的令状	a writ of fieri facias
分租租契	under-lease
承转租人	under-lessee
承付票	promissory note
执行重收权或没收租赁权	enforce the right of re-entry or forfeiture
临时救济	interim relief
高等法院开庭期	sittings of High Court
休庭期	vocation
法律顾问	legal advisor
披露文件	disclosure of documents
撤销仲裁裁决	vacation of award
其他和补充条款	miscellaneous and supplementary provisions
（基于事实）做出并公布裁决	make an award
超出范围的裁决	excessive award
欠薪支付裁决	backpay award
（留待执行的）终局裁决	final award
域外裁决	foreign award
同一事项已经仲裁裁决的答辩	arbitrament and award
总额财产裁决，一次性财产裁决	award in gross
多数裁决，非一致同意的裁决	majority award
时效	time limit; prescription; limitation
时效中止	suspension of prescription/limitation
时效中断	interruption of limitation/prescription
时效延长	extension of limitation
时效取得	acquisitive prescription

续表

术语	英译
时效终止	lapse of time; termination of prescription
一审法院	court of first instance
申请强制执行	apply for enforcement of the valid court documents
藐视法庭	contempt of court
复原性救济	restitutionary relief
施行救济	dispense remedy
优势证据	preponderant evidence
反驳证据	rebuttal evidence
具体证据的相关性	relevance of specific evidence
审前动议	pretrial motion
退庭评议	retire to deliberate
对抗制或抗辩制	adversary system
陪审制度	jury system
对物权	in rem
互争权利诉讼	interpleader
达成和解	reach a settlement agreement
勘验物证或现场	inspecting or examining physical evidence on site
原告	claimant
证明标准	standard of proof
代替性证据	secondary evidence
遣散费	severance payments
资产负债状况说明书	statement of affairs
分租	sublet
分权共有人	tenant in common
汤林命令（和解令的一种）	Tomlin order
上诉复审	appellate review
宣誓证人	deponent
个人送达	personal service; service in person
邮寄送达	service by mail
公告送达	service by publication
张贴送达	service by posting

续表

术语	英译
替代送达	substituted service
送达文书	service documents
签收单	acknowledgement of receipt
同住的成年人	cohabiting adults
送达证明	proof of service
刑事附带民事诉讼	adhesion / adhesive procedure

第二节　核心术语的表达和理解

1. complaint

complaint 可译为"民事起诉状",是民事诉讼文书的一种,起诉人应在其中简要说明法院具有管辖权的根据并阐明要求获得法律救济的请求。起诉状应和传票令一起被送达被告人。

依据美国的《联邦刑事诉讼规则》,刑事控告书是指由受害人、警察、地区检察官或其他利害关系人向有管辖权的联邦司法官提出的说明某一犯罪行为已经发生的文书,其中应说明构成其所指控罪行的重要事实。虽然提出控告书旨在指控犯罪,但在诉讼中正式的起诉书应为大陪审团起诉书或检察官起诉书。

2. petition

petition 可译为"申诉"或"申请",是向法院或其他官方机构提交的正式书面文件,请求其行使职权以纠正不法行为、授予某种特权或许可、就特定事项采取司法措施等。例如,美国《宪法》第 1 条修正案和英国的《权利法案》都确认公民有申诉权,以及债权人或债务人有权向破产法院提出破产申请。

在英国,离婚或宣告婚姻无效的程序、破产程序、在上议院和枢密院进行的程序都是以申请开始的。此外,原诉呈请(originating petition)也是在高等法院衡平分庭提起诉讼的方式之一。

3. defendant, respondent, the accused, defender, libelee

defendant 是"被告"的通用语,可用于一般民事或刑事案件的初审中,与其相对的"原告"为 plaintiff,如"She overturned the conviction, saying the defendant was entrapped."(她指控被告是被陷害的,推翻了判决)。

respondent 用于上诉审、申请获得特别命令或离婚、遗嘱验证等衡平法案件中,与其相对的"原告"(或"上诉人")有 appellant, petitioner, applicant 等。

the accused 是指刑事被告,与之相对的"原告"有 plaintiff, prosecution。

defender 是苏格兰专门用语中的被告,与其相对的"原告"为 pursuer。

libelee 专指海事或离婚案件的被告,与其相对的"原告"为 libelant,如"The man is the libelee in the divorce case."。

4. pleading

pleading 意为"诉讼文件"或"诉状"。诉讼当事人交替向法庭及对方提交书面文件,以提出诉讼请求、陈述诉讼理由或进行答辩。

在英国高等法院的诉讼程序中,"起诉状""被告答辩状""原告答辩状"分别为 statement of claim, statement of defence, reply。在美国,普通法中严格的诉状体系已得到大大简化,其作用也已大大降低,对事实及争议点的限定通过披露程序(discovery)及审前会议(pretrial conference)进行。根据《联邦民事诉讼程序规则》,诉状包括起诉状(complaint)、答辩状(answer)、反诉答辩状(reply to a counterclaim)、交叉诉讼答辩状(answer to a cross-claim)、第三方起诉状(third party complaint)及第三方答辩状(third party answer)。在诉讼过程中提交或使用的动议/申请书(motion)、律师辩论意见书(brief)、宣誓书(affidavit)等属于广泛意义上的法庭文件,而不属于诉状。

5. burden of proof

burden of proof 意为"举证责任"。案件一方当事人提出诉求时,应该向法庭提供证据,即"谁主张,谁举证"。承担此责任的当事人如果想得到某种解释,就必须提供证据。若当事人提供足够的证据来请求法院对问题进行审议,那么该责任就已完成。

在民事诉讼中,证明标准是优势证据或清晰且具有说服力的证据。两者都是合理怀疑之外程度较轻的举证责任。优势证据只意味着一方当事人相对于另一方拥有更多有力的证据,即便是最低程度上的优势。清晰且具有说服力的证据指具有高度盖然性(high probability)的事实要件。

6. summary judgment

summmary judgment 意为"即决判决",也有译者将其译为"建议程序"(很多学者对此提出反对意见,两者存在较大差异)。即决判决制度允许法官可以不经开庭审理而对全部或部分案件直接做出实体性的、有拘束力的判决。

7. default judgment

default judgment 意为"缺席判决"。缺席判决是指被告不出席审判或不应诉答辩,法院据此做出不利于被告、满足原告在起诉状中要求的救济的判决。传票中必须明示被告应诉和答辩的期间,并应告知被告不出席审判并对诉讼提出抗辩将导致法院做出缺席判决。

缺席判决的前提是登记有关当事人缺席的事实,即被请求积极救济判决的当事人不应诉或未能行使诉讼规则规定的其他抗辩,且该事实已被宣誓书或其他方法明确。缺席判决可分为自愿的撤销诉讼(voluntary dismissal)和非自愿的撤销诉讼(involuntary dismissal)。

8. Erie Doctrine

Erie Doctvine 意为"伊利原则"。伊利原则是美国民事诉讼法中关于纵向法律选择(vertical choice of law)问题的一项基本法律原则,该原则旨在解决联邦法和州法法律冲突中的法律适用问题。它有两个目标：阻止诉讼当事人通过有意挑选某一法院进行诉讼以获得利于自己的判决（forum shopping）；避免法律实施时的不公允（inequitable administration of the laws）。

9. counterclaim

counterclaim 可译为"反诉"或"反诉请求"，是指本诉被告针对本诉原告所提起的独立的反请求，它可以分为强制性反诉（compulsory counterclaim）和任意性反诉（permissive counterclaim）。

10. cross-claim

cross-claim 可译为"交叉请求"，又称为"交叉诉讼"，是指共同诉讼人中的一个当事人可以在诉讼文书中对另一个共同诉讼人提出诉讼请求。提出的交叉请求可以是基于作为本诉或反诉之诉讼标的的交易或事件而产生的请求，也可以是与作为本诉之诉讼标的的财产权有关的请求。被交叉请求人有可能替交叉请求人负全部或部分责任。

11. impleader

impleader 可译为"引入诉讼"，是指在诉讼开始后的任何时候，被告以第三人对其被诉的权利请求负有全部或部分责任为由，起诉第三人而将其作为新的被告引入原来的诉讼。此时被告成为第三当事人原告（third-party plaintiff），被引入已开始的诉讼中的人成为第三当事人被告（third-party defendant）；当被反诉时，原告作为反诉被告也有权引入第三当事人被告。

12. answer

answer 译为"答辩"。对起诉状进行答辩是被告的责任。答辩状应简明扼要记载对原告各种请求的抗辩，且必须自认或者否认对方主张。答辩具有期限限制。美国联邦法院规定被告的答辩时限为 20 天，而州法院规定的答辩时限则根据法律和地方法院规则可能是 10 天、15 天、30 天或 60 天。

被告答辩有三种形式：否认（denial）、积极抗辩（affirmative defense）和独立救济请求（independent prayer for relief）。

13. deposition

deposition 常被译为"庭外作证"或"庭外质询"，是一种在正式开庭前进行证据开示的方式。不同于文件交换、书面证言交换等各国诉讼制度都有的证据开示方式，庭外质询是美国、加拿大民事诉讼中独有的制度，也是常常让参与美国诉讼的中国当事人感到困惑的程序。

14. long arm jurisdiction

long arm jurisdiction 可译为"长臂管辖权"，是指当被告的住所不在法院所在的州，但和该州有某种最低限度联系，而且所提权利要求的产生又和这种联系有关时，就该项权利而言，该州对于该被告有属人管辖权，可以在州外对被告发出传票。例如，1997 年美国司法部颁布的《反托拉斯法国际实施指南》规定：如果外国的交易对美国商业产生了重大的和可预见的后果，不论它发生在什么地方，均受美国法院管辖。

美国伊利诺伊州于1955年制定的《长臂管辖权令》是最早的长臂管辖权法。北达科他州在1967年颁布了类似法案，后在1971年6月又将其写入该州民事诉讼程序中。与此同时，先后有35个州也同意类似的法案，如明尼苏达州、南达科他州、蒙大拿州等。

15. preliminary injunction

preliminary injuction 译为"临时禁令"，是由一方当事人申请并由法院做出的、为了防止对方当事人为某种特定行为而对其采取的一种临时性的限制措施，其目的在于确保以后的判决能够得到执行或确保当事人的利益不受到损害。

临时禁令和永久禁令（permanent injunction）相对应，永久禁令属于判决内容，在判决时做出，而临时禁令一般在诉讼前期采用，与最终判决结果无关，仅是一种临时限制措施。申请临时禁令是当事人的一项程序性权利，当事人必须提供相应担保，如果措施错误，被采取措施的当事人有权要求赔偿。中国的民事诉讼法中的诉讼保全措施与之相似。

临时禁令的听证活动十分重要，原告在听证过程中提出的证据可不在审判时重复，而且法院还有权根据案件情况决定是否将听证活动和审判活动结合。

16. relief, remedy, redress

三个词语均有"司法救济"的含义。

relief 主要是指衡平法上的救济，如以强制令或合同、协议的强制履行等方式进行的救济。remedy 则主要指普通法上的救济，是法律规定的执行、保护、恢复权利的方法，或补救权利所受侵害的方法。

redress 既可指衡平法上的救济，也可指普通法上的救济，可替代 remedy 和 relief，如在"Money damages, as opposed to equitable relief, is the only redress available."中，redress 是指普通法上的救济，等同于 remedy。

17. court, tribunal

在英国司法中，既有 Court of Appeal, High Court, Crown Court, Family Law Court，也有各种各样的 Employment Tribunal, Traffic Penalty Tribunal, Tax Tribunal 等。

court 和 tribunal 都可译为"法院""法庭"，但两者之间存在差异。英国的法院体系中主要采用的是 court。上议院（House of Lords）是英国最高等级的上诉法院。上诉法院（Court of Appeal）在等级序列中仅次于上议院。高等法院（High Court of Justice）是上诉法院的下级法院，受上议院和上诉法院裁决约束。皇家法院（Crown Court）是刑事案件的初审法院，受上议院和上诉法院的约束。郡法院（County Court）和治安法院（Magistrate's Court）是级别最低的法院，受上议院、上诉法院和高等法院约束，没有法院受它们裁决约束。

tribunal 就是与法院相比正式程度较低的司法机构。tribunal 采用与 court 相似的方式裁决纠纷，但有不同的规则和程序，并且在严格意义上 tribunal 只处理民事法范畴内某个专门领域的纠纷或案件。tribunal 处理专门、特别的小型案件，而其余案件则由法官进行正式法庭处理并做出相应裁决。无论是 court 还是 tribunal，都是受政府主导的司法机构，具有司法效力。

18. review

法律文本中，review 有两个意思：一是指为了纠正错误而再次进行的审查，尤指上诉审法院或上级行政机关对下级法院的判决或对下级行政机关的决定是否正确、合法而进行的复审或复议；二是由司法机关对下级法院的诉讼程序、立法的通过、政府行为等的合法性或合宪性进行的审查，即 judicial review。例如：

① 对驳回申请、不予公告的商标，商标局应当书面通知商标注册申请人。商标注册申请人不服的，可以自收到通知之日起十五日内向商标评审委员会申请复审。

Where a trademark registration application is rejected or publication is denied, the Trademark Office shall notify the applicant in written form. The applicant may apply to the Trademark Appeal Board for a review within 15 days after receiving the notice.

常见短语有 administrative review（行政复审或司法审查）、application for judicial review（申请司法审查程序）、architectural review（建筑设计审查）、bill in the nature of a bill of review（复审诉状性质的诉状）、bill of review（复审诉状）、bill of review for error apparent（因明显错误而请求复审的诉状）、board of review（审查委员会或复议委员会）、commission of review（复查委任令）等。

19. verdict

陪审团就提交其审理的事项所做的正式裁决的英文为 verdict，它包括：一般裁决（general verdict），用以确定民事案件中是原告胜诉还是被告胜诉，或刑事案件中被告人是有罪还是无罪；特别裁决（special verdict），是指陪审团仅对案件中的特定事项做出裁决，而将该事实适用的法律问题留给法官解决。

《元照英美法词典》将 verdict 译成"（陪审团）裁断"和"（无陪审团审判时）法官的裁决"，但这两个译词都不好，前者未能遵守学术界的共识而翻译成"例陪审团裁决"，后者则没有注意到"法官"和"裁决"二词是不搭的（屈文生、丁沁晨，2017）。

verdict 的常见搭配及汉译见表 6-2。

表 6-2 verdict 的常见搭配及汉译

搭配	汉译
reasons for the verdict	裁决理由
return a verdict	做出……的裁决
the verdict of the jury	陪审团的裁决
unanimous verdict	一致裁决
verdict of acquittal	无罪的裁决
verdict of not guilty	无罪裁决
verdict of guilty	有罪裁决

20. judgment

《布莱克法律词典》中 judgment 的第 2 条释义是 "A court's final determination of the rights and obligations of the parties in a case",即法庭对案件各方当事人权利和义务的终局裁判。该英文定义传递的信息与"判决"基本对等:英文定义中的 court 一词说明 judgment 的主体是法院;the rights and obligations of the parties in a case 说明 judgment 适用于解决案件的实体法律关系;final determination 说明 judgment 系终局裁判。由此看来,"判决"基本可与 judgment 对应。与 judgment 有关的常见短语见表 6-3。

表 6-3 judgment 相关短语

短语	汉译
deliver judgment on	宣告判决
give a judgment	做出判决
judgment by / in default	缺席判决
satisfaction of the judgment	判决的履行
summary judgment	即决判决
satisfy the judgment	履行判决
declaratory judgment	确权判决
invalidating judgment	除权判决
final and binding judgment/ irrevocable judgment	终局判决

21. decree

decree 译作"判决",尤指衡平法院根据公平和良心原则的裁判。衡平法中的 decree 分为 final decree 和 interlocutory decree 两类。普通法与衡平法程序融合后,一般用 judgment 代替 decree。此外,decree 只用于民事案件,判决也不一定是终局的。

中国香港律政司的《英汉法律词汇》将 decree 统一译作"判令",如 decree of divorce(离婚判令)、final decree(最后判令)、decree of nullity marriage(婚姻无效判令)、decree of nullity(无效判令)、judicial decree(司法判令)等。

decree 主要解决的是实体法律关系,而 order 主要在诉讼过程中做出,处理的是程序法律关系。

22. summons

summons 可作名词,意思是"传票,传唤状,出庭通知";summons 也可作动词,作"传唤"理解。作为名词使用,单数是 a summons,如"He was given/served with a summons to appear in court."(他收到一份出庭传票)。复数是 summonses,如"The Russian law enforcement office declined to accept the summonses, US prosecutors said."(美国检察官说,俄罗斯执法人员拒绝接受传票)。

summons 作为动词,第三人称单数是 summonses,过去式是 summonsed,如"She

was summonsed for speeding."。

把 summons 直接转为动词使用，是 17 世纪以后的事情。之前几百年，summons 只用作名词，动词用 summon。

23. subpoena

subpoena 作名词，意为"传票""传唤状""强制作证传票""强制调取证"等，如 serve a subpoena on a witness（向证人送达传票）。

subpoena 也可作动词，意为"传唤"，如"The court subpoenaed her to appear as a witness."（法庭传她到庭作证）。

subpoena 的含义具有强制性，比如，要求证人出庭作证，如果证人不出庭，就是藐视法庭，要承担后果。

24. contempt of court

contempt of court 译为"藐视法庭"，可替代 judicial contempt，是指当事人拒不执行法院的命令或判决。比如，在民事案件审理过程中，法院要求被告人当庭签署文件，被告人拒不签署；法院判决丈夫支付子女抚养费，丈夫拒不执行。前者是当庭拒不执行法庭命令，称作 direct contempt of court（直接藐视法庭）；后者是背后不执行法院判决，称作 indirect contempt of court（间接藐视法庭）。

如出现上述情况，法院可以藐视法庭为名，另行起诉被告人，要求其签署文件或者执行判决。这一程序为藐视法庭诉讼（contempt proceedings）。法院可判处被告人罚款或监禁，直到其同意执行。

启动藐视法庭程序是为了让被告人服从法院命令或执行法院判决，所以适用普通的民事案件程序，称作民事藐视法庭程序（civil contempt of court proceeding）。

25. process, procedure, proceeding

三个词都与诉讼、法律程序有关。

process 有"传票，令状"的意思，如 service of process（传票送达）。

procedure 比较有概括性，指诉讼遵循的程式、规则。《布莱克法律词典》将其定义为"1) The body of law …; 2) A particular method or practice in carrying on civil litigation."。由此可见，它指的是诉讼法、特定的诉讼方法或做法。比如，civil procedure 虽然译为"民事诉讼"，但它不是指某一起具体的诉讼，而是一般意义上的"诉讼"。这点与 proceeding 不同。

proceeding 的字面意思是"程序"，最常见的翻译是"诉讼"，即在法院中开展的程序。相对于 procedure 而言，proceeding 更为具体，如提起某个具体的刑事诉讼（criminal proceeding）或其中的组成部分。proceeding 还可以指其他程序，如行政程序、仲裁程序等。

proceeding 与 action 的区别也要引起注意，proceeding 的含义更广，覆盖 action 的含义。基于这一点，有观点认为法律文件中经常出现的 action or proceeding 的搭配（如：any legal action or proceeding arising out of this agreement）是没有必要的，因为 action 的含

义被包含在proceeding里面。不过美国有的地方（如纽约州）会对action和proceeding给出不同含义，所以为准确起见，文件的起草或翻译还是要把二者保留或翻译出来。

26. find, hold

find的适用对象是事实，故事实认定用finding(s) of fact，而hold的适用对象是法律，故法律认定用holding of law或conclusions of law。

严谨的法学著作或裁判文书内不会有诸如a court holds（应为finds）on questions of fact的说法；同样美国上诉法院也不会使用诸如it affirms a finding of fact的说法，上诉法院能裁定维持原判的只有holding，因为上诉法院只负责审查法律认定（holding of law）是否有误，对于初审法院做出的事实认定（finding of fact）是不负责审查的。

在《布莱克法律词典》中，finding的定义是"A determination by a judge, jury, or administrative agency of a fact supported by the evidence in the record, usu., presented at the trial or hearing."（法官、陪审团或行政机关依庭审或听证会上出示的证据对事实做出的裁判）。

"Because the court finds that the jury's finding is supported by the evidence, the court holds that Gibbons is entitled to recover punitive damages from Allred & Co." 就完美诠释了find和hold的用法。

第三节 常见句型结构

1. 诉讼参与人的各种表达

诉讼文本中最常见的就是诉讼参与人的各种表达。不同于普通文本，法律文本非常讲究诉讼参与人名称的对应，如原告和被告（刑事诉讼中则为公诉人、被告人和受害人等）、上诉人和被上诉人、申请人和被申请人等。因此译者在翻译时需要注意诉讼参与人名称的对应性，对此，李克兴（2011）曾做过归纳，见表6-4。

表6-4 诉讼参与人的各种表达

Part A 甲方	Party B 乙方
plaintiff 原告	defendant 被告
accuser 原告，控告者	defender 被告，答辩人，被申请人
applicant 申请人，呈请人	respondent 答辩人，被申请人，被告
petitioner 申请人	respndent 答辩人，被申请人，被告
claimant 原告，索赔人	respondent 答辩人，被申请人，被告
appelant/appealer 上诉人	appellee 被上诉人

2. ……满足要求或满足诉求……

一般译为satisfy the claim，在民事案件中较为常用。例如：

② A Trustee's account was established to <u>satisfy possible claims</u> resulting from the social plan established to compensate staff for eventual disadvantages in connection with the transfer of separation.

设立了一个受托人账户，以<u>满</u>足为补偿工作人员因调动或离职可能受到的损失而制定的该安置计划所可能产生的<u>要求</u>。

③ In contrast to an avoidance proceeding, but rather a contribution from directors to <u>satisfy the claims</u> of all creditors

此外，与撤销权程序不同，所追求的并非是对公司资产的追偿，而是由董事出<u>资清偿</u>所有债权人的<u>债权</u>。

例③的译文根据具体情境增补了债权债务关系的相关信息，并没有直接翻译为"满足要求"。同样的还有传票中经常出现的结构：

④ If you fail to <u>satisfy</u> the claim or to return the Acknowledgement within the time stated …

如果你未能在规定的时间<u>满</u>足原告的诉求或交回确认书……

3. … count …

由于法系和各国法律文化之间的差异，法律术语翻译有时很难找到直接对应的表达（这也是本书"常见的句型结构"部分存在中英文结构交叉问题的原因），但译者又不得不翻译，所以难免需要创造一些表达结构，如"… count …"。

民事起诉书中会有 count 1 foreseeability, count 2 negligence hiring 等表述结构，这里的 count 与汉语的"诉讼请求"不是对应关系。诉讼请求是原告向被告主张的法律上的利益，如返还标的物等。按照李克兴（2011）的说法，count 不但包含诉讼请求，还有"陈述"的意思，译为"诉项"较合适。在刑事诉讼中，译者可以将 count 译为"罪状，罪项"，也有人建议将其译为"诉因"，相当于 charge。

4. … 受理 …

"受理"可译为 entertain，指的是法院对公民、法人或者其他组织的起诉进行审查后，对符合法律规定的起诉条件的案件决定立案审理，从而引起诉讼程序开始的诉讼行为。起诉和受理是两种不同性质却又密切联系的诉讼行为，前者是原告的诉讼行为，是受理前提；后者是法院的诉讼行为，是起诉的结果。

《民事诉讼法》中有 26 句与受理结构相关，一般都译为 entertain，如第三十六条：

⑤ 人民法院发现<u>受理</u>的案件不属于本院管辖的，应当移送有管辖权的人民法院，受移送的人民法院应当<u>受理</u>。

If a people's court finds that a case it has <u>entertained</u> is not under its jurisdiction, it shall refer the case to the people's court that has jurisdiction over the case, and the people's court to which the case is transferred shall <u>entertain</u> the case。

中国香港地区的《高等法院条例》英文版本中也有类似用法。例如：

⑥ 上诉法庭或原讼法庭如具有司法管辖权可受理强制令或强制履行令的申请，则可在授予强制令或强制履行令之外再判给损害赔偿，或判给损害赔偿以代替强制令或强制履行令。

Where the Court of Appeal or the Court of First Instance has jurisdiction to entertain an application for an injunction or specific performance, it may award damages in addition to, or in substitution for, an injunction or specific performance.

再如：

⑦ 判决是就某项诉因做出的，而由于公共政策或其他类似的理由，该项诉因是不可能获最高法院受理的。

The judgment was in respect of a cause of action which for reasons of public policy or for some other similar reason could not have been entertained by the Supreme Court.

显然中英文中的受理结构用法是对应的，而不是如有些版本中将"受理"译为 accept。语料库检索表明，accept 多译为"接受"或"接纳"。例如：

⑧ In a case where any tenant or sub-tenant is willing to accept such an order, make an order for the grant of a new tenancy or new tenancies in respect of such part or parts of the premises as the Tribunal thinks just and equitable having regard to those reasonable requirements and all the circumstances of the case.

在租客或分租客愿意接纳有关命令的情况下，审裁处经顾及各项合理需要及申请个案的一切情况后，须按其认为公正及公平，就处所的一个或多个部分而做出授予一项或多项新租赁的命令。

5. ……有权……

对"有权"的翻译需要结合具体法条中的含义来确定，有时译为 have the right to do，有时译为 is entitled to，有时还不直接翻译出来。《民事诉讼法》条文中有 29 处涉及"有权"结构，如第十四条：

⑨ 人民检察院有权对民事诉讼实行法律监督。

The people's procuratorates shall have the right to exercise legal supervision over civil proceedings.（该条文中就译为 have the right to，强调权利的使用）

再如《民事诉讼法》第四十四条：

⑩ 审判人员有下列情形之一的，应当自行回避，当事人有权用口头或者书面方式申请他们回避。

Under any of the following circumstances, a judge shall voluntarily disqualify himself or herself, and a party shall be entitled to request disqualification of such a judge verbally or in writing.（该译文中的有权就翻译为 be entitled to，强调具有相关资格）

中国香港地区《高等法院条例》中同样有类似的表达方式，一般"有权"译为 be entitled to，而"有权力"则译为 have power/right to。例如：

⑪ 被告人包括获送达任何传讯令状或法律程序文件的人，或就任何法律程序获送达通知书的人，或<u>有权</u>出席任何法律程序的人。

Defendant includes any person served with any writ of summons or process, or served with notice of, or <u>entitled to</u> attend, any proceedings。（该条文中就使用了 be entitled to do，强调具有相关资格）

再看另一例：

⑫ 聆案官<u>具有权力</u>做出由于衡平法执行而委任接管人的命令，并如某强制令是该命令所附带或连带的，则聆案官亦<u>具有权力</u>授予以该范围为限的强制令。

A master shall <u>have power to</u> make an order for the appointment of a receiver by way of equitable execution and to grant an injunction if, and only so far as, the injunction is ancillary or incidental to such order。（该条文中"具有权力"应该侧重权力的行使，故而译为 have power to do）

6. ……和解……

诉讼和解是指在民事诉讼过程中，当事人双方在自行协商的基础上达成解决争议的协议，并请求法院结束诉讼程序的一种制度。

对于民事诉讼文本中的"和解"，有版本译为 compromise，也有版本译为 settlement，但后者较为恰当。如《民事诉讼法》第五十条：

⑬ 双方当事人可以自行<u>和解</u>。

Both sides of a civil action may reach a <u>settlement</u> themselves.（settlerment 侧重于争端解决，而不因为妥协而达成一致）

再如第二百三十条：

⑭ 一方当事人不履行<u>和解</u>协议的，人民法院可以根据对方当事人的申请，恢复对原生效法律文书的执行。

If either party fails to fulfil the <u>settlement</u> agreement, the people's court may, at the request of the other party, resume the execution of the legal document which was originally effective.

中国香港地区的《高等法院条例》中同样有类似表达。例如：

⑮ 调解指获授权人员为了就申索达成<u>和解</u>而发起或承担进行的商议或行动。

Conciliation means a discussion or action initiated or undertaken by an authorized officer for the purpose of reaching a <u>settlement</u> of a claim.

7. 英文民事起诉书正文中常见的固定结构

英文民事起诉书正文中常见的固定结构举例如下：

⑯ Now comes the Plaintiff ... by and through his or her attorney ... and as for his or her complaint, states as follows ...

兹有原告_____仅由他/她的律师_____代理，就其起诉状作如下陈述……

⑰ Comes now, plaintiff above named and hereby complaints of Defendant and for cause of action alleges ...

上述原告向法院呈递诉状起诉被告，提出如下诉讼理由……

⑱ This is an action for damages based on ... in violation of ....

这是一起因违反……基于……所引起的伤害赔偿诉讼……

⑲ Jurisdiction of this court is based on ...

本院的管辖权是依据……

⑳ Jurisdiction over state law claims herein is based on ...

本院对于州法律上的请求管辖权是依据……

㉑ Venue lies in this Distric pursuant to ...

依据……审判地位于本地区……

㉒ Wherefore, Plaintiff prays for judgements as follows ... / Wherefore, Plaintiff respectfully requests that this Court grant the following relief ...

为此，原告请求法院作出如下判决……

第四节　翻译实例分析

1. 级别管辖的规定

第十八条　基层人民法院管辖第一审民事案件，但本法另有规定的除外。

Article 18　A Basic People's Court shall have jurisdiction as the court of first instance over civil cases, unless otherwise provided in this Law.

第十九条　中级人民法院管辖下列第一审民事案件：

Article 19　An Intermediate People's Court shall have jurisdiction as courts of first instance over the following civil cases:

a. 重大涉外案件；

a. Major cases involving foreign elements;

b. 在本辖区有重大影响的案件；

b. Cases that have major impacts in the area of its jurisdiction; and

c. 最高人民法院确定由中级人民法院管辖的案件。

c. Cases under the jurisdiction of the intermediate people's courts as determined by the Supreme People's Court.

第二十条 高级人民法院管辖在本辖区有重大影响的第一审民事案件。

Article 20 A Higher People's Court shall have jurisdiction as the court of first instance over civil cases that have major impacts on the areas of its jurisdiction.

第二十一条 最高人民法院管辖下列第一审民事案件：

Article 21 The Supreme People's Court shall have jurisdiction as the court of first instance over the following civil cases：

a. 在全国有重大影响的案件；

a. Cases that have major impacts on the whole country; and

b. 认为应当由本院审理的案件。

b. Cases that the Supreme People's Court deems should be adjudicated by itself.

本段是民事诉讼法中对级别管辖的规定，即 jurisdiction by levels of courts。首先要明确的是实行四级两审终审制度，四级法院的英文表达分别是 Basic People's Court，Intermediate People's Court，Higher People's Court，Supreme People's Court。

三个条文中的"重大"都译为 major，以便统一，而两次提及的"本辖区"都译为 the areas of its jurisdiction。第十九条中的重大涉外案件不能简单理解为涉及外国人，译成英文后要补充相关信息，即译为 involving foreign elements。

2. 地域管辖的规定

第二十二条 对公民提起的民事诉讼，由被告住所地人民法院管辖；被告住所地与经常居住地不一致的，由经常居住地人民法院管辖。

Article 22 A civil lawsuit brought against a citizen shall be under the jurisdiction of the people's court located in the place where the defendant has his domicile; if the defendant's domicile is different from his habitual residence, the lawsuit shall be under the jurisdiction of the people's court located in the place of his habitual residence.

对法人或者其他组织提起的民事诉讼，由被告住所地人民法院管辖。

A civil lawsuit brought against a legal person or an organization shall be under the jurisdiction of the people's court located in the place where the defendant has its domicile.

同一诉讼的几个被告住所地、经常居住地在两个以上人民法院辖区的，各该人民法院都有管辖权。

Where the domiciles or habitual residences of several defendants in the same lawsuit are in the areas under the jurisdiction of two or more people's courts, all of those people's courts shall have jurisdiction over the lawsuit.

第二十三条 下列民事诉讼，由原告住所地人民法院管辖；原告住所地与经常居住地不一致的，由原告经常居住地人民法院管辖：	Article 23 The civil litigations described below shall be under the jurisdiction of the people's court located in the place where the plaintiff has his domicile; if the plaintiff's domicile is different from his habitual residence, the lawsuit shall be under the jurisdiction of the people' court located in the place of the plaintiff's habitual residence. The relevant civil litigations are:
a. 对不在中华人民共和国领域内居住的人提起的有关身份关系的诉讼；	a. Litigations concerning the status of persons who do not reside within the territory of the People's Republic of China;
b. 对下落不明或者宣告失踪的人提起的有关身份关系的诉讼；	b. Litigations concerning the status of persons whose whereabouts are unknown or whom have been declared missing;
c. 对被劳动教养的人提起的诉讼；	c. Litigations brought against the persons who are undergoing reeducation through labor; and
d. 对被监禁的人提起的诉讼。	d. Litigations brought against persons who are in imprisonment.
第二十四条 因合同纠纷提起的诉讼，由被告住所地或者合同履行地人民法院管辖。	Article 24 A lawsuit brought about a contract dispute shall be under the jurisdiction of the people's court located in the place where the defendant has his domicile or where the contract is performed.

本段文字选自民事诉讼法中的地域管辖部分，即 territorial jurisdiction。其中有前面提及的"民事诉讼"（civil litigation）、"被告"（defendant）、"身份关系"（status of person）、"住所"（domicile）、"经常居住地"（habitual residence）、"宣告失踪"（be declared missing）、"劳动教养"（reeducation through labor）、"监禁"（in imprisonment）。"对……提起的诉讼"统一译为 litigations brought against。

3. 对抗制度

Most knowledgeable observers would agree that the Anglo-American adversary tiral system is a thing of wonder. One wonders whethter it is properly designed to reach its announced goal, the ascertainment of relevant truth. Beyond that, one wonders how it ever works at all.	大多数知识渊博的观察者会认同英美法系的对抗审判制度是值得怀疑的。有人怀疑它是为了达到宣称的目标，即因对相关实施的确认而设计合理。除此之外，还有人怀疑它究竟如何起作用。

There is nothing very scientific about the process of litigation. As on highly experienced trial lawyer, who believed in being frank, once described it, "The way we administer justice is by an adversary proceeding, which is to say, we set the parties fighting." A trial is a competition of inconsistent versions of facts and theories of law.

对抗制里没有什么很科学的诉讼程序，一个有丰富经验的律师，一个相信坦诚的人，曾经这样描述：我们通过抗辩程序实现公平，也就是说，我们让当事人争斗。庭审是一场对事实和法律理论的不同见解的比赛。

本段选自英美法系中有关对抗制度的解释，整体难度不大，有术语 adversary trial system, adversary proceeding, litigation 等。另外有两点需要注意："… is a thing of wonder" 中，对 wonder 的理解需要结合上下文，不能简单地将其理解为"奇迹"；在英国法律环境下宜将 trial lawyer 理解为"出庭律师"。

4. 答辩状

答辩人与原告之间不存在直接的合同关系。答辩人于 2019 年 6 月 10 日与××第三建筑公司订立了一份口头合同，由××第三建筑公司负责把答辩人的一个高压电表柜拆除。原告是受××第三建筑公司的委托来拆除高压电表柜的，与答辩人之间不存在直接合同关系。

原告的伤害赔偿应由××第三建筑公司负责，其一，根据我国法律和有关司法解释规定，××第三建筑公司对其职工在履行合同的范围内所受到伤害应负责任，原告的伤害并不是由于合同客体以外的事物造成的……其三，受××第三建筑公司委托的原告在拆除高压电表柜的过程中，存在着严重违反操作程序的行为，未尽一个电工应尽的注意义务。

The respondent does not have a direct contractual relationship with plaintiff. The respondent entered into an oral contract with ×× No 3 Construction Company on June 10, 2019, whereby ×× No 3 Construction Company shall be responsible for removing the high-voltage meter cabinet. The plaintiff was engaged in removing the high-voltage meter cabinet as entrusted by ×× No 3 Construction Company and therefore has no direct contractual relationship with the respondent.

The liabilities for compensating the plaintiff for the damage shall be born by ×× No 3 Construction Company for the following reasons. Firstly, pursuant to PRC laws and relevant judicial interpretations, ×× No 3 Construction Company shall be liable for any injuries suffered by its employees to the extent of the contract performance. The injuries of the plaintiff were not caused by anything other than the object of the contract… Thirdly, the plaintiff, who was entrusted by ×× No 3 Construction Company, seriously violated the operational procedure in removing the high-voltage meter cabinet and failed to pay due attention thereto.

答辩状是被告、被上诉人或者被申请人对原告、上诉人、申请人的辩驳文书,针对的是起诉书、上诉书或者申请书。本段文字围绕原告基于合同而提起的赔偿请求展开。相关术语不难,如"答辩人"(the respondent)、"原告"(plaintiff),"订立了一份口头合同"(enter into an oral contract with)、"操作程序"(the operational procedure)等。

对于上诉案件,法院做出的判决一般有四种情况:维持原判(to affirm the judgment of the first instance)、推翻下级法院判决(to overrule the judgment of the first instance)、改变下级法院判决(to modify the judgment of the first instance)、将案件发回重审(to remand the case for retrial)。

5. 国际油污损害民事责任公约

Where the owner, after an incident, has constituted a fund in accordance with Article V, and is entitled to limit his liability.	当船舶所有人在事件发生之后已按第五条规定设立一项基金并有权限制其责任范围时,则:
a. No person having a claim for pollution damage arising out of that incident shall be entitled to exercise any right against any other assets of the owner in respect of such claim;	a. 对上述事件造成的油污损害提出索赔的任何人不得就其索赔对船舶所有人的任何其他财产行使任何权利;
b. The Court or other competent authority of any Contracting State shall order the release of any ship or other property belonging to the owner which has been arrested in respect of a claim for pollution damage arising out of that incident, and shall similarly release any bail or other security furnished to avoid such arrest;	b. 各缔约国的法院或其他主管当局应下令退还由于对该事件造成的油污损害提出索赔而扣留的属于船舶所有人的任何船舶或其他财产,对为避免扣留而提出的保证金或其他保证金也同样应予以退还;
c. The foregoing shall, however, only apply if the claimant has access to the Court administering the fund and the fund is actually available in respect of his claim.	c. 但上述规定只在索赔人能向管理基金的法院提出索赔,并且该基金对他的索赔确能支付的情况下才适用。

因为本书没有单独的国际法相关章节,因而在相应部门法收录了部分与民事相关的文本。本段文字是国际油污损害民事责任的规定。其中有一些术语,如 constitute a fund(设立一项基金)、in respect of such claim(究其索赔)、the Contracting State(缔约国)、other competent authority(其他主管当局)、release(退还)、the foregoing(上述规定)。

就句子结构而言,a 款和 b 款的英文结构相对复杂,如 a 款中,having a claim for pollution damage 作为修饰部分,解释 no person,其后的 arising out of that incident 又做 pollution damage 的修饰成分,这是典型的"葡萄藤"结构。在翻译法律文本时,译者在掌握术语的基础上还要能够熟练地切分句子,以便于理解和翻译。

练习 1

上诉人因租赁合同一案，不服第 12 号《民事判决书》，现依法提起上诉。

上诉事实和理由：

首先，上诉人对本案的基本和主要观点：

上诉人认为，根据《合同法》倡导的当事人意思高度自治和契约自由的理念，以及目前司法实践中的主流执法观念，上诉人与被上诉人之间共存在三份合同，均应认定为有效合同。该三份合同的主体、标的物、价款基本一致。

① 一审法院认定上诉人与被上诉人签订的房屋租赁合同为无效合同，于法无据。

② 法院以被上诉人已履行了合同大部分义务，上诉人在双方订立合同时已在使用租赁房屋为由认定上诉人先履行抗辩权不能成立，这明显违反了《合同法》有关先履行抗辩权的规定。

其次，上诉人基于并不完全认可的一审法院判决的几点抗辩观点：

① 一审法院以 2017 年后上诉人与被上诉人之间存在事实租赁关系为由，判决上诉人比照 2016 年合同的租金标准承担租金，于法无据。

② 一审法院对被上诉人未履约的 13 平方米问题的判决存在明显的执法错误。

③ 鉴于一审法院孤立执法（只处理 2016 年合同）的情况，上诉人在 2016 年以后已经给付的租金就不止贰万元。

④ 即便在一审法院只处理 2016 年合同的情形下，对有关装潢不予补偿，亦不公平。

综上所述，上诉人认为，上诉人与被上诉人之间共存在三份合同。被上诉人和一审法院对该三份合同在明知和已经查明的情况下，却有意割裂当事人之间的完整民事法律关系，从而造成一审判决存在片面、孤立执法，加重当事人的讼累。一审判决存在执法尺度、执法理念的不统一、不协调（如对 13 平方米未追究违约责任）。一审判决还存在越权司法、违法裁量等问题。为此，上诉人恳请二审法院，能在基于依法查明本案全部事实的基础上均衡执法，做出公正的裁判！

练习 2

That Plaintiff and Defendant are in compatible. Whereof, Plaintiff prays judgment as follows:

① That Plaintiff be granted an absolute decree of divorce from the Defendant, that the bonds of matrimony now and heretofore existing between the parties be dissolved; and that the parties hereto be released from all the obligations therefore;

② That Plaintiff be awarded as his sole and separate property all that property he had prior to the marriage to include the residence located at 420 Old Fannin Road, Rankin County, the State of Mississippi and his personal jewelry, car and effects; that Defendant shall be awarded as her sole and separate all that property she had prior to the marriage and her personal jewelry, belongings, and effects.

③ For such other and further relief as to the court may seem just and proper in the premises.

练习3

委托事项：代为答辩、出庭；提出反诉，调查取证，并向有关法院递送有关证据；进行和解；接受法庭调解；接受、放弃或变更诉讼请求；准备上诉和提出上诉；申请再审；申请在审理中或者审理前的证据保全及财产保全措施；申请强制执行法庭有效文件；接收送达的法庭文件；签收裁决、判决、传票及任何其他的法庭文件；处理与所有上述事务有关的相应问题。

练习4

The initial step in the court's analysis is to determine whether the harm suffered by the Plaintiff's decedent was reasonably foreseeable to the defendants. The Plaintiff alleges that the defendants knew at some point that Jackson: had a criminal background; had been convicted of burglary in the third degree, larceny in the third degree and disorderly conduct; had used marijuana at some point; had attempted suicide; had exhibited violent and self-abusive behavior. It is not reasonably foreseeable that a person convicted of burglary and disorderly conduct will later commit assault, battery and murder. Similarly, it is not forceable that a person who has used marijuana or attempted suicide will subsequently commit such brutal, violent acts.

第七章
仲裁的基本知识和翻译

仲裁（arbitration），又称为 alternative dispute resolution（ADR），是指买卖双方在纠纷发生之前或之后，签订书面协议，自愿将纠纷提交双方所同意的第三者予以裁决，以解决纠纷的一种方式。显然仲裁庭的管辖权来源于当事人之间的协议，仲裁庭仅可就当事人业已同意提交仲裁的纠纷行使管辖权。若一方当事人违反仲裁协议开始诉讼，另一方当事人可以向法院申请中止诉讼程序（anti-suit injunction）。仲裁庭的管辖权范围也限定于仲裁协议的约定，仲裁庭不得超越当事人赋予的管辖权范围进行裁判。

仲裁协议有两种形式：一种是在争议发生之前订立的，它通常作为合同中的一项仲裁条款出现；另一种是在争议发生之后订立的，它是把已经发生的争议提交给仲裁的协议。这两种形式的仲裁协议的法律效力相同。

有不少涉外合同存在中英文两种版本，基于双方的谈判力等原因，相关合同中未能明确约定仲裁事宜，当两种版本的表述出现分歧时，对于以哪一版本为准会产生分歧。

因为仲裁条款约定不符合法律规定或翻译不同而产生法律纠纷的案件不在少数。如在《关于江苏×××化工有限公司与 Liven Agrichem Pte Ltd.（利跃农化有限公司）买卖合同纠纷的请示案》中，案涉合同第十九条仲裁条款的中英文表述如下：

> 任何由此合同产生或与此合同相关的争议，包括合同的存在性、有效性或终止的任何问题，参考并最终在中国根据国际商会现行的仲裁规定仲裁解决。这些规定视同本条款的参考。

> Any dispute arising out of or in connection with this contract, including any question regarding its existence, validity or termination, shall be referred to and finally resolved by arbitration in China in accordance with the Arbitration Rules of Singapore International Arbitration Center for the time being in force which rules and deemed to be incorporated by reference into this clause.

中文部分的主要内容是在中国适用国际商会现行的仲裁规则仲裁，而英文部分的主要内容为在中国适用新加坡国际仲裁中心现行的仲裁规则仲裁，内容截然不同。

中国最高人民法院认为，本案当事人没有约定确定仲裁条款效力的准据法，但中英文两个版本均约定在中国进行仲裁。根据《中华人民共和国涉外民事关系法律适用法》第十八条规定，当事人可以协议选择仲裁协议适用的法律。当事人没有选择的，适用仲裁机构所在地法律或者仲裁地法律。在涉案仲裁条款的中英文两个部分约定不一致且当事人事后亦未达成补充协议的情况下，应当认定涉案仲裁条款的内容约定不明确，无法执行。

再如，在《关于××服务公司请求确认其与沧州××钢管股份有限公司签订的ZX090201-08〈购销合同〉中仲裁协议效力无效的请示案》中，案ZX090201-08《购销合同》采用了中英文对照的形式，对其中约定的仲裁条款，中文表述为"在履行协议过程中，如发生争议，双方应友好协商解决，若通过友好协商未能达成协议，则提交中国国际贸易促进委员会对外贸易仲裁委员会，根据该会仲裁程序暂行规定进行仲裁。若一方不服裁决，则再由新加坡国际仲裁法按照该会仲裁程序的有关规定进行仲裁"。然而英文中则没有"若一方不服裁决，则再由新加坡国际仲裁法按照该会仲裁程序的有关规定进行仲裁"的相应部分。对于国内仲裁机构的约定，英文的表述是"the case in dispute shall be submitted to China International Trade Arbitration Commission, Shanghai Branch"。中英文版本的差异直接导致仲裁当事一方向法院申请确认该仲裁条款无效，彻底改变案件结果。

最初××服务公司先向中国国际经济贸易仲裁委员会申请仲裁，仲裁委员会向××服务公司发函要求说明中英文表述不一致的缘由。后来申请人和被申请人均确认以中文版本为准。中国最高法院认为，当事人既未约定仲裁协议的适用法律，也未约定仲裁地，按照《最高人民法院关于适用〈中华人民共和国仲裁法〉若干问题的解释》第十六条，应适用我国法律。但购销合同中的中文表述违反了我国"一裁终局"的原则，仲裁协议被认定为无效。

企业之间的商事纠纷数量多、频率高，且适用法律和争议解决机制的可约定性较强。这也使得适用法律和争议解决机制成为企业合同谈判中的重点谈判内容。一般而言，企业之间的商事纠纷可以通过仲裁、法院、第三方调解机构调解解决。根据对2015—2017年走出国门企业的调研，在走出去的企业中有超过一半的企业选择通过国际常设仲裁机构解决争议。

目前全球影响力比较大的国际常设仲裁机构包括国际商会（International Chamber of Commerce，简称ICC）的下设独立仲裁机构国际仲裁院（International Court of Arbitration，简称ICA）、伦敦国际仲裁院（London Court of International Arbitration，简称LCIA）、斯德哥尔摩商会仲裁院（Arbitration Institute of the Stockholm Chamber of Commerce，简称"SCC"仲裁院）、新加坡国际仲裁中心（Singapore International Arbitration Center，简称SIAC）、中国国际经济贸易仲裁委员会（China International Economic and Trade Arbitration Commission，简称CIETAC）等。

除上述传统国际仲裁机构外，美国仲裁协会（American Arbitration Association，简称AAA）、解决投资争端国际中心（International Centre for Settlement of Investment Disputes，简称ICSID）、北京仲裁委员会（Beijing Arbitration Commission，简称BAC）等仲裁机构也发展迅速，但仍以区域性业务为主。

国际商事法庭也逐步发展起来，荷兰、新加坡等国都设立了国际商事法庭，中国最高人民法院也于2018年设立国际商事法庭，并分别在深圳和西安设立了第一国际商事法庭和第二国际商事法庭。国际商事法庭的后续发展对法律翻译从业者来说也值得关注。

第一节　常用术语

仲裁的常用术语见表7-1。

表7-1　仲裁的常用术语及其英文表达

术语	英译
中国国际商会仲裁院	Arbitration Institute of the China Chamber of International Commerce
接受仲裁申请	accept arbitration application
管理仲裁案件	administrate arbitration case
受案范围	jurisdiction
转让	transfer
失效	expiry
无效	invalidity
未生效	ineffectiveness
被撤销	rescission
仲裁庭	arbitration tribunal
仲裁裁决	arbitration award
营业地	place of business
注册地	place of registration
住所地	domicile
惯常居住地	habitual residence
放弃异议	waiver of right to object
仲裁申请、答辩、反请求	request for arbitration, defense and counterclaim
案件秘书	case manager
程序管理	procedural administration
主合同	principal contract
从合同	ancillary contract
仲裁通知	notice of arbitration
不能履行	incapable of being performed

续表

术语	英译
鉴定	authenticate
延缓	adjourn
缔约国	contracting state
书面协定	agreement in writing
仲裁条款	arbitration clause
互换电函	exchange of letters or telegrams
程序规则	rules of procedure
原裁决之正本	duly authenticated original award
正式副本	duly copy
提供担保	give security
撤销裁决	set aside the award
中止裁决	suspension of the award
一裁终局	single ruling system
司法行政部门	judicial administrative department
特别规定	special stipulation
公证行为	notarial act
诉讼保全	preservative measures in litigation
承诺书	note of acceptance
不得向人民法院起诉	shall not bring the suit in a people's court
有效证明书	certificate of validity
公证证明书	certificate of notary
驳回上诉	reject the appeal
维持原判	sustain the original judgment
重审	retrial
被申请人	respondent
追加当事人	joinder of additional parties
仲裁程序	arbitral proceeding
合并仲裁	consolidation of arbitration
紧急仲裁员	emergency arbitrator
首席仲裁员	presiding arbitrator
询问式或辩论式	inquisitorial or adversarial approach

续表

术语	英译
进行合议	hold deliberations
开庭	oral hearing
缺席审理并做出判决	proceed with the arbitration and make a default award
庭审笔录	record of oral hearing
质证	examination of evidence
调解	conciliate
调解书	conciliation statement
法律强制性规定	a mandatory provision of the law
部分裁决	partial award
费用承担	allocation of fees
仲裁庭组成	formation of the arbitral tribunal
其他证明文件	other supporting documents
程序变更	change of procedure
仲裁员的选定或指定	nomination or appointment of arbitrator

第二节 核心术语的表达和理解

1. arbitration

arbitration 意为"仲裁",是指争议双方在争议发生前或争议发生后达成协议,自愿将争议交给第三方(即仲裁员)来审理并做出裁决的争议解决方法。与仲裁直接相关的常用术语有 submit for arbitration(提交仲裁)、arbitration agreement(仲裁协议)、umpire(首席仲裁员)、award(仲裁裁决)、arbitrator(仲裁员)、arbitration association(仲裁协会)、arbitration clause(仲裁条款)、arbitration board(仲裁庭)等。

典型的仲裁条款如下:

① Any dispute arising from or in connection with the Contract shall be settled through friendly negotiation. In case no settlement is reached, the dispute shall be submitted to China International Economic and Trade Arbitration Commission (CIETAC), Shenzhen Commission, for arbitration in accordance with its rules in effect at the time of applying for arbitration. The arbitral award is final and binding upon both parties.

凡因本合同引起的或与本合同有关的任何争议应协商解决。若协商不成,应提交中国国际经济贸易仲裁委员会(CIETAC)深圳分会,按照申请仲裁时该会当时施行的仲裁规则进行仲裁。仲裁裁决是终局的，对双方均有约束力。

2. institutional arbitration, ad hoc arbitration

按照组织形式不同，仲裁可以分为机构仲裁（institutional arbitration）和临时仲裁（ad hoc arbitration）。

机构仲裁，有时又称为常设仲裁（permanent arbitration），是一种由当事人合意选择仲裁机构解决其争议的国际商事仲裁。常设仲裁机构是指有固定的组织形式、固定的仲裁地点、固定的仲裁规则以及一定的仲裁员名单的仲裁机构。审理争议时，由双方当事人从仲裁员名单中选定仲裁员组成仲裁庭审理争议。目前，世界上各种常设仲裁机构多达130多个。

ad hoc arbitration 中，按照拉丁语，ad 是 to 或 towards 的意思，hoc 是 this 的意思，将其直译过来为"为此，特此"。因此，ad hoc arbitration 就具有了"为此仲裁，特此仲裁"之意，又译为"特设仲裁"。

设立在荷兰海牙的国际法院分为常设法庭（permanent court）和特设法庭（ad hoc court）。如果 ad hoc arbitration 不与 institutional arbitration 并列，而是与 permanent arbitration 并列，我们就可以用"特设仲裁"和"常设仲裁"来翻译。

3. 仲裁地

选择仲裁地意味着将仲裁程序置于该地法律体系之内，依据该地法律展开并受该地法院监督。仲裁地不同于庭审地（place of hearings）、仲裁庭合议地（place of deliberation）等地点。前者是抽象法律概念，后两者属于地理或空间上的概念。仲裁地在英文中有多种表达方式，包括 place of arbitration, arbitral seat, arbitral situs, locus arbitration, arbitral forum。仲裁法和仲裁规则中最为常用的是前两种：UNCITRAL Model Law on International Commercial Arbitration 中用的是 place of arbitration, ICC Arbitration Rules（2017）中用的也是 place of arbitration；English Arbitration Act 1996 和 HKIAC Arbitration Rules（2013）用的则是 seat of arbitration, LCIA Arbitration Rules（2014）用了两种，即 arbitral seat 和 seat of arbitration。

仲裁地通常由当事方在仲裁协议中进行约定。对仲裁地的约定最好明确城市的名称。例如，LCIA 示范条款即注明"The seat, or legal place, of arbitration shall be（City and/or Country）"。在没有明确约定时，仲裁地依据仲裁规则加以确定。多数情况下，仲裁规则将此权力授予仲裁庭或仲裁机构。例如，UNCITRAL Arbitration Rules 第 18（1）条规定"If the parties have not previously agreed on the place of arbitration, the place of arbitration shall be determined by the arbitral tribunal having regard to the circumstances of the case."。

但也有仲裁规则会规定优先适用某个仲裁地。例如，LCIA Arbitration Rules（2014）第 16.2 条规定"In default of any such agreement, the seat of the arbitration shall be London（England）, unless and until the Arbitral Tribunal orders …"。

仲裁地选定具有重要法律意义：首先，可以确定仲裁程序的管辖法律。UNCITRAL Model Law, English Arbitration Act 等法律均规定，该法适用于仲裁地位于该国境内的仲裁。其次，确定协助并监督仲裁程序的法院，如请求法院审查仲裁庭的管辖权决定，请求法院指定或移除仲裁员，向法院申请临时保全措施，向法院申请撤销仲裁裁决等。最后，可以帮助确定仲裁裁决的国籍，从而判断是否适用《纽约公约》。《纽约公约》第1（1）条规定"This Convention shall apply to the recognition and enforcement of arbitral awards made in the territory of a State other than the State where the recognition and enforcement of such awards are sought … "。

4. arbitration agreement

仲裁协议（arbitration agreement）指当事人在合同中订明的仲裁条款或以其他方式达成的提交仲裁的书面协议。按照规定，仲裁协议应当采取书面形式。书面形式包括合同书（contract）、信件（letter）、电报（telegram）、电传（telex）、传真（fax）、电子数据交换（electronic data interchange）、电子邮件（e-mail）等可以有形地表现所载内容的形式。在仲裁申请书和仲裁答辩书交换中，若一方当事人声称有仲裁协议而另一方当事人不做否认表示，则视为存在书面仲裁协议。

5. res judicata

res judicata 为拉丁语，译为"既决事项，既判力，一事不再理"。一般认为，既判力原则属于请求的可受理性（admissibility of claim）范畴，是有合法管辖权的法院就案件做出终局判决后，在原当事人之间不得就同一事项、同一诉讼标的、同一请求再次提起诉讼。法院做出的发生法律效力的判决是最终的决定。

6. expedited procedure rules

expedited procedure rules 译为"快速程序规则"。2016 年 11 月，ICA 发布了最新的《仲裁规则》，新规则自 2017 年 3 月 1 日正式实施。此次规则修改的最大亮点是引入快速程序规则。根据新的规则，仲裁协议签订于 2017 年 3 月 1 日之后，争议总金额不超过 200 万美元，适用快速程序。

当事人可以约定不适用快速程序，ICA 也可以根据个案具体情况决定不适用。与此同时，当事人也可以自愿选择（opt in）快速程序，不受仲裁协议签订时间及争议金额大小的限制。

7. Internaitonal Center for Settlement of Investment Disputes，ICSID

ICSID 译为"解决投资争端国际中心"。ICSID 秘书处 2011 年 5 月 24 日登记的案号为"ARB/11/15"的伊佳兰公司诉中华人民共和国仲裁案（EkranBerhad v. People's Republic of China）是中国政府第一次作为被申请人在 ICSID 登记的国际投资仲裁案。

因海南省万宁市人民政府依据当地地方性法规收回了伊佳兰公司下属公司 Sino Malaysia Art & Culture 投资的国有土地使用权，伊佳兰公司随后向 ICSID 提起仲裁，请求赔偿和补偿相关损失。该案涉及《中华人民共和国政府和马来西亚政府关于相互鼓励和保护投资协定》，最终因双方达成和解，以伊佳兰公司撤诉结案。

与前案相反，中国平安人寿保险公司诉比利时王国投资条约仲裁案（Ping An Life Insurance Company of China, Limited and Ping An Insurance Group Company of China,

Limited v. Kingdom of Belgium, ICSID Case No. ARB/12/29），是中国企业在 ICSID 起诉东道国政府的第一起案件，同时也是比利时在 ICSID 第一次作为被申请人，受到广泛的关注。在与比利时政府协商、调解 3 年无成果后，中国平安人寿保险公司将比利时政府推向被告席，并就投资损失补偿事宜，向 ICSID 寻求救济。

8. arising from, arising out of, in connection with, relating to

在国际仲裁中，仲裁机构的管辖权来自争议，但仲裁机构无权处理所有争议，除了仲裁地准据法认为不具有可仲裁性的事项外，当事人也可以通过仲裁条款或仲裁协议排除仲裁庭对于一些事项的管辖。在确定管辖权的时候，对词句文义进行严格解释是普通法系国家看重的。

就常用语义来说，arising from 和 arising out of 几乎完全相同，from 更多地强调源头，而 out of 则有"由内而外"的意思。按照美国上诉法院的理解，out of 表明了所有根源于或起源于该合同的争议，无论是否隐含了关于合同本身解释和履行的问题。

美国法院曾经认为 arising under the contract 的词义更严格，表明了只有关于合同解释和履行的争议才能进行仲裁。含义范围最广的是 in connection with，relating to 和 in connection with 同义。

9. challenges to jurisdiction of the tribunal

challenges to jurisdiction of the tribunal 译为"管辖权异议"，是指一方当事人认为仲裁机构仅就部分请求或反请求享有管辖权的主张，属于部分异议。

一方当事人主张仲裁协议无效或提交仲裁的所有争议事项均在仲裁协议范围之外时，属于全部异议，如：一方当事人主张其并非仲裁协议的当事人，因而不受该仲裁协议的拘束；该仲裁协议缺乏书面这一形式要件；提交仲裁的争议事项在相关法律下不具有可仲裁性。

10. 范围

《仲裁法》和相关的法律文本中会有描述仲裁范围或受理范围之类的文字，语料库检索发现英文版的《仲裁法》中"范围"有三种译法，即 scope, extent, jurisdiction。例如：

② 约定的仲裁事项超出法律规定的仲裁范围的……

Matters agreed upon for arbitration are beyond the scope of arbitration prescribed by law …

③ 裁决的事项不属于仲裁协议的范围或者仲裁委员会无权仲裁的……

The matters of the award are beyond the extent of the arbitration agreement or not within the jurisdiction of the arbitration commission …

④ ……属于仲裁委员会的受理范围

the arbitration must be within the jurisdiction of the arbitration commission …

显然，同一部法律条文中出现三种译法，违反了法律翻译的一致性原则，特别是例

③,译者可选择用 scope 来代替 extent。例如,《纽约公约》第五条中有"范围"一词的表述:

⑤ The award deals with a difference not contemplated by or not falling within the terms of the submission to arbitration, or it contains decisions on matters beyond the scope of the submission to arbitration.

裁决所处理之争议非为交付公断之标的或不在其条款之列,或裁决载有关于交付公断范围之外事项之决定者。

再如:

⑥ The English High Court decision of Bond v Mackay and others [2018] EWHC 2475 (TCC) concerned a situation where, when a claimant sought to bring further issues before an arbitral tribunal, the court was asked to determine whether those issues fell within the scope of the matters referred to the arbitrator and therefore within his jurisdiction.

英国高等法院在"Bond v Mackay and others [2018] EWHC 2475 (TCC)"一案中的裁定涉及这样一种情形,即当申请人请求向仲裁庭提出更多事由时,法庭需要确定这些事由是否属于提交仲裁庭事项范围,因而属于其管辖范围。

11. if any

if any 通常的含义是 if there is/are any at all,可译为"如果有的话"。实践中,有的企业在英文仲裁条款中就约定"Arbitration if any to be settled in country (or region)"译为"如果提起仲裁,在某国(或某地区)进行"。

第三节 常见句型结构

仲裁条款的起草特别是多语种仲裁条款的起草,直接影响仲裁条款效力,决定着争议合同或者协议是否能够被提交给相关的仲裁机构。本节收录了一些国内和国际主要仲裁机构推荐的标准仲裁条款。

有效的仲裁条款必须包含两个要素,即将争议提交仲裁的意思表示和仲裁适用的规则。当然国内仲裁机构 CIETAC,上海国际仲裁中心(SHIAC),香港国际仲裁中心(HKIAC)的示范条款都明确了仲裁机构,而 ICC, LIAC, UNCITAL 的示范条款都没有明确仲裁机构。那么约定仲裁机构是否有必要呢?这要根据仲裁地的准据法。如果用 ICC 或 LIAC 示范条款的仲裁准据法是英国法的话,不约定仲裁机构,仲裁条款也有效。

但中国的仲裁法对没有仲裁机构管理的临时仲裁是不认可的。因此,如果采用 ICC 的示范条款,而仲裁地在中国,没有约定仲裁协议的准据法而使用仲裁地法中国法的话,中国法院是不会认可该仲裁协议的效力的。即使仲裁裁决被做出,也会不被承认和执行。

根据国外仲裁规则在中国领土上做出的裁决(不包括中国香港与澳门地区,因为有特殊规定），在理论上可能被认为是内国裁决（domestic arbitration award），从而可能不受《纽约公约》保护，但是最高人民法院在2013年3月的《最高人民法院关于申请人安徽省龙利得包装印刷有限公司与被申请人BP Agnati S. R. L. 申请确认仲裁协议效力案的复函》认可选择国际商会仲裁院仲裁、管辖地为上海的仲裁协议有效。在起草国际仲裁条款时，起草者最好加上仲裁机构，以减少不必要的纠纷和降低成本。

1. CIETAC 的官方仲裁条款

⑦ 凡因本合同引起的或与本合同有关的任何争议，均应提交中国国际经济贸易仲裁委员会，按照申请仲裁时该会现行有效的仲裁规则进行仲裁。仲裁裁决是终局的，对双方均有约束力。

Any dispute arising from or in connection with this Contract shall be submitted to China International Economic and Trade Arbitration Commission (CIETAC) for arbitration which shall be conducted in accordance with the CIETAC's arbitration rules in effect at the time of applying for arbitration. The arbitral award is final and binding upon both parties.

2. SHIAC 的官方仲裁条款

⑧ 凡因本合同引起的或与本合同有关的任何争议，均应提交上海国际经济贸易仲裁委员会/上海国际仲裁中心进行仲裁。

Any dispute arising from or in connection with this Contract shall be submitted to Shanghai International Economic and Trade Arbitration Commission/Shanghai International Arbitration Center for arbitration.

3. HKIAC 的官方仲裁条款

⑨ 凡因本合同所引起的或与之相关的任何争议、纠纷、分歧或索赔，包括合同的存在、效力、解释、履行、违反或终止，或因本合同引起的或与之相关的任何非合同性争议，均应提交由香港国际仲裁中心管理的仲裁，并按照提交仲裁通知时有效的《香港国际仲裁中心机构仲裁规则》最终解决。

Any dispute, controversy, difference or claim arising out of or relating to this contract, including the existence, validity, interpretation, performance, breach or termination thereof or any dispute regarding non-contractual obligations arising out of or relating to it shall be referred to and finally resolved by arbitration administered by the Hong Kong International Arbitration Centre (HKIAC) under the HKIAC Administered Arbitration Rules in force when the Notice of Arbitration is submitted.

4. SIAC 的官方仲裁条款

⑩ 凡因本合同引起的或与本合同有关的任何争议,包括合同的存在、效力和终止,均应提交由新加坡国际仲裁中心,(下称"新仲"),依据仲裁开始时最新施行的《新加坡国际仲裁中心仲裁规则》(下称"新仲规则"),以新加坡为仲裁地,通过仲裁方式最终解决。新仲规则视为本仲裁条款的一部分。

Any dispute arising out of or in connection with this contract, including any question regarding its existence, validity or termination, shall be referred to and finally resolved by arbitration administered by the Singapore International Arbitration Centre (SIAC) in accordance with the Arbitration Rules of the Singapore International Arbitration Centre (SIAC Rules) for the time being in force, which rules are deemed to be incorporated by reference in this clause.

5. ICC 的官方仲裁条款

⑪ 凡产生于或与本合同有关的一切争议均应按照国际商会仲裁规则由依据该规则指定的一名或数名仲裁员终局解决。

All disputes arising out of or in connection with the present contract shall be finally settled under the Rules of Arbitration of the International Chamber of Commerce by one or more arbitrators appointed in accordance with the said Rules.

该条款根据欧美法律可能不存在争议,但根据中国法律规定,该条款却有可能导致仲裁协议无效。中国《仲裁法》规定:仲裁协议对仲裁事项或者仲裁委员会没有约定或者约定不明确的,当事人可以补充协议;达不成补充协议的,仲裁协议无效。上述国际商会标准条款并没有明确约定仲裁委员会,如果双方没有达成补充协议,那么该仲裁协议无效。这就有可能造成双方不能通过仲裁解决纷争或者仲裁裁决得不到执行。为此国际商会针对中国的情况重新拟定了如下条款:

⑫ All disputes arising out of or in connection with the present contract shall be submitted to the International Court of Arbitration of the International Chamber of Commerce and shall be finally settled under the Rules of Arbitration of the International Chamber of Commerce by one or more arbitrators appointed in accordance with the said Rules.

凡产生于或与本合同有关的一切争议均应提交国际商会国际仲裁院并按照国际商会仲裁规则由依据该规则指定的一名或数名仲裁员终局解决。

6. LCIA 的官方仲裁条款

⑬ 凡因本合同引起的或与本合同有关的任何争议,包括合同的存在、效力和终止,均应提交伦敦国际仲裁院,并按照伦敦国际仲裁院规则终局解决,伦敦国际仲裁院规则视为本仲裁条款的一部分。

Any dispute arising out of or in connection with this contract, including any question regarding its existence, validity or termination, shall be referred to and finally resolved by arbitration under the LCIA Rules, which Rules are deemed to be incorporated by reference into this clause.

7. UNCITRAL 的官方仲裁条款

⑭ 任何争议、争执或请求，凡由于本合同而引起的或与之有关的，或由于本合同的违反、终止或无效而引起的或与之有关的，均应按照《联合国国际贸易法委员会仲裁规则》仲裁解决。

Any dispute, controversy or claim arising out of or relating to this contract, or the breach, termination or invalidity thereof, shall be settled by arbitration in accordance with the UNCITRAL Arbitration Rules as at present in force.

第四节　翻译实例分析

1. 仲裁裁决书

仲裁裁决书	Arbitration Award
双方当事人：	Parties：
申诉方/反诉被诉方：卖方	Claimant/counter-defendant：Seller
被诉方/反诉申诉方：买方	Defendant/Counter-claimant：Buyer
仲裁地：	Place of arbitration：
事实：	Facts：
1994年，双方当事人根据某种协议规格规定签署了3份买卖一种产品的合同。在收到货运单据后，买方即按合同规定，支付了全部合同价的90%。	In 1994, the parties concluded three contracts for the sale of a product according to certain contract specifications. The Buyer paid 90% of the price payable under each of the contracts upon presentation of the shipping documents, as contractually agreed.
按第一和第三份合同提供的产品符合协议规格，第二批货物的规格在装运前就有过争议。产品抵达目的地后被重新检验，买方发现其不符合协议规格。为了便于脱手，买方对货物进行了某种处理，最终将产品卖给第三方，损失惨重。	The product delivered pursuant to the first and third contracts met the contract specifications. The conformity of the second consignment was dispute prior to its shipment. When the product was again inspected upon arrival, it was found that it did not meet the contract specifications. The product was eventually sold by the Buyer to third parties at considerable loss, after having undergone a certain treatment to make it more saleable.

卖方提请仲裁，要求收回10%的合同余款。买方提起反诉，声称应从卖方所索费用中扣除买方估计应由卖方赔偿买方的一笔费用，即直接损失费、财务成本费、所损失的利润及利息费。

（1）适用的法律

a. 鉴于合同未含有关实体法的任何条款，故法律问题应根据国际商会仲裁规则第13条第3款决定。根据该条规则，仲裁员们应适用它们认为适合的法律冲突规则所规定的准据法则。

b. 这是一份由国籍不同的卖方和买方签署的在第三国交货的合同。买卖规定为船上交货，故风险在卖方所在国便转给买方。由此，卖方所在国似乎就成为与买卖关系最近的管辖地。

c. 有关国际货物买卖适用法律的1995年6月15日的《海牙公约》在涉及销售合同时，将卖方现行居住地法律视为准据法。买方所在国加入了《海牙公约》，卖方所在国则没有。尽管如此，法律冲突法的总趋势却是适用合同主要业务的债务人现行所在地的国内法。在销售合同中，此债务人为卖方。基于这些因素，卖方所在国的法律似乎便成了规定买卖双方之间合同的准据法。

The Seller initiated arbitration proceedings to recover the 10% balance remaining due under the contracts. The Buyer filed a counterclaim alleging that the Seller's claim should be set off against the amounts which the Buyer estimates to be payable to the buyer by the seller, i.e., the direct losses, financing costs, lost profits and interest.

(1) Applicable Law

a. The contract contains no provisions regarding the substantive law. Accordingly that law has to be determined by the Arbitrators in accordance with Art. 13 (3) of the ICC rules. Under that article, the Arbitrators will apply the law designated as the proper law by the rule of conflicts which they deem appropriate.

b. The contract is between a Seller and a Buyer of different nationalities for delivery in a third country. The sale was F.O.B. so that the transfer of risks to the Buyer took place in the country of Seller. The country of Seller accordingly appears as being the jurisdiction to which the sale is most closely related.

c. The Hague Convention on the law applicable to international sales of goods dated 15 June 1995 (Art. 3) regarding sales contracts, refers as governing law to the law of the Seller's current residence. The country of the Buyer has adhered to The Hague Convention, not the country of the Seller. However, the general trend in conflicts of law is to apply the domestic law of the current residence of the debtor of the essential undertaking arising under the contract. That debtor in a sales contract is the Seller. Based on those combined findings, the law of the country of the Seller appears to be the proper law governing the Contract between the Seller and the Buyer.

d. 至于卖方所在国法律的适用规则，仲裁员们依据的是双方当事人各自陈述的理由，以及仲裁员们从一位独立咨询人处所得的信息。根据国际商会仲裁规则第 13 条最后一段规定，仲裁员们也将考虑相关的贸易惯例。

（2）反诉的可受理性

a. 仲裁庭认为，1980 年 4 月 11 日的《关于国际货物销售的联合国公约》（通称《维也纳公约》）是现行贸易惯例的最好渊源，即使买卖双方所在国均不是公约的成员国。倘若买卖双方所在国均为公约成员国，在本案中，该公约不仅可被考虑作为贸易惯例适用，而且还可作为法律适用。

b.《维也纳公约》已在 17 个国家生效，考虑用它适用于国际货物销售中的不符规格事项有通用惯例，应属合情合理。《维也纳公约》第 38 条第 1 款规定买方负有"当场检查或叫人检查货物"的责任。买方应在注意或应当注意到瑕疵后的合理期限内通知卖方货物不符合同的规格；否则，他将丧失就上述不符规格而提起索赔的权利。第 39 条第 1 款规定："若买方在交货后两年之内没有通知卖方，无论如何，买方都将丧失在货物不符规格问题上的申诉权利，除非此种不符规格构成了对长期单保的违背。"

d. As regards the applicable rules of the law of the country of the Seller, the Arbitrators have relied on the Parties' respective statements on the subject and on the information obtained by the Arbitration from an independent consultant. The Arbitrators, in accordance with the last paragraph of Art. 13 of the ICC rules, will also take the relevant trade usage into account.

（2） Admissibility of the Counterclaim

a. The Tribunal finds that there is no better source to determine the prevailing trade usage than terms of The United Convention on the International Sale of Goods of 11 April 1980, usually called the Vienna Convention. This is also even though neither the country of the Buyer nor the country of the Seller are parties to that Convention. If they were, the Convention might be applicable to this case as a matter of law and not only as reflecting the trade usage.

b. The Vienna Convention, which has been given effect to in 17 countries, may be fairly taken to reflect the generally recognized usage regarding the matter of the non-conformity of goods on international sales. Art. 38（1）of the Convention puts the onus on the Buyer to "examine the goods or cause them to be examined promptly". The buyer should then notify the Seller of the nonconformity of the goods within a reasonable period as of the moment he noticed or should have noticed the defect; otherwise, he forfeits his right to raise a claim based on the said non-conformity. Art. 39（1）specifies in the respect that: "In any event the buyer shall lose the right to rely on a lack of conformity of the goods if he has not given notice thereof to the seller within a period of two years from the date on which the goods were handed over, unless the lack of conformity constituted a breach of guarantee covering a longer period."

c. 本案中买方在合理的期限内已对货运做过检查，因为在货物抵达之前，曾请一位专家去检查过。买方也应被认定在合理期限内，即在专家报告公布后8天内，就产品瑕疵做过通报。

c. In the circumstances, the Buyer had the shipment examined within a reasonable time-span since an expert was requested to inspect the shipment even before the goods had arrived. The Buyer should also be deemed to have given notice of the defects within a reasonable period, which is eight days after the expert's report had been published.

d. 仲裁庭认为，就本案情况而言，买方遵守了上述《维也纳公约》的要件规定。这些要件要比卖方所在国的法律的规定灵活许多。卖方所在国法律所规定的买方通知卖方的时限特别短、特别具体，在这点上，似乎是通用的贸易惯例的一种例外。

d. The Tribunal finds that, in the circumstances of the case, the Buyer has complied with the above-mentioned requirements of the Vienna Convention. These requirements are considerably more flexible than those provided under the law of the country of the Seller. This law, by imposing extremely short and specific time requirements in respect of the giving of the notice of defects by the Buyer to the Seller appears to be an exception on this point to the generally accepted trade usage.

e. 仲裁庭裁决全部如下：卖方应获得其全部所主张的金额，扣除买方在反诉中提出的抵消部分数额。

e. The Tribunal awarded the Seller the full amount of its claim and set it off against part of the counterclaim filed by the Buyer.

所选例子是有关货物销售争议的仲裁书，涵盖仲裁裁决书的典型要素：仲裁当事人、仲裁地、事实查明、适用的法律、反诉的可受理性、仲裁裁决等。熟悉裁决书的体例和组成部分后，我们在法律翻译过程中选词时一定要注意保持法言法语。英译中的conclude（签署）、prior to its shipment（装运前）、third parties（第三方）、initiate arbitration proceedings（提请仲裁）、file a counterclaim（提起反诉）、the proper law（准据法则）、admissibility（受理）等都体现出词汇的专业性。

裁决书中两次出现的仲裁庭"认为"都被准确地译为find，find侧重事实查明，而hold强调法律适用问题。两次仲裁庭"认为"后面的内容看似是法律适用问题，实质上是在查明事实。仲裁庭裁决部分的英译并未与中文保持格式上的一致，而是遵循英文表达习惯，译为"The Tribunal awarded the Seller the full amount of its claim and set it off against part of the counterclaim filed by the Buyer."。其中，一定要注意到award不是普通英语中"奖励"的意思，否则会出现理解偏差。

2. 实体性问题

Prior to discussing the substantial issues, the judge firstly highlighted the importance of complying with the requirements imposed by Order 73 rule 5 (4) of Rules of High Court for an application to challenge an award on the ground of serious irregularity and for leave to appeal on a question of law. The judge noted that non-compliance carried the risk of applications being struck out immediately as abuse of process, since the aim of the Ordinance was to facilitate the fair and speedy resolution of disputes by arbitration without unnecessary expense, and the Ordinance was based on the principles that parties should be bound by their agreement to resolve a dispute by arbitration and to be bound by an arbitral award as being final. Resolution of disputes relating to the binding effect of an arbitration agreement and the arbitral award should be resolved without undue delay and unnecessary costs.

在讨论实体性问题之前，法官首先强调了遵守《高等法院规则》第 73 号令第 5 条第 4 款规定所涉的两项要求的重要性，即以严重失常行为为由质疑仲裁裁决，以及基于法律问题提起上诉。法官指出，由于《条例》的目的是通过仲裁促进公平和迅速地解决争议而避免产生不必要的费用，并且《条例》以当事人应受其通过仲裁解决争议之协议的约束，并受终局仲裁裁决约束为原则，因此不遵守要求可能会因滥用程序而存在申请被当即驳回的风险。与仲裁协议和仲裁裁决的约束力有关的争议应在无不当迟延和无非必要费用的情况下予以解决。

"实体性问题"和"实体法"的译法比较类似，都是用 substantial。对首字母大写的 Order 的翻译需要根据上下文来确定，本段中 order 指的是《高等法院规则》第 73 号令。challenge an award 短语中 award 译为"裁决"，而 challenge 不是"回避"的意思，应译为"质疑"。

第一句中真正的难点是 serious irregularity，我们需要运用相关法律知识来理解。在英国法中，仲裁是"一裁终局"的争议解决方式，即仲裁裁决做出后立即生效而不能向法院上诉。

世界上大多数国家也均认可仲裁的"一裁终局"，《1996 年英国仲裁法》规定了三种允许对仲裁裁决提起上诉的情况：仲裁庭缺乏实体管辖权（substantive jurisdiction）；仲裁庭、仲裁程序或仲裁裁决存在严重失常的情况；仲裁庭对仲裁裁决中所涉及的法律问题认定不准确。

后面几句的译文根据逻辑关系进行了相应的调整，把"因此不遵守要求可能会因滥用程序而存在申请被当即驳回的风险"后置。

3. 仲裁地问题

With regard to the application for leave to appeal on questions of law under section 6 of Schedule 2 of the Ordinance, CPC argued that Schedule 2 did not in fact apply to the arbitration clause. The judge noted that for Schedule 2 to apply, section 100 of the Ordinance requires the arbitration clause to provide that arbitration was a domestic arbitration. However, the DP Contract provided for arbitration in accordance with Cap. 341 (i.e. the predecessor of the current Ordinance) which permitted both domestic and international arbitrations. Thus, the judge was of the view that without expressly providing for resolution of disputes by domestic arbitration, the DP Contract did not fall within the ambit of section 100 of the Ordinance, for the Schedule to apply.

关于根据《条例》附表2第6条的规定就法律问题提出上诉的申请，CPC主张附表2实际上并不适用于仲裁条款。法官指出，就附表2的适用而言，《条例》第100条要求仲裁条款规定仲裁是本地仲裁。但是，DP合同根据《仲裁条例》第341章（即现行"条例"的前身）规定仲裁允许国内和国际仲裁。因此，法官认为，就附表的适用而言，在没有明确规定通过国内仲裁解决争议的情况下，DP合同不属于《条例》第100条的适用范围。

　　on questions of law 是仲裁文本中的常见表达，译为"法律问题"；"Schedule 2"不是"计划安排"的意思，而是表示"附表"；domestic arbitration 译为"本地仲裁"，而不是"国内仲裁"；the judge was of the view 译为"法官认为"；expressly 在法律文本中都译为"明确地"。

　　最后一句话中"did not fall within the ambit of section 100 of the Ordinance"可以等同于"did not fall within the scope of section 100 of the Ordinance"。

4. 合同的适用范围问题

DP further argued that Schedule 2 applied by virtue of section 101 (1) of the Ordinance, pursuant to which the arbitration agreement contained in the main contract would apply to the sub-contract, where the whole or part of the construction operations to be carried out under the main contact was sub-contracted and there was an arbitration clause in that sub-contract. The judge noted that the WSD Contract contained an arbitration agreement which expressly provided for domestic arbitration. However, the unusual feature was, as per the arbitrator's finding in the arbitral award, there was

DP进一步主张，附表2可依据《条例》第101条第1款而得以适用。而根据该附表，主合同所包含的仲裁协议将适用于分包合同，而主合同下将要进行的全部或部分建设工作是被分包了的，并且分包合同中有仲裁条款。法官指出，WSD合同包含明确规定本地仲裁的仲裁协议。然而，根据仲裁裁决中仲裁员的裁定，不寻常的特征是LW和CPC之

only a verbal contract between LW and CPC under which LW sub-contracted the works under the WSD Contract to CPC (the CPC Contract), but the terms of the CPC Contract did not provide for and made no reference to the existence of an arbitration agreement. Thus, the judge held that the CPC Contract did not fall within 101 of the Ordinance, for the Schedule to apply to the CPC Contract. Since the Schedule did not apply to the CPC Contract, the Schedule could not apply to the DP Contract between CPC and DP by operation of section 101.

间只存在口头合同。根据该合同，LW把WSD合同下的工作分包给了CPC（CPC合同），但CPC合同的条款没有规定并且没有提及仲裁协议的存在。因此法官认为，就附表适用于CPC合同而言，CPC合同不属于《条例》第101条的适用范围。由于附表不适用于CPC合同，附表不能通过第101条适用于CPC和DP之间的DP合同。

该段文字逻辑性较强，层层推理，得出结论，是裁定文书中的说理部分，译者需要通读全文后再尝试按照其中的逻辑关系翻译。在英文法律文本中 argue, find, hold, note 等表示"认为，主张，指出"。"However, the unusual feature was, as per the arbitrator's finding in the arbitral award" 句中的 as per 意为"依据"或"按照"。本段文字中多次出现 provide, 在其他法律文本中也多译为"规定"。made no reference to 译为"提及，提到"。

5. 条款效力和受理范围

不同于允许当事人就法律问题向英国法院提起上诉的《1996年英国仲裁法》，仲裁地在中国香港的仲裁之当事人一般不当然享有就法律问题对裁决提起上诉的权利。这项权利连同其他特别诉诸法院的权利，被规定在《条例》附表2中。根据中国香港法律，希望享有这些权利的各方必须根据《条例》第99条明确"选择"加入附表2的规定。因此，香港法院很少处理就法律问题对仲裁裁决提起上诉的申请。

Different to English Arbitration Act 1996 under which parties are allowed for an appeal to the English courts on a point of law, parties to arbitrations seated in Hong Kong, China do not, in general, have an automatic right to appeal an award on a question of law. Such rights, along with other special rights of recourse to the courts, are set out in Schedule 2 to the Arbitration Ordinance. Under Hong Kong, China law, parties wishing to enjoy such rights must expressly "opt in" to the provisions of Schedule 2 pursuant to section 99 of the Ordinance. As a result, it is rare for the Hong Kong court to deal with an application for leave to appeal an arbitral award on a question of law.

仲裁中有不少争议聚焦于仲裁条款效力和受理范围问题。an appeal to the English courts on a point of law 在前面的例子中多次出现，下半句 do not ... have an automatic right to... 可译为"不当然/自动享有……权利"。

rights of recourse to the courts 中的 recourse 在有些语境中被理解为追索权，此处译为"诉诸法院的权利"；are set out in Schedule 2 中的 set out 相当于 stipulated，即"规定"；an applicaton for leave to appeal an arbitral award 中 leave 是名词，相当于 permission，所以宜译为"对仲裁裁决提起上诉申请"。

翻译练习

练习1

All disputes arising out of the performance of, or relating to this Contract, shall be settled amicably through negotiation. In case no settlement can be reached through negotiation, the case shall then be submitted to China International Economic and Trade Arbitration Commission for arbitration in accordance with its arbitration rules. The arbitral award is final and binding upon both parties.

练习2

Arbitration. Any dispute, controversy, or claim arising out of, in connection with, or relating to the performance of this Agreement or its termination shall be settled by arbitration in the Commonwealth of Massachusetts, pursuant to the rules of the American Arbitration Association. Any award shall be final, binding and conclusive upon the parties and a judgment rendered thereon may be entered in any court having jurisdiction thereof.

练习3

当事人可以约定将争议提交中国国际经济贸易仲裁委员会或仲裁委员会分会/仲裁中心进行仲裁；约定由中国国际经济贸易仲裁委员会进行仲裁的，由仲裁委员会仲裁院接受仲裁申请并管理案件；约定由分会/仲裁中心仲裁的，由所约定的分会/仲裁中心仲裁院接受仲裁申请并管理案件。约定的分会/仲裁中心不存在、被终止授权或约定不明的，由仲裁委员会仲裁院接受仲裁申请并管理案件。如有争议，由中国国际经济贸易仲裁委员会做出决定。

练习4

当事人约定将争议提交中国国际经济贸易仲裁委员会仲裁但对本规则有关内容进行变更或约定适用其他仲裁规则的，从其约定，但其约定无法实施或与仲裁程序适用法的强制性规定相抵触者除外。当事人约定适用其他仲裁规则的，由中国国际经济贸易仲裁委员会履行相应的管理职责。

The High Court's decision

Davis QC (sitting as Deputy High Court judge) disagreed with the arbitrator's finding that the clause 2 (i) dispute was not within the initial reference to arbitration. The court noted that the reasons behind the arbitrator's award were difficult to follow and that the court was essentially rehearing the matter of jurisdiction. In this respect the principal issue appeared to be whether a dispute under clause 2 (i) was outside the matters referred to the arbitrator because the arbitration had initially proceeded on the basis of disputes under different clauses of the BG Deed. The judge disagreed with such an approach. He instead found that the court should take a "broad view of the factual matrix" in determining what had been referred, including the wider factual background such as correspondence leading up to the appointment of the arbitrator and the acceptance of the appointment.

Against that context, the judge accepted the claimant's argument that the matter referred to the arbitrator was correctly seen as a claim for "compensation", "whether that be under clause 2 (i), 5 or 6". Thus, the fact that a breach of clause 2 (i) was not initially referred to from the outset did not mean that it was outside the arbitrator's jurisdiction.

第八章

刑法的基本知识和翻译

中国现行刑法，即《中华人民共和国刑法》（以下简称《刑法》），是 1979 年通过并实施的，其后为适应经济社会发展又进行了 11 次修正，第 11 次修正案是 2020 年 12 月 26 日通过的。

美国的实体刑法虽然源于英国普通法，但它属于成文法。美国的刑法由州议会和国会确定。大多数州都有一部全面的实体刑法典，一般由刑事责任总则、定义特定罪行的法律，以及定义免除义务和行为正当理由的法律组成。约 2/3 的州全部或者部分采用 20 世纪五六十年代美国法学会（American Law Institute）拟定的《刑法范典》（Model Penal Code）。

虽然美国各州都有相对独立的法律体系，对犯罪的定义和分类都不尽相同，但也有相通之处，比如犯罪可以分为重罪（felony）和轻罪（misdemeanor）。重罪以处以一年以上有期徒刑为准；一般轻罪以处以一年以下有期徒刑为准，还可以包括罚款、缓刑、社区服务、赔偿等处分。当事人拥有陪审团听证及使用公辩律师的权利，一般如骚乱（disturbance）、轻盗窃罪（petty larceny）、轻微攻击（simple assault）等，根据犯罪实际情况，都有可能属于轻型犯罪。如果罪名成立，且是初犯，算是轻罪，会被处以一年以下有期徒刑或罚金，或两者并处。

每种犯罪还可以细分为若干等级，以区分严重或者恶性程度。以美国明尼苏达州的性犯罪（criminal sexual conduct）为例，第四级会被处以十年监禁或两万美元以下罚金，或者并处。第三级一般会被处以十五年以下监禁或三万美元以下罚金，或者并处；第二级和第一级主要针对威胁使用暴力或者使用暴力的情形，第二级会被处以七年半到二十五年的监禁或三万五千美元以下的罚金，或者并处；第一级则会被处以十三年到三十年的监禁或四万美元以下的罚金，或者并处。

英国根据罪行严重程度把犯罪行为分为三等：叛国罪（treason）、重罪（felony）和轻罪（misdemeanor）。在早期，达到死刑的罪为重罪，后来又被进一步分为死刑罪和普通重型罪。盗窃财物价值达 500 英镑以上者可以被定为普通重型罪，定罪后只需服刑一年以下或者处以罚金的案件视为轻罪案件，而现在这种重罪和轻罪的区分被取消了。

刑法的核心术语主要集中在三个方面：犯罪（crime）、刑罚（punishment）和刑事责任（criminal liability）。

第一节 常用术语

刑法的常用术语见表 8-1。

表 8-1 刑法的常用术语及其英文表达

术语	英译
犯罪构成要件	the essential elements of crime
行为要求	act requirement
精神状态	mental state
因果关系	causation
作为	commission
不作为	omission
特殊目的	specific intent
恶意	malice
明知	knowledge
放任	recklessness
过失	negligence
严格责任	strict liability
实际因果关系	actual causation
近因	proximate causation
负刑事责任	bear criminal responsibility
间歇性精神病人	person whose mental illness is of an intermittent nature
应当从轻或者减轻处罚	shall be given a lighter or mitigated punishment
免于处罚	be exempted from punishment
不法侵害	unlawful infringement
防卫过当	undue defense
紧急避险	commit an act in an emergency to avert an immediate danger
犯罪中止	discontinuation of a crime
共同犯罪	joint crime
犯罪集团的首要分子	ringleader who organizes or leads a criminal group
主犯	principal
从犯	accomplice
按照他的犯罪情节	in the light of the circumstances of the crime one commits

续表

术语	英译
企业、事业单位、机关或团体	enterprise, institution, state organ, or organization
管制	public surveillance
拘役	criminal detention
有期徒刑	fixed-term imprisonment
无期徒刑	life imprisonment
死刑	the death penalty
剥夺政治权利	deprivation of political rights
没收财产	confiscation of property
驱逐出境	deportation
具结悔过	make a statement of repentance
主管部门	the competent department
羁押	be held in custody
选举权和被选举权	the right to vote and to stand for election
担任国家机关职务的权利	the right to hold a position in a state organ
自首	voluntary surrender
强制措施	compulsory measures
司法机关	the judicial organ
重大立功	perform major meritorious services
正当防卫	self-defense; justifiable defense
妨碍司法	obstruction of justice
窝赃逃犯	harbor a fugitive
妨碍起诉	hinder prosecution
犯罪未遂	inchoate offense
教唆	solicitation
同谋	conspiracy
抗辩事由	defense
精神病	insanity
胁迫	duress
杀人	homicide
恶意预谋	malice aforethought
重罪谋杀	felony murder

续表

术语	英译
致死武器理论	deadly weapon rule
转移意图	transferred intent
一级谋杀	first degree murder
二级谋杀	second degree murder
预谋	premeditation
极端轻率谋杀	depraved heart murder
共同重罪犯	co-felon
非预谋杀人罪	manslaughter
非预谋故意杀人	voluntary manslaughter
无故意非预谋杀人	involuntary manslaughter
激情杀人	heat of passion
殴击罪	battery
企图伤害罪	assault
非法拘禁	false imprisonment
绑架罪	kidnapping
纵火罪	arson
贿赂罪	bribery
入室盗窃罪	burglary
挪用/盗用罪	embezzlement
间谍罪	espionage
伪造罪	forgery
文字诽谤罪	libel
伪证罪	perjury
诽谤罪	slander
入侵私人土地罪	trespass
走私	smuggle goods
金融机构	banking institution
伪造货币	counterfeit currencies
虚假出资	make a false capital contribution
伪造、变造或转让	forge, alter or transfer
财务会计报告	financial and accounting report

续表

术语	英译
与走私罪犯通谋	conspire with criminals of smuggling
抽逃其出资	surreptitiously withdraw the contributed capital
组织、领导或积极参加	form, lead or actively participate
擅离岗位	discharge his official duties
电力、燃气或者其他易燃易爆设备	electric power, gas facility or any other inflammable or explosive equipment
招股说明书	the prospectus on share offer
认股书	subscription form
索取他人财物	demand money or property from another person
非法收受他人财物	illegally accept another person's money or property
收受回扣或手续费	accept rebates or service charges
谋取不正当利益	seek illegitimate benefits
决水、爆炸、投毒	breach a dike, cause explosion, spread poison
持有违禁品	possession of contraband
私藏赃物	receipt of stolen property
生产、销售劣药	produce or sell medicines of inferior quality
不符合卫生标准的食品	not up to hygiene standards
非法吸收公众存款	illegally take in deposits from the general public
伪造、变造金融票证	forge or alter financial bill
扰乱金融秩序	disrupt the financial order
汇票和本票	bills of exchange and promissory notes
股票或公司、企业债券	stocks or corporate and enterprise bonds
内幕信息	inside information
勒索财物	extort money or property
窃取、刺探或收买	steal, spy or buy
敲诈勒索公私财物	extort public or private money or property by blackmail
抢夺罪	forcible seizure of money or property
报复陷害	retaliate against or frame up
假公济私	use his public office for private ends
拘留所或看守所	detention house or a custody house
捏造事实诽谤他人	invent stories to defame sb.

续表

术语	英译
侮辱他人	humiliate another person
拐卖	abduct and traffick
捏造事实诬告陷害他人	invent stories to implicate another person
限制人身自由	restrict their personal freedom
聚众哄抢公私财物	gather to forcibly seize public or private money or property
盗窃、利诱或胁迫	steal, lure or coercion
聚众打砸抢	gather to commit beating, smashing or looting
聚众斗殴	gather to engage in affrays
引诱、教唆或欺骗	lure, aid and abet or cheat
渎职罪	dereliction of duty
泄露国家秘密	divulge State secret
枉法裁判	twist the law when rendering judgments or orders
徇私枉法	bend the law for selfish ends
徇私舞弊	malpractice for personal gain
徇情枉法	twist the law for a favor
黑社会性质的组织	an organization in the nature of criminal syndicate
编造并传播虚假信息	fabricate and spread false information

第二节 核心术语的表达和理解

1. act, law, statute

act 主要是指由立法机关制定的法律（the formal product of a legislative body），常用作单一法律的名称，可译为"××法"，如《刑法》（Criminal Law Act）、《反不当竞争法》（Anti-Competitive Act）。

law 既可指单部法律或法规，又可表示一般和抽象的含义，但它一般不用作某个特定的法律命令名称，如《国际商品销售统一法规编纂》（Uniform Law on the International Sale of Goods）、《忏悔者爱德华法律汇编》（Laws of Edward the Confessor）、《合同法》（Law of Contract）。

statute 是指制定法，与判例法相对。立法机关制定的 act 既可称为 law，也可称为 statute，如《伊丽莎白法令》（Statute of Elizabeth）、《林肯法令》（Statute of Lincoln）、《防止欺诈法》（Statute of Frauds）、《刑法》（Penal Statute）。

2. homicide, killing, manslaughter

homicide 是指一个人的作为或不作为导致或促使他人的死亡，为中性词，只描述客观行为，而对其道德或法律性质并没有做出判断，如过失杀人（negligent homicide）、正当杀人（justifiable homicide）、可免责的杀人（excusable homicide）、恶意杀人（felonious homicide）、应受惩罚的杀人罪（culpable homicide）（指苏格兰法律中还未达到谋杀罪程度的杀人罪）。

killing 不是严格意义上的法律术语，可指一切杀人行为，包括他杀（homicide）和自杀（suicide）两种，如意外杀人（killing by misadventure）、非故意杀人（accidental killing）。

manslaughter 是指非预谋杀人罪，指无预谋恶意地非法终止他人生命的行为。普通法将非预谋杀人罪分为非预谋故意杀人（voluntary manslaughter）和无故意非预谋杀人（involuntary manslaughter），前者的处罚重于后者。

3. assault, battery

assault 是指英美刑法中的企图伤害罪，或指侵权法中的威胁、恐吓。assault 强调企图（attempt to commit a violent injury）；battery 强调实施，意思是完成对这种威胁的实施。所以 assault 与 battery 经常一起出现，意思是"企图伤害罪与殴击罪"，可简称为"殴击罪"。

4. murder

在美国刑法里，谋杀罪（murder）可分为一级谋杀罪（first degree murder）和二级谋杀罪（second degree murder）。

一级谋杀罪是被告在从事杀人行为时具备恶意，经过深思熟虑（deliberation/specific intent to kill）与预谋（premeditation）。此种谋杀罪的行为人并非冲动性杀人，而是蓄意策划，具备强烈杀人意图，因此一级谋杀罪是美国刑法中最严重的犯罪，被告恶行也最重大。

二级谋杀罪也是一种非法谋杀（unlawful killing），行为人同样在实施行为时具备恶意，但二级谋杀罪的恶意要件并非是像一级谋杀罪那样需要经过深思和预谋，只要被告具备杀人意图（intent to kill）、对被害人身体进行重大伤害的意图（an intent to inflict great bodily injury），或对于被害人生命漠不关心（a reckless indifference to human life）所构成的间接故意，即符合二级谋杀罪的主观要件。二级谋杀罪的主观恶行没有一级谋杀罪重大，被告可以用自陷己醉（voluntary intoxication）和事实错误（mistake of facts）作为抗辩事由。

5. principal, principal in the second degree

美国刑法里面主犯和从犯分为四种：一级主犯（principal）、二级主犯（principal in the second degree）、事前从犯（accessary before the fact）和事后从犯（accessary after the fact）。直接帮助主犯从事犯罪活动的是二级主犯，并且不论是事前协助过主犯，比如帮助主犯拿东西或者开车，还是事后帮助过主犯，比如协助主犯逃跑或者毁灭证据。

6. intentional crime, negligent crime

intentional crime 意为"故意犯罪"。明知自己的行为会产生危害社会的结果（entail harmful consequences），并且希望（wish）或者放任（allow）这种结果产生，因而构成犯罪的，是故意犯罪。

negligent crime 意为"过失犯罪"。应当预见自己行为可能发生危害社会的结果，因为疏忽大意（negligence）而没有预见，或者已经预见而轻信能够避免，以致发生这种结果的，是过失犯罪。

7. ringleader

ringleader 意为"首要分子"。首要分子在中国刑法里是指在犯罪集团或者聚众犯罪中起组织（organize）、策划（plot）、指挥（direct）作用的犯罪分子。

8. entrapment

entrapment 可译为"诱惑执法，钓鱼执法，警察圈套"，是指执法人员为获取相关案件的证据，制造陷阱，诱惑犯罪人，使其上当受骗，从而将其逮捕，对其提起刑事控诉的行为。

1932年美国的"索里尔斯案"最先确立"警察圈套"辩护事由。在该案中被告经不住警方代理人的再三请求，给其卖了酒并被其抓捕，并被控告违反了禁酒法。联邦高院判决，被告在面临向政府代理人卖酒而违反禁酒法的指控时可以使用"警察圈套"的抗辩理由。

9. embezzlement

embezzlement 意为"侵占罪"。侵占罪是指行为人在犯罪当时具有合法占有该财产的权利，却非法将占有改成持有。例如，公司高级主管管理公司的现金财产，其占有这些现金是合法占有，并为公司利益及需要来支付公司费用与账单，但如果高级主管将公司的现金资产占为己有，挪用公款，就可能构成侵占罪。

10. larceny

larceny 源自法语，意为"盗窃"，是指行为人取得自己无权占有的东西，只要行为人拿取该物品时不具有合法权利即构成犯罪，即使事后行为人取得所有权人的同意仍然会构成盗窃罪。

11. self-defense

self-defense 意为"正当防卫"。正当防卫是一种阻却违法事由（justification），必须是被害人真诚且合理地相信有必要去实施武力来对抗非法的行为。同时行为人也不可以是一开始的攻击者，举例来说，防卫者 A 不可以先挑衅或刻意激怒行为人 B，让 B 对自己做出攻击行为后，再以正当防卫的名义来攻击 B，这是不可以的。这也就是清白无瑕（clean hands）原则。

12. burglary

burglary 意为"侵入住宅罪"，也译为"夜盗罪"，其认定需要满足以下四点：

一是 breaking，指的是行为人打开关起来的门而进入屋内，如果进入时门没关则不算是 breaking；

二是 entering，只要被告身体的任一部分或手足的延伸（如包）进入了屋子就算；

三是 dwelling house of another，以占有权而非所有权来认定，因此若是房东侵入已经租给房客的住宅仍然有可能构成侵入住宅罪；

四是 with the intention to commit a felony inside，必须是行为人在进门时就有此意图。

中国有类似罪行，即非法侵入他人住宅罪，但不能用这个词来套译 burglary，因为根据中国刑法，非法侵入他人住宅是指未经主人同意，无正当理由擅自闯入他人居住的场所，影响他人生活，或住宅主人要求退出，但无理取闹拒不退出的行为。

13. blackmail, extortion, racketeering

这三个术语均表示"敲诈勒索"，但 blackmail 一般是指不使用暴力而是通过威胁，如通过威胁泄露对对方有害的资料而索取钱财；extortion 是指通过暴力、地位、权利等索取金钱；racketeering 则类似于 fraud，是指以欺骗或威胁手段勒索钱财。

14. abettor, instigator

abettor 和 instigator 在概念上都指"教唆犯"，但 abettor 的原形 abet 作为动词在程度上与后者有一定的差异。abettor 可指协助、帮助某人做某事（尤其是坏事），但一般都指较轻的违法行为；instigator 可以是教唆、唆使某人犯较严重的罪行，如煽动兵变（mutiny）。

15. defalcation, embezzlement, encroachment

三个词都可以译为"侵吞，侵占"，但其内涵有所不同：defalcation 是指挪用公款罪（侵吞、侵占公家或其托管的金钱）；embezzlement 是指侵吞任何钱物；encroachment 是指侵吞他人的不动产，如土地。

16. affray, nuisance

affray 和 nuisance 都可指"滋事罪"：前者主要是指聚众打架斗殴之类的滋扰；后者则特指做一些让公众普遍讨厌的事情，如在夜间大声喧哗扰民。

17. traffick, smuggle

中国《刑法》中与毒品有关的罪名一共约有 12 条，常见的有非法持有毒品罪（illegal possession of drugs），容留他人吸毒罪（provide venues for drug users），走私、贩卖、运输和制造毒品罪（smuggle, sell, traffick and produce drugs）等。其中 traffick 译为"运输"，侧重于境内，而 smuggle 强调跨越国家边境，译为"走私"。

18. offense, crime

juvenile offense 是指未成年人犯罪。在表示"罪"时，我们要注意区分 offense 和 crime。

offense 更倾向于指违法和犯较轻罪，还可以指民法中的违法行为，与故意侵权基本相同，因此 offender 可以译为"违法者，犯罪者"。

crime 是指刑法中规定的犯罪（a social harm that law makes punishable; the breach of a legal duty treated as the subject-matter of a criminal proceeding），译为"罪犯"。

19. deception, deceit, fraud

deception 本身不是罪行，却与多种罪行相关，如诈骗财产、保险单等，以诈骗行为获取报偿；但在英国法律中指不诚实地获取他人财产，或利用语言、行为或意思表达获得金钱上的好处。

deceit 多指可以予以起诉的民事侵权行为，指故意以虚假陈述或因无知传播虚假陈述使他方当事人相信，从而导致他方当事人遭受损失的违法行为。

fraud 多指民事侵权行为，也可以指犯罪，即为获得物质利益而通过陈述或行为所做的虚假表示，如预付费欺诈（advance-fee fraud）、邮件诈骗（mail fraud）。

20. robbery, forcible seizure

robbery 是指"抢劫罪"。forcible seizure 是指"抢夺罪"。

两者定罪量刑有较大的差异，抢夺不强调暴力，而是乘人不备，依靠的是突然、快速和敏捷，所以译者在翻译的时候应注意区分。

第三节 常见句型结构

除了因为使用大量术语让读者或译者感到晦涩难懂外，刑法文本中有一些特殊句型结构也会带来理解障碍，因为这些句型在普通英语文本中较少出现，让人感到生疏难解，这也是法律翻译让很多人望而生畏的原因之一。

幸运的是这些句型结构不多，在各类型文本中重复出现，因此一旦掌握使用率极高。此外，法律文本要求一致性，对词汇和句型多样性的要求比较低。

1. ……有下列情形之一的……

《刑法》第二百六十三条规定：

① 以暴力、胁迫或者其他方法抢劫公私财物的，处三年以上十年以下有期徒刑，并处罚金；<u>有下列情形之一的</u>，处十年以上有期徒刑、无期徒刑或者死刑，并处罚金或者没收财产……

Whoever robs public or private property by violence, coercion or other methods shall be sentenced to fixed-term imprisonment of not less than 3 years but not more than 10 years and shall also be fined; <u>whoever falls under any of the following categories</u> shall be sentenced to fixed-term imprisonment of not less than 10 years, life imprisonment or death and shall also be fined or sentenced to confiscation of property ...

汉语句子省略了"有下列情形之一的（人）"中的主语，英译增补了 whoever 使之成为一个符合语法的句子。

如《刑法》第二百六十四条规定：

② 盗窃公私财物，数额较大或者多次盗窃的，处三年以下有期徒刑、拘役或者管制，并处或者单处罚金；数额巨大或者有其他严重情节的，处三年以上十年以下有期徒刑，并处罚金；数额特别巨大或者有其他特别严重情节的，处十年以上有期徒刑或者无期徒刑，并处罚金或者没收财产；<u>有下列情形之一的</u>，处无期徒刑或者死刑，并处没收财产……

Whoever steals a relatively large amount of public or private property or commits theft repeatedly shall be sentenced to fixed-term imprisonment of not more than 3 years, criminal detention or public surveillance and shall also, or shall only, be fined; if the amount is huge, or if there are other serious circumstances, he shall be sentenced to fixed-term imprisonment of not less than 3 years but not more than 10 years and shall also be fined; if the amount is especially huge, or if there are other especially serious circumstances, he shall be sentenced to fixed-term imprisonment of not less than 10 years or life imprisonment and shall also be fined or be sentenced to confiscation of property; <u>whoever falls under any of the following categories</u> shall be sentenced to life imprisonment or death, and shall also be sentenced to confiscation of property …

再如《刑法》第二百九十二条规定：

③ 聚众斗殴的，对首要分子和其他积极参加的，处三年以下有期徒刑、拘役或者管制；<u>有下列情形之一的</u>，对首要分子和其他积极参加的，处三年以上十年以下有期徒刑……

Where people are gathered to engage in affrays, the ringleaders and the active participants shall be sentenced to fixed-term imprisonment of not more than 3 years, criminal detention or public surveillance; the ringleaders and the active participants <u>who fall under any of the following categories</u>, shall be sentenced to fixed-term imprisonment of not less than three years but not more than 10 years …

2. 情节严重的，情节特别严重的，（尚未）造成严重后果的

"情节严重的"译为 if the circumstances are serious；"情节特别严重的"译为 if the circumstances are especially serious。中国刑法条文中包含"情节严重的"条文有132例，由此可见其使用率极高。"严重"和"特别严重"属于模糊语，目的是增强条文的弹性和包容性，以应对复杂的现象，英译时要对其进行保留。

如《刑法》第一百零七条规定：

④ 境内外机构、组织或者个人资助境内组织或者个人实施本章第一百零二条、第一百零三条、第一百零四条、第一百零五条规定之罪的，对直接责任人员，处五年以下有期徒刑、拘役、管制或者剥夺政治权利；<u>情节严重的</u>，处五年以上有期徒刑。

Where an organ, organization or individual inside or outside of the territory of China provides funds to any organization or individual within the territory of China to commit the crime as prescribed in Article 102, 103, 104 or 105, the person who is directly responsible for the crime shall be sentenced to fixed-term imprisonment of not more than 5 years, criminal detention, public surveillance or deprivation of political rights; <u>if the circumstances are serious</u>, he shall be sentenced to fixed-term imprisonment of not less than 5 years.

再如《刑法》第三百八十条规定：

⑤ 战时拒绝或者故意延误军事订货，情节严重的，对单位判处罚金，并对其直接负责的主管人员和其他直接责任人员，处五年以下有期徒刑或者拘役；造成严重后果的，处五年以上有期徒刑。

Where a unit, during wartime, refuses to accept orders for military supplies or intentionally delays the provision of such supplies, if the circumstances are serious, it shall be fined, and the persons who are directly in charge and the other persons who are directly responsible for the offence shall be sentenced to fixed-term imprisonment of not more than 5 years or criminal detention; if the consequences are serious, they shall be sentenced to fixed-term imprisonment of not less than 5 years.

《刑法》全文中包含"情节特别严重的"条文共有 44 例，虽然数量明显少于"情节严重的"，但掌握其固定翻译还是有较大的意义。

如《刑法》第四百四十六条规定：

⑥ 战时在军事行动地区，残害无辜居民或者掠夺无辜居民财物的，处五年以下有期徒刑；情节严重的，处五年以上十年以下有期徒刑；情节特别严重的，处十年以上有期徒刑、无期徒刑或者死刑。

Any serviceman who, during wartime, cruelly injures innocent residents in an area of military operation or plunders their money or property shall be sentenced to fixed-term imprisonment of not more than 5 years; if the circumstances are serious, he shall be sentenced to fixed-term imprisonment of not less than 5 years but not more than 10 years; if the circumstances are especially serious, he shall be sentenced to fixed-term imprisonment of not less than 10 years, life imprisonment or death.

"（尚未）造成严重后果的"在《刑法》中共有 40 例，一般都译为 causing (no) serious consequences 或 if there are (no) serious consequences。

《刑法》第一百一十四条规定：

⑦ 放火、决水、爆炸、投毒或者以其他危险方法破坏工厂、矿场、油田、港口、河流、水源、仓库、住宅、森林、农场、谷场、牧场、重要管道、公共建筑物或者其他公私财产，危害公共安全，尚未造成严重后果的，处三年以上十年以下有期徒刑。

Whoever commits arson, breaches a dike, causes explosion, spreads poison or uses other dangerous means to sabotage any factory, mine, oilfield, harbour, river, water source, warehouse, house, forest, farm, threshing ground, pasture, key pipeline, public building or any other public or private property, thereby endangering public security but causing no serious consequences, shall be sentenced to fixed-term imprisonment of not less than 3 years but not more than 10 years.

再如《刑法》第一百二十三条规定：

⑧ 对飞行中的航空器上的人员使用暴力，危及飞行安全，<u>尚未造成严重后果的</u>，处五年以下有期徒刑或者拘役；<u>造成严重后果的</u>，处五年以上有期徒刑。

Whoever uses violence against any person on board an aircraft and thereby endangers air safety, <u>if there are no serious consequences</u>, shall be sentenced to fixed-term imprisonment of not more than 5 years or criminal detention; <u>if there are serious consequences</u>, he shall be sentenced to fixed-term imprisonment of not less than 5 years.

从这三个句型中，我们可以发现"情节"译为 circumstance，而"结果"译为 consequence。"情节严重的"的译法较为固定，而"（尚未）造成严重后果的"有两种译法，即 causing（no）serious consequences 和 if there are（no）serious consequences，译者可以根据句型需要选择使用。

3. 法律禁令句型"不得"

用"不得"表达禁止性规范，庄重严肃，简洁明快。"不得"一般译为 shall not，一般不译为 may no。译者要注意根据实际情况选择程度不同的否定表达方式。

如《刑法》第三条规定：

⑨ 法律明文规定为犯罪行为的，依照法律定罪处刑；法律没有明文规定为犯罪行为的，<u>不得</u>定罪处刑。

For acts that are explicitly defined as criminal acts in law, the offenders shall be convicted and punished in accordance with law; otherwise, they <u>shall not</u> be convicted or punished.

再如《刑法》第七十九条规定：

⑩ 对于犯罪分子的减刑，由执行机关向中级以上人民法院提出减刑建议书。人民法院应当组成合议庭进行审理，对确有悔改或者立功事实的，裁定予以减刑。非经法定程序<u>不得</u>减刑。

If punishment to a criminal is to be commuted, the executing organ shall submit to a People's Court at or above the intermediate level a written proposal for commutation of punishment. The People's Court shall form a collegiate panel for examination and, if the criminal is found to have shown true repentance or performed meritorious services, issue an order of commutation. However, <u>no</u> punishment <u>shall</u> be commuted without going through legal procedure.

又如《刑法》第八十二条规定：

⑪ 对于犯罪分子的假释，依照本法第七十九条规定的程序进行。非经法定程

序不得假释。

Parole shall be granted to a criminal through the procedure prescribed in Article 79 of this Law. No parole shall be granted without going through legal procedure.

"不得"译为 no ... shall,与中文相呼应,简洁而庄重,在语义和语用上都能充分表达禁止性含义。

4. "处"字句

"处"字句是《刑法》条文中使用最多的句型,法律语料库检索显示一共有630次提及"处"字,排除"处罚"等固定搭配295例、"判处"91例,还有244例。用"处"字句表示禁止性规范有两个特点:其一,在语义上,与"不得"不同的是,它用具体的制裁来表示禁令。其二,在结构上,主语往往为"的"字结构,突出犯罪主体或犯罪行为,简洁庄重。谓语部分的"处"字强调对犯罪主体或犯罪行为的处置。

"处"字句一般为被动句,为使行文简洁,实施主体(司法机关)一般不出现。有时为了使语义明确,实施主体也可以出现,通常译为 be sentenced to 句式。

如《刑法》第一百零三条规定:

⑫ 组织、策划、实施武装叛乱或装武暴乱的,对首要分子或者罪行重大的,处无期徒刑或者十年以上有期徒刑;对积极参加的,处三年以上十年以下有期徒刑;对其他参加的,处三年以下有期徒刑、拘役、管制或者剥夺政治权利。

Among those who organize, plot or carry out the scheme of splitting the State or undermining unity of the country, the ringleaders and the others who commit major crimes shall be sentenced to life imprisonment or fixed-term imprisonment of not less than 10 years; the ones who take an active part in it shall be sentenced to fixed-term imprisonment of not less than 3 years but not more than 10 years; and the other participants shall be sentenced to fixed-term imprisonment of not more than 3 years, criminal detention, public surveillance or deprivation of political rights.

5. "是"字句

"是"字句规定什么行为是犯罪,语气坚决,庄重简练。与"处"字句不同的是,它不表述具体的处罚,常常译为 refer to,用来解释说明。在刑法语料库中"是"字出现81次。

如《刑法》第二十二条规定:

⑬ 为了犯罪,准备工具、制造条件的,是犯罪预备。

Preparation for a crime refers to the preparation of the instruments or the creation of the conditions for a crime.

再如《刑法》第二十五条规定:

⑭ 共同犯罪是指二人以上共同故意犯罪。

A joint crime refers to an intentional crime committed by two or more persons jointly.

又如《刑法》第十四条规定：

⑮ 明知自己的行为会发生危害社会的结果，并且希望或者放任这种结果发生，因而构成犯罪的，是故意犯罪。

An intentional crime refers to an act committed by a person who clearly knows that his act will entail harmful consequences to society but who wishes or allows such consequences to occur, thus constituting a crime.

有时为了强调构成，"是"译为constitute，以罪名为宾语，如《刑法》第四百二十条：

⑯ 军人违反职责，危害国家军事利益，依照法律应当受刑罚处罚的行为，是军人违反职责罪。

Any act committed by a serviceman in transgression of his duties, an act that endangers the military interests of the State and should therefore be subjected to criminal punishment in accordance with law, constitutes a crime of a serviceman's transgression of duties.

有时"是"译为mean，其实可以用refer to代替mean，如《刑法》第四百五十一条：

⑰ 本章所称战时，是指国家宣布进入战争状态、部队受领作战任务或者遭敌突然袭击时。

The word "wartime" as used in this Law means the time when the State declares the state of war, the armed forces receive tasks of operations or when the enemy launches a surprise attack.

6. 禁止句型

刑法为了反映和引导社会大众对一些行为的否定评价，会用禁止句型来限定一些行为，告诫人们如果有类似行为，不仅会触发人们的道德谴责，还会招致国家刚性法律、刑法的惩罚。因此《刑法》条文中会有一些禁止句型，通常译为prohibit或forbid。为了体现同一性和一致性，译法最好统一。

如《刑法》第一百五十一条规定：

⑱ 走私珍稀植物及其制品等国家禁止进出口的其他货物、物品的，处五年以下有期徒刑，并处或者单处罚金；情节严重的，处五年以上有期徒刑，并处罚金。

Whoever smuggles precious and rare species of plants and the products thereof, the import and export of which is forbidden by the State, shall be sentenced to fixed-term imprisonment of not more than 5 years and shall also, or shall only, be fined; if the circumstances are serious, he shall be sentenced to fixed-term imprisonment of not less than 5 years and shall also be fined.

再如《刑法》第三百二十六条规定：

⑲ 以牟利为目的，倒卖国家禁止经营的文物，情节严重的，处五年以下有期徒刑或者拘役，并处罚金；情节特别严重的，处五年以上十年以下有期徒刑，并处罚金。

Whoever, for the purpose of profit, resells the cultural relics, the sale of which is prohibited by the State, if the circumstances are serious, shall be sentenced to fixed-term imprisonment of not more than 5 years or criminal detention, and shall also be fined; if the circumstances are especially serious, he shall be sentenced to fixed-term imprisonment of not less than 5 years but not more than 10 years and shall also be fined.

7. "以……为目的"句型

该类结构描述某个犯罪的主观意图，以实现对一些意图的否定性评价，从而将以此为意图的行为和其他行为区分开来，同时从刑法上来予以消极评判。《刑法》语料库显示，"以……为目的"的句型共有24例，集中表现为"以营利为目的""以牟利为目的""以非法占有为目的"等。

如《刑法》第一百五十二条规定：

⑳ 以牟利或者传播为目的，走私淫秽的影片、录像带、录音带、图片、书刊或者其他淫秽物品的，处三年以上十年以下有期徒刑，并处罚金；情节严重的，处十年以上有期徒刑或者无期徒刑，并处罚金或者没收财产；情节较轻的，处三年以下有期徒刑、拘役或者管制，并处罚金。

Whoever, for the purpose of making profits or dissemination, smuggles pornographic movies, videotapes, magnetic tapes, pictures, books or periodicals or other pornographic materials shall be sentenced to fixed-term imprisonment of not less than 3 years but not more than 10 years and shall also be fined; if the circumstances are serious, he shall be sentenced to fixed-term imprisonment of not less than 10 years or life imprisonment and shall also be fined or be sentenced to confiscation of property; if the circumstances are minor, he shall be sentenced to fixed-term imprisonment of not more than 3 years, criminal detention or public surveillance, and shall also be fined.

再如《刑法》第二百一十七条规定：

㉑ 以营利为目的，有下列侵犯著作权情形之一，违法所得数额较大或者有其他严重情节的，处三年以下有期徒刑或者拘役，并处或者单处罚金；违法所得数额巨大或者有其他特别严重情节的，处三年以上七年以下有期徒刑，并处罚金……

Whoever, for the purpose of making profits, commits any of the following acts of infringement on copyright shall, if the amount of illegal gains is relatively large, or if there are other serious circumstances, be sentenced to fixed-term imprisonment of not more than 3 years or criminal detention and shall also, or shall only, be fined; if the amount of illegal gains is huge or if there are other especially serious circumstances, he shall be sentenced to fixed-term imprisonment of not less than 3 years but not more than 7 years and shall also be fined …

比较第一百五十二条和第二百一十七条的译文，我们发现"营利"和"牟利"译为 making profits。营利是指以金钱、劳务等为资本而获得经济上的利益，谋取利润。"营"在这里是"谋取"的意思。"营利"有两个近义词——"牟利"和"谋利"，说的都是"谋取利益"。比如，老板经常告诫下属：采购公物，千万不可从中牟利。这句话也可以这样说：采购公物，千万不可从中营利。"营利"为中性词，"牟利"为贬义词，但是在刑法中都表现为通过犯罪行为去追求利润，二者的意义几近相同。

营利目的和牟利目的是相关犯罪的犯罪构成必要要件，是认定犯罪的重要依据。《刑法》分则的相关条款都明确将营利目的和牟利目的规定为构成犯罪的必要要件。

营利目的和牟利目的也有利于辨别行为性质和确定罪名，正确认定罪与非罪、此罪与彼罪的界限。以营利为目的和以牟利为目的在认定犯罪方面仍起到几乎相同的语境作用和指引作用。因此，我们应将"营利"和"牟利"统一，以避免引起误解或者被过度解读，从而增加没有必要的语言模糊性。

除"以营利/牟利为目的"外，还有"以非法占有为目的"，结构也较为类似。

《刑法》第二百二十四条规定：

㉒ 有下列情形之一，以非法占有为目的，在签订、履行合同过程中，骗取对方当事人财物，数额较大的，处三年以下有期徒刑或者拘役，并处或者单处罚金；数额巨大或者有其他严重情节的，处三年以上十年以下有期徒刑，并处罚金；数额特别巨大或者有其他特别严重情节的，处十年以上有期徒刑或者无期徒刑，并处罚金或者没收财产……

Whoever, during the course of signing or fulfilling a contract, commits any of the following acts to defraud money or property of the other party for the purpose of illegal possession, if the amount involved is relatively large, shall be sentenced to fixed-term imprisonment of not more than 3 years or criminal detention and shall also, or shall only, be fined; if the amount involved is huge, or if there are other serious circumstances, he shall be sentenced to fixed-term imprisonment of not less than 3 years but not more than 10 years and shall also be fined; if the amount involved is especially huge or if there are other especially serious circumstances, he shall be sentenced to fixed-term imprisonment of not less than 10 years or life imprisonment and shall also be fined or be sentenced to confiscation property ...

"以勒索财物为目的"和"以出卖为目的"的译法同上，如《刑法》第二百三十九条规定：

㉓ 以勒索财物为目的偷盗婴幼儿的，依照前款的规定处罚。

Whoever steals a baby or an infant for the purpose of extorting money or property shall be punished in accordance with the provisions of the preceding paragraph.

8. 刑法中的但书

在中国《刑法》中，有些条文的后半部分规定了与该条文前半部分相反或者是例外的情况，并用"但是"一词把两者连接起来，组成一个转折式的偏正复句。前半部分是正句，是条文的正意所在；后半部分为偏句，是说明、限制正句的，以引起人们的特别注意。这种现象就是刑法理论中的"但书"规定。《刑法》中"但书"句型共有20例，从第七十条开始到第二百七十二条结束，其中有几例的"但书"是条件句，译为 if，其余的一般都译为 however，也有译为 but。

如《刑法》第七条规定：

㉔ 中华人民共和国公民在中华人民共和国领域外犯本法规定之罪的，适用本法，但是按本法规定的最高刑为三年以下有期徒刑的，可以不予追究。

This Law shall be applicable to any citizen of the People's Republic of China who commits a crime prescribed in this Law outside the territory and territorial waters and space of the People's Republic of China; however, if the maximum punishment to be imposed is fixed-term imprisonment of not more than 3 years as stipulated in this Law, he may be exempted from the investigation for his criminal responsibility.

再如《刑法》第一百四十九条规定：

㉕ 生产、销售本节第一百四十一条至第一百四十八条所列产品，不构成各该条规定的犯罪，但是销售金额在五万元以上的，依照本节第一百四十条的规定定罪处罚。

Whoever produces or sells products listed in Articles 141 through 148 of this Section, if the case does not constitute the crime as mentioned in these Articles respectively but more than 50,000 *yuan* is earned from sales, shall be convicted and punished in accordance with the provisions of Article 140 of this Section.

第四节 翻译实例分析

1. 正当防卫

正当防卫是排除犯罪性的行为,也就是说,这种行为在表面上给合法权利造成了损害,实质上却是保护了合法权益。因此,中国刑法明文规定这种行为不构成犯罪。根据刑法,为了使国家、公共利益、本人或者他人的人身、财产和其他权利避免受到正在进行的不法侵害,而采取的制止不法侵害的行为,对不法侵害人造成损害的,属于正当防卫,不负刑事责任。

Justifiable defense is the act being exempted from crimes, namely, this act appears to cause damage to lawful rights and interests, but in essential it protects lawful rights and interests. Therefore, Chinese Criminal Law definitely prescribes that this act doesn't constitute crimes. According to the Criminal Law, an act that a person commits to stop an unlawful infringement in order to prevent the interest of the state and the public, or his own or other people's individual rights, rights of property or other rights from being infringed upon by the on-going infringement, thus harming the perpetrator, is justifiable defense, and he or she shall not bear criminal responsibility.

美国刑法里,刑事案件中的辩护理由除了不在犯罪现场(alibi)之外,还有自我防卫(self-defense),又写成 the defense of others(他我防卫)、defense of home and property(家庭财产防卫)等。这几个理由都被包含在中国刑法的正当防卫中。

正当防卫是法律给予积极评价的行为,其犯罪性被排除在外(be exempted from)。"中国刑法明文规定"中的"明文"理解为"明确地,清楚地",译为 definitely。"合法"译为 lawful,"非法的"译为 unlawful,所以"合法权益"译为 lawful rights and interests,"不法侵害"译为 unlawful infringement。

2. 重罪

At the time the American colonies broke away from England, over 200 different felonies were recognized under English law, and each of the felonies was subject to capital punishment. Many of the felonies of that period, though capital offenses today we would classify as no more than misdemeanors. Eighty percent of the executions were for property offenses, and some involved only petty theft. Executions were public affairs, attend by huge crowds, and often carried out as cruelly as possible.

美国刚脱离英国殖民统治的时候,所沿用的英国法律中有200多条重罪,每个重罪都对应着死刑。许多可以判处死刑的重罪,按照我们今天的标准来看不过是一些轻罪。80%的死刑都是侵犯财产罪,甚至包括一些小偷小摸行为。执行广受公众关注,会有许多人围观,执行时也是极尽残忍之道。

felony是英美法系中的规定，中国刑法中没有直接对应的罪名，而是借用通行译法直接译为"重罪"；而misdemeanor则是与之相对的"轻罪"。petty theft是指小的偷盗行为。

3. 精神病人的刑事责任

精神病人在不能辨认或者不能控制自己行为的时候造成危害结果，经法定程序鉴定确认的，不负刑事责任，但是应当责令他的家属或者监护人严加看管和医疗；在必要的时候，由政府强制医疗。

If a mental patient causes harmful consequences at a time when he is unable to recognize or control his own conduct, upon verification and confirmation through legal procedure, he shall not bear criminal responsibility, but his family members or guardian shall be ordered to keep him under strict watch and control and arrange for his medical treatment. When necessary, the government may compel him to receive medical treatment.

该段文字是《刑法》第十八条的内容，主要规范精神病人不承担刑事责任的情形。其中造成危害结果的两种状态分别翻译为unable to recognize his own conduct和unable to control his conduct。"鉴定确认"需要被翻译出来，译为verification。

后半句的"严加看管"和"医疗"分别译为keep him under strict watch and control和arrange for his medical treatment。"医疗"作动词理解，意思是"送其接受治疗"。

另一个难点在于对"强制医疗"的理解，"强制"译为compel，而不是force，可以减少暴力的色彩。按照《韦氏法律词典》的解释，compel侧重权威或法律带来的压力，而force则表示compel by physical means often against resistance。

4. 仿造和变造

有下列情形之一，伪造、变造金融票证的，处五年以下有期徒刑或者拘役，并处或者单处二万元以上二十万元以下罚金；情节严重的，处五年以上十年以下有期徒刑，并处五万元以上五十万元以下罚金；情节特别严重的，处十年以上有期徒刑或者无期徒刑，并处五万元以上五十万元以下罚金或者没收财产。

Whoever commits any of the following acts of forging or altering financial bills shall be sentenced to fixed-term imprisonment of not more than 5 years or criminal detention and shall also, or shall only, be fined not less than 20,000 *yuan* but not more than 200,000 *yuan*; if the circumstances are serious, he shall be sentenced to fixed-term imprisonment of not less than 5 years but not more than 10 years and shall also be fined not less than 50,000 *yuan* but not more than 500,000 *yuan*; if the circumstances are especially serious, he shall be sentenced to fixed-term imprisonment of not less than 10 years or life imprisonment and shall also be fined not less than 50,000 *yuan* but not more than 500,000 *yuan* or be sentenced to confiscation of property.

该段文字是《刑法》第一百七十七条的内容，理解的第一个难点在于"伪造"和"变造"的差异。金融票证的伪造是指无权限人假冒出票人或虚构人名义进行签章和其他记载事项的行为，签章的变造属于伪造（即票据上的伪造包括票据的伪造和票据上签章的伪造）；票据的变造是指采用技术手段改变票据上已经记载事项的内容，或增加、减少票据记载事项的内容，从而达到变更票据权利义务关系的目的。因此，译者在翻译"伪造"和"变造"时需要加以区别，分别将其译为 forge 和 alter，以实现语义和语用上的匹配。

第二个难点是对"并处五万元以上五十万元以下罚金或者没收财产的"理解和翻译。并处包括两种情况，即"并处五万元以上五十万元以下罚金"与"并处没收财产"，前半句的"处"直接被融合在 fine 中，后半句的"处"则通过 be sentenced to 体现出来。

Punishments originally consisted of either fine, the infliction of bodily harm, or execution. The primary forms of corporal punishment were branding, flogging and mutilation. Still another early form of punishment was banishment—exclusion from the community. All of these early forms of punishment have persisted through modern times and are to be found today in at least some parts of the world. In our part of the world, however, many of these early forms of punishment have been completely or largely eliminated and new forms of punishment have replaced them.

A person who sets fire to and destroys an unoccupied dwelling house belonging to another or who sets fire to and destroys an unoccupied structure, mine, train, electric car, or another vehicle, vessel, or aircraft for public transport on water, on land, or in the air which belongs to another shall be sentenced to imprisonment for not less than three years but not more than ten years.

A person who endangers public safety by setting fire to and destroying a thing belonging to him that is specified in the preceding paragraph shall be sentenced to imprisonment for not less than six months but not more than five years.

A person who negligently sets fire to and destroys a thing specified in Paragraph 1 shall be sentenced to imprisonment for not more than six months, short-term imprisonment, or a fine of not more than three hundred *yuan*; a person who negligently endangers public safety by setting fire to and destroying a thing specified in Paragraph 2 shall be subject to the same punishment.

练习 3

被判处管制、拘役、有期徒刑、无期徒刑的犯罪分子，在执行期间，如果认真遵守监规，接受教育改造，确有悔改表现的，或者有立功表现的，可以减刑；有下列重大立功表现之一的，应当减刑：

① 阻止他人重大犯罪活动的；
② 检举监狱内外重大犯罪活动，经查证属实的；
③ 有发明创造或者重大技术革新的；
④ 在日常生产、生活中舍己救人的；
⑤ 在抗御自然灾害或者排除重大事故中，有突出表现的；
⑥ 对国家和社会有其他重大贡献的。

练习 4

虽然今天刑法中违法的概念已经明确，但并不是一成不变的。把一部分违法行为看作犯罪是历史不断发展的结果。社会在接受犯罪这个概念的过程中经历过几个重要的决定，在今天其中一些还在不断接受着检验。社会必须确认有一些行为应当视为对公众总体的侵害，而不是针对个人的侵害。

练习 5

Like many States, Missouri has periodically sought to improve its administration of the death penalty. Early in the 20th century, the State replaced hanging with the gas chamber. Later in the century, it authorized the use of lethal injection as an alternative to lethal gas. By the time Mr. Bucklew's post-conviction proceedings ended, Missouri's protocol called for lethal injections to be carried out using three drugs: sodium thiopental, pancuronium bromide, and potassium chloride. And by that time, too, various inmates were in the process of challenging the constitutionality of the State's protocol and others like it around the country.

Ultimately, this Court answered these legal challenges in Baze v. Rees, 553 U. S. 35 (2008). Addressing Kentucky's similar three-drug protocol, the chief justice, joined by justice alito and justice Kennedy, concluded that a State's refusal to alter its lethal injection protocol could violate the Eighth Amendment only if an inmate first identified a "feasible, readily implemented" alternative procedure that would "significantly reduce a substantial risk of severe pain".

第九章

刑事诉讼法的基本知识和翻译

刑事诉讼法的英译为 Criminal Procedure Law，美国的 Federal Rules of Criminal Procedure 译为"联邦刑事诉讼规则"。

在中国，刑事诉讼法是规范公安机关、人民检察院、人民法院等国家机关的职权活动，打击犯罪，保障犯罪嫌疑人、被告人的合法权益不受侵犯，保护刑事被害人及其他公民正当权益的基本法，其根本目标是实现刑事司法公正、维护社会的公平与正义。其中不少术语会和民事诉讼法的内容重叠，比如"管辖""立案""送达"等。

在内地，检察机关有权对公安机关的监督限于批准警察的逮捕申请（批捕）和审查起诉期间对案卷的审查（review）；审查中如果发现公安机关提供的证据不充分，可以退回公安机关补充侦查（return the case to the police for more investigation）。拘留证（arrest warrant）由公安机关直接签发；拘留嫌疑人之后3天（最多30天），公安机关要请检察院决定是先放回去，还是继续关押。法院直到审判阶段才介入。香港地区整体上沿袭了英国法律，包括刑事诉讼法在内的香港地区各类法律均与大陆法系法律存在较大差别。在香港审判刑事案件的法院包括裁判法院、区域法院、原讼法庭（Court of First Instance）、上诉法庭（Court of Appeal）和终审法院。之所以把 Court of First Instance 和 Court of Appeal 译为"原讼法庭"和"上诉法庭"而非"原讼法院"和"上诉法院"，主要是因为两者均属于香港高等法院。

美国的刑事案件处理一般由以下程序构成：逮捕（arrest）、提审或传讯（arraignment）、提审后程序（after the arraignment）、庭审（trail）、判决（verdict）和上诉（appeal）。具体庭审程序还可以细分为筛选陪审员（choosing a jury）、开场陈述（opening statements）、证人作证（witness testimony and examination）、最后辩论（closing arguments）、指示陪审团（jury instruction）、陪审团评议和裁决（jury deliberation and verdict）。美国的拘留证是由法院签发的，拘留之后两三天由法官决定是先放回去（即保释）还是继续关押。警察实施拘留之后便进入公诉阶段。

第一节 常用术语

刑事诉讼法的常用术语见表9-1。

第九章 刑事诉讼法的基本知识和翻译

表 9-1 刑事诉讼法的常用术语及其英文表达

术语	英译
犯罪中止	desistence of crime
犯罪团伙	criminal gang
犯罪构成	constitution of a crime
犯罪动机	criminal motive
犯意	criminal intent
从重处罚	give a severer punishment
公开法庭审理	file in open court
终审裁定	final order
第一次出庭	first appearance
结论,(陪审团)裁决	finding
自白书	statement of confession
恶意证人	hostile witness
公诉书	information
利害关系人	interested person
缺席判决	judgment in default
维持	affirm
推翻	reverse
发回	remand
法庭判决意见书	opinion
陪审团成员审选	jury array
候选陪审员	jury panel
书面训诫	mandamus
开庭陈述	opening statement
撤销假释	parole revocation
初始管辖权	original jurisdiction
假释违反行为	parole violation
不予起诉	no true bill
无因回避	peremptory challenge
起诉状	petition
辩诉交易	plea bargaining
预审	preliminary hearing

续表

术语	英译
大陪审团起诉报告	presentment
推定判刑	presumptive sentence
审前羁押	pretrial detention
审前释放	pretrial release
程序性抗辩	procedural defense
合理怀疑	reasonable doubt
搜查令	search warrant
判决前听审	sentencing hearing
传票	subpoena
缓解监禁（缓刑）	suspended sentence
重新审判	trial de novo
无条件释放	unconditional release
调卷令状	writ of certiorari
人身保护令状	writ of habeas corpus
陪审团裁决	verdict
工具不能犯	impossibility of instruments
对象不能犯	object impossibility
故意犯罪	intentional crime
惯犯	habitual criminal
过失犯罪	criminal negligence
缓刑	probate execution
既遂犯	accomplished crime
监禁	imprisonment
间接故意	indirect intent
教唆未遂	attempt of solicitation
结果犯	consequential offense
结果加重犯	aggregated consequential offense
结合犯	combinative crime
连续犯罪	continuing crime
量刑	sentence criterion
累犯	recidivist; repeat offender

续表

术语	英译
情节加重犯	aggravated offence by circumstance
偶犯	casual offender
刑事责任能力	criminal capacity
检察官指控	criminal complaint/charge
大陪审团指控	grand jury indictment
认罪	plead guilty
不认罪	plead not guilty
社区矫正	community correction
人民陪审员	people's assessor
审判委员会	judicial committee
鉴定结论	expert conclusion
刑讯逼供	extort confession by torture
不得毁灭、伪造证据	not to destroy or falsify evidence
监视居住	residential surveillance
检察委员会	the procuratorial committee
勘验、搜查	inquest or search
附带民事诉讼	incidental civil action
保证（对法庭做出的保证，比如付保释金）	assurance
社区服务令	community service order（CSO）
数种刑罚	concurrent sentences
强化改造令	intensive correction order
不得保释期间	non-parole period
违法者负担	offender levy
量刑前报告	pre-sentence report
伴随合法逮捕后的搜索	search incident to lawful arrest
诱供	inducement; induced confession; to induce confession
翻供	recantation; retraction; to retract/recant confession
骗供	tricked confession; trick sb. into confession
套口供	trapped confession; to trap a suspect into confession
串供	collaboration/collusion among witnesses
录供	take down a confession

续表

术语	英译
供认	confession；to confess to a crime
不打自招	voluntary confession；confess without being pressed
疲劳审讯	sleep deprivatio

第二节　核心术语的表达和理解

刑事诉讼法与刑法的关系是程序法与实体法的关系。刑法规定了犯罪与刑罚问题，是刑事实体法；刑事诉讼法则规定追诉犯罪的程序、追诉机关、审判机关的权力范围、当事人，以及诉讼参与人的诉讼权利和相互的法律关系，是刑事程序法。

程序法是为实现实体法而存在的，但本身具有独立的品格。刑事诉讼法规范涉及国家权力与个人权利的分配关系，直接关系到公民的自由、财产等各项权利的实现程度。

伴随着诉讼民主化的发展历程，刑事诉讼程序发生的变化很大，承担不同诉讼职能的国家机关之间也存在职责分配的变化。刑事诉讼法所规定的程序内容在不断的变化中走向程序正义，引导刑事程序法治的实现。因此，对刑事诉讼法律文本的理解和翻译很重要。

1. magistrate judge, district judge

在美国司法制度中，这两个短语可分别译为"治安官"和"地区法官"。在美国的大多数州，magistrate judge 由联邦地区法院任命，是联邦驻各州的初级法官，负责处理车辆违章或破坏治安的案件，主持刑事案件的预审（第一次听证会），签发逮捕令、搜查令，决定是否准予保释，以及处理小额民事案件。

district judge 为联邦地区法官，一般情况下他们是联邦政府设在各个联邦司法区（judicial districts）的初审法院里的法官，而并非各州某区法院的法官（个别州除外，如佛罗里达州自己设地区法院）。

2. district attorney

district attorney 一般译作"地区检察官"，也译为"检控官"。美国各州的每一个司法区都有负责公诉的公职官员，所以译为"地区检察官"。但有些州的司法区域不按照地区划分，负责的官员称为 prosecuting attorney/officer，public attorney 或 state's attorney。比这个职位高的就是州司法部长（attorney general），每个州都有这个职位；在联邦政府，attorney general of the United States 译为"司法部长"。

3. privilege against self-incrimination

privilege against self-incrimination 译为"不自证其罪特权"，也写为 right against self-incrimination 或 right to remain silent。该规则最早起源于英国 12 世纪早期，美国宪法第五修正案及州宪法中也有类似条款。它规定在任何刑事案件中应根据证据论罪，被告享有不得被迫证明自己有罪的特权，但仅限于不提供作为证据的口供，不适用于笔迹、指纹等物证。

4. double jeopardy

double jeopardy 可译为"双重追诉，双重危险，双重危境"，有时写为 double jeopardy clause，译为"一事不再理"。该原则是英美法系的一条基本原则。美国宪法第五修正案具体规定了这一原则，即任何人不因同一罪行而受两次审判，任何已被释放或已被宣判无罪的人均不能因同一罪行而再次被置于"生命或肢体的危险"之中。

5. bound over

bound over 译为"具结候审"，是指法院发现有充分理由说明被告有犯罪行为而采取的强制措施，即将被告交给拘留所拘押等候审理，接下来的法律程序是具结候审听证（bind-over hearing/ preliminary hearing）。

6. writ

writ 是古英语固有词，是指法庭或司法机关的各种书面命令或令状，也可指"权力"或"权限"，如 one's writ（某人的权限）、one's writ runs（某人在某方面或某种程度上的权限）、writ large（明显的，夸大的）等。

常见的令状有传票（writ of summons）、权利令状（writ of right）、审查令（writ of review）、保护令（writ of protection）、人身保护令（writ of habeas corpus）。

7. indictment

indictment 是指大陪审团起诉书，即指控刑事犯罪的正式书面文件，原先由大陪审团经宣誓向法院提出。1933 年英格兰部分废除了大陪审团。大陪审团被废除之前，如果发现有刑事犯罪，须先向大陪审团提出申请公诉书（bill of indictment），大陪审团对支持指控的证人进行询问，如果大陪审团的多数成员认为犯罪已得到充分证明，应将犯罪人交付法庭审判，即在申请公诉书上签署"准予起诉"（true bill），则公诉书获得批准，犯罪人处于被起诉的地位，并将被安排传讯（arraignment）；如果大陪审团的多数成员认为犯罪未得到充分的证明，即在申请公诉书上签署"不予起诉"并将被控告人释放。

以前在普通法中大陪审团起诉书用于对叛国罪、重罪、包庇叛国罪或包庇重罪的犯罪和具有公共性质的轻罪提起控诉。现在，公诉书只适用于应由小陪审团审判的严重犯罪，对应由具有简易裁判权的法院专属管辖的其他罪行不适用。

8. information, indictment, presentment, complain

对应于"起诉书"，英美法中有 information, indictment, complaint 三个术语。前两个是刑事方面的，information 与中国"刑事诉讼起诉书"的概念对等，而 indictment 是英美法特有的概念，是指由大陪审团给出的起诉书。complaint 则指民事起诉状。

presentment 译为"起诉报告"，是大陪审团在未有申请公诉书的情况下根据自己对案件的调查和了解主动提出的书面报告，相当于申请公诉书。如果译者"刑民不分"，也不了解两大法系的区别，就容易错译、误译。

9. Fruit of the Poison Tree Doctrine

Fruit of the Poison Tree Doctrine 是"毒树果实原则",即所谓的证据排除法则(exclusionary rule),指在调查过程中通过非法手段取得的证据,因为证据的来源(树)受到污染,那么任何从它获得的证据(果实)也是被污染的,在诉讼审理的过程中将不能被采纳。

10. Miranda Warning

Miranda Warning 也写作 Miranda Rights,译为"米兰达告诫""米兰达忠告""米兰达公约"或"米兰达宣言",是指美国警察(包括检察官)根据美国联邦最高法院在"米兰达诉亚利桑那州案"一案的判例来确立的规则。

在讯问刑事案件犯罪嫌疑人之前,警察必须明白无误地告知嫌疑人有权援引宪法第五修正案,即刑事案件犯罪嫌疑人有"不被强迫自证其罪的特权",有权行使沉默权和要求得到律师协助的权利。

全文如下:

You have the right to remain silent. Anything you say can and will be used against you in a court of law. You have the right to talk to a lawyer and have him present while you are questioned. If you cannot afford to hire a lawyer, one will be appointed to represent you before questioning, if you wish one. (你有权保持沉默,否则你所说的一切都可以在法庭上作为指控你的不利证据。审问之前,你有权与律师谈话,得到律师的帮助和建议。受审时,你也有权让律师在场。如果你想聘请律师但负担不起,法庭将为你指定一位律师。)

11. trial

trial 是指庭审。庭审分为法官审(bench trial)和陪审团审(jury trial)两种。按照美国联邦宪法规定,被告有权决定是法官审还是陪审团审。

如果决定是法官审,检察官要将证据与被告律师分享,以让对方准备庭审。

如果是陪审团审,由从普通公民中筛选出来的人组成陪审团,按照合法进入庭审的证据和证词认定事实。法官的主要作用是作为一个裁判,在辩方和检察官的对抗过程中裁定哪些证据、证人、证词可以进入庭审。法官的另外一个作用是向陪审团全体成员解释法律,陪审团不理解、有疑问时可以问法官。

陪审团适用法官解释的法律,基于陪审团自己认定的事实,一般情况下全体一致认定原告是否构成犯罪。陪审团不能与被告辩护律师或者检察官进行问答,或者进行其他形式的互动。陪审团不能不经法院批准,而擅自试图获得其他证据、造访当事人、察看犯罪现场。

12. prosecution and pretrial service

prosecution and pretrial service 译为"起诉和审前服务"。经过初步调查,警察认为确有犯罪发生,也抓到了嫌疑人,就会请公诉部门决定是否指控(charge)。若决定指控,就带嫌疑人见法官(initial appearance),让法官决定继续侦查期间是否有合理根据(probable cause)继续关押嫌疑人,如果没有则嫌疑人可被保释;若获得保释,嫌疑人要遵守保释条件（bail conditions），如执行宵禁（curfew）、参加戒毒（drug rehabilitation program）、接受心理辅导（counseling）、定期向审前服务部门汇报情况等，保证审判时按时到庭（appear in court）。

美国很多州接下来还有个初步听证（preliminary hearing）的程序，控辩双方各传证人，法官决定是否有合理根据相信发生了犯罪。如果认为无合理根据便驳回起诉（dismiss the case）。在交给法院审理前，有些州还有一个大陪审团审查证据的程序，查看如果起诉证据是否充分。

13. adjudication

adjudication 通常译为"审判，裁判"，但此处应作狭义解释，即只包括定罪与否的裁判，不包括量刑，因为审判流程中还有一个环节是"量刑和制裁"。

在中国，定罪（conviction）和量刑（sentencing）合并进行，统称审判阶段：在同一次审理中，控辩双方既出示有无犯罪的证据（incriminating and exonerating evidence），也出示犯罪轻重的证据（mitigating and aggravating evidence），法官在最后宣判时既确定有罪无罪（guilty or not guilty），也确定处罚（punishment/penalty/sanction）。

在美国，审判阶段仅决定是否有罪（被告人认罪或独任法官认定有罪），量刑在另外一次听证中确定。

14. sentencing and sanctions

sentencing and sanctions 译为"量刑和制裁"。在美国，被告人认罪，或者经法官或陪审团认定有罪之后，法庭隔一段时间会再举行一次听证，即量刑听证，以决定处罚方式。处罚的种类有死刑（capital punishment / death sentence）、终身监禁（life imprisonment）、监禁（imprisonment）、缓刑（probation）、罚金（fine）、返还财物（restitution）等。

在量刑听证上，法官会听取考察部门（probation officer）的量刑前报告（pre-sentencing report），了解被告人的成长历史、犯罪背景等，作为量刑参考。有的司法辖区有量刑指南（sentencing guidelines），里面有详细的计算公式，规定什么情况加刑几个月或减刑几个月。法官的自由裁量权（discretion）往往很小，有的司法辖区会给法官较大的自由裁量权。

中国刑罚的种类和美国差不多，有些叫法不同：有期徒刑（fixed term imprisonment），相当于美国的 imprisonment；无期徒刑（non-fixed term imprisonment），相当于美国的 life imprisonment (with parole)，即"（可以获得假释的）终身监禁"。

15. presentence report

presentence report 译为"判前报告"，是判决前法官要求对已经被定罪的被告所做的调查报告，包括被告的教育背景、职业背景、社会经历、过去居住地情况、疾病史、以往的犯罪记录、未来处境等信息，以及负责撰写报告的法庭官员对被告的犯罪动机和目的的看法和处理建议。

16. correction

correction 译为"矫正",是量刑后的执行阶段。对于判刑的人来说,这就意味着坐牢(serve their sentence in jail/prison)。关押的地方可能是 jail(看守所),也可能是 prison(监狱)。监狱分为不同安全级别(security level),通常为五级。级别不同,看管的严密程度不同。在监狱表现好,罪犯就会获得减刑,服刑达一定时间后,可以获得提前释放。

被假释的犯人接受考察人员的监管。服刑人员还可以通过别的方式获得宽大处理(clemency)。被判缓刑的人要接受考察人员的监管,提供社区服务(作为处罚)或遵守一定的条件。

17. summon, summon for interrogation

"被取保候审的犯罪嫌疑人、被告人应当遵守以下规定:……在传讯的时候及时到案"中,"传讯"译为 summon。

刑事诉讼法中还存在另一个概念,即"传唤",如"对于不需要逮捕、拘留的犯罪嫌疑人,可以传唤到犯罪嫌疑人所在市、县内的指定地点或者到他的住处进行讯问"。

传讯是指人民检察院或公安机关传唤犯罪嫌疑人或被告人于指定时间到指定场所接受讯问,其对象是犯罪嫌疑人或被告人;而传唤除了针对犯罪嫌疑人或被告人外,还适用于人民法院对自诉人出庭的要求,因此传讯可以理解为传唤犯罪嫌疑人、被告人来接受讯问。

因此,"传讯"应译为 summon,而"传唤"则译为 summon for interrogation。

18. entrust, authorize

"委托"的翻译有功能对等的英文法律术语,但《刑事诉讼法》的英译文却用了不具有法律意义的普通词来替代,或误用了法律概念不同的术语,如第三十三条规定:

① ……还可以<u>委托</u>一至二人作为辩护人。下列的人可以被<u>委托</u>为辩护人……

… may <u>entrust</u> one or two persons as his defenders. The following persons may be <u>entrusted</u> as defenders …

再如《刑事诉讼法》第三十四条规定:

……告知被告人有权委托辩护人……

… he shall be informed that he may <u>appoint</u> a defender …

两个法条中"委托"分别译为 entrust 和 appoint。即使不考虑法律文本所要求的一致性,两个词语本身也存在问题。一般情况下,entrust 确是译为"委托",如"He's entrusted his children to me for the day."(他委托我照看一天孩子)。但这种委托非法律术语,可理解为"托付"或"拜托",而 appoint 意为"指派""任命",两者都不同于法律意义上的"委托"。

法律上的"委托"是建立代理法律关系的行为,一旦建立委托关系,必将在委托人和受托人之间确立委托代理关系,对双方具有约束力。刑事诉讼法中犯罪嫌疑人和被告人有权委托律师,这种委托必须通过签订委托代理协议正式确立,委托后律师作为代理人或辩护人,所为的法律行为将直接约束犯罪嫌疑人或被告人,它对应的英文法律术语应为 authorize。

19. testimony, evidence

美国的法庭审判以证人当庭作证为基本要求。在控辩双方做完开庭陈述后,法官会问"Is the prosecution ready to present its case?"。在公诉人举证完毕后(after the prosecution rests its case),法官会询问被告"Is the defense ready to present its case?"。所以,"举证"译为 present its case。而这里的 case 不能被理解成"案件",而是诉讼中支持一方的系列事实或者论点。

美国控辩双方应向法庭提交物证、书证等,"物证"译为 physical evidence,而不是 material evidence。material evidence 应该译为"重大证据,实质性证据"。"书证"译为 documentary evidence,而"质证"则可以译为 challenge the evidence。

在中国庭审中,控辩双方在证人不出庭作证的情况下,可以提交证人证言(witness statements)。美国法庭要求证人出庭作证,即要有现场证人(live witness)。live testimony 则译为"当庭作证"。

20. examination, cross examination

我们在美剧的法庭场景中可以经常看到检察官或辩护人依次传唤自己证人到庭,首先自己发问,让证人把知道的(有利于己方)事情说一遍,这轮是询问(examination),也称为"直接询问"(direct examination)、"主询问"(examination-in-chief)等。提问只能问开放性问题(open-ended question),不可以问诱导性问题(leading question)。在特殊情况下,若己方的证人不配合,辩护人则请求法官将该证人确认为敌对证人(hostile witness),之后就可以用诱导性问题发问。

中国法庭不允许使用诱导性问题,否则会有诱供(elicit a confession)嫌疑。

21. probable cause

在美国刑事诉讼法中,与排除合理怀疑标准(beyond a reasonable doubt)有紧密关系的术语为 probable cause, reasonable suspicion, reasonable doubt。probable cause 译为"合理依据"。

"Reasonable suspicion refers to the level of suspicion required to justify law enforcement investigation, but not arrest or search which is a lower level of suspicion or evidence than probable cause. An officer has reasonable suspicion when the officer is aware of specific, articulate facts, together with rational inferences from those facts, which, when judged objectively, would lead a reasonable person to believe that criminal activity occurred or was occurring." 中的 reasonable suspicion 译为"合理怀疑"。

"Reasonable doubt, such a doubt as would cause a careful person to hesitate before acting in matters of importance to himself/herself." 中的 reasonable doubt 也译为"合理怀疑"。

合理依据所要求的证据标准不同于要证明有罪所要求的证据标准,后者必须是实质性的。合理依据与合理推论有关，不是一个基于严格要求的技术判断。美国在判例实践中确立的标准坚持认为，当权力机构知晓的真实情况足以使人合理地注意到某种犯罪已经发生或正在发生时，便意味着存在合理依据，其证据强度约为50%以上。

22. speedy trial

speedy trial 译为"快速审理"，是美国公民的宪法权利。美国宪法第六修正案规定：在所有刑事起诉中的被告皆享有迅速及公开审判之权利，以避免因审判程序久延而严重影响被告权益。然而，何谓"迅速"并不明确。

美国联邦最高法院虽曾于1972年指出较为明确的快速审判方式，但仍有诸多疑义。美国国会遂于1974年制定《联邦速审法案》（Federal Speedy Trial Act），要求案件的审理期限为70天，以期能兼顾公众与被告之利益，将案件迅速审结。

23. due process

due process 译为"正当法律程序"。美国宪法规定：非经正当法律程序，不得剥夺任何人的生命、自由和财产。这就是著名的正当法律程序条款。正当程序是英美法系中重要的宪政和法治原则，其本质上是一种对政府行为和权利的检验和审查。美国的正当程序制度是法院运用司法权力对政府行为和权利进行广泛干预的重要手段，其目的是保障个人权利，是一项重要的司法审查制度。

24. exclusionary rule

exclusionary rule 译为"非法证据排除规则"。非法证据排除规则源于英美法系，于20世纪初产生于美国。排除规则的要求是对于直接或间接违反美国宪法第四、第五或第六修正案而获得的证据，控方不得在审理中用其来证明被告人有罪。若法庭不恰当地采纳了违反排除规则的证据，将会导致判决的撤销。美国的非法证据排除规则是作为法律的强制要求发挥作用的，即以非法手段取得的证据在刑事诉讼中将自动被排除或导致不可采信。

25. jail, prison

在美国，监狱有不少名称，如 county jail, state penitentiary 等，执行监禁的场所有囚室（cell）或监房（ward）、牢房（jail/gaol）、看守所或拘留所（detention center）、监狱（prison）等。刚抓到的罪犯一般被关押在 detention center；已经起诉但尚未定罪的嫌疑人一般被关在 jail；已经定罪或者判刑的囚犯特别是重大犯罪者，一般会被送往 prison 或 penitentiary 服刑。

jail 一般是由县或郡的治安部门或警察局（sheriff department）管理；而 prison 或 penitentiary 是由州政府或联邦政府管理。目前英国已经不太用 penitentiary 一词，但美国还常用。

26. opinion

opinion 是指判决书中的意见。判决书的意见有很多种，译者需要根据搭配和实际语境判断采用哪种说法。

majority opinion 表示超过半数的多数法官意见，具有强制力；而 plurality opinion 是指未超过半数的多数法官意见,不具有强制力,即当没有绝对半数通过时,判决结果称为多数意见。

concurring opinion 译为"附和意见"。如果审理法院同意多数法官的最终判决但是有不同的理由,就可以写一个赞同判决但理由有异的意见来陈述这个结论是怎么得出的。

dissenting opinion 译为"反对意见"。反对意见制度符合客观事实的要求,有助于强化法官的个人责任感和法院系统自身对案件的深入认识与反思。

第三节 常见句型结构

1. "可以"结构

"可以"作为能愿动词包含两层含义:一是表示可能或者能够,即使不会,通过用心观察是可以学会的;二是表示许可,如凭借校园卡可以进出学校图书馆。

法律文本中,"可以"通常作能愿动词,表示许可,多用于授权性规范。刑事诉讼法是规范刑事诉讼过程中国家司法机关与犯罪嫌疑人、被告人等刑事诉讼当事人及其他诉讼参与人的权利和义务的法律,一方面通过授权性规范明确国家司法机关和不同的诉讼参与人在诉讼中可以做什么,另一方面明确禁止他们做什么。刑事诉讼文本中,"可以"一词的授权对象包括警察、司法机关、当事人、辩护人或代理人及其他诉讼参与人。

在翻译相关条款中的"可以"时,译者容易误解以致误译,因为"可以"和"可以不"作为指示的两个向度在司法实践中是异向延伸的。司法机关在"可以"和"不可以"之间的选择直接关系当事人的利益,正确理解"可以"显得特别重要。《刑事诉讼法》通过"可以"一词给公安、司法部门授权82次,给当事人授权30次,给辩护人或代理人授权14次,给其他诉讼参与人授权3次。但是对于具体条款中的"可以"阐述的是权利还是义务,有学者存在不同看法(刘方权、黄小芳,2008)。《中国法律法规汉英平行语料库(大陆)》的检索信息显示,"可以"都译为may,也有译者将有些理解为义务规定的"可以"译为must。

如《刑事诉讼法》第四十五条:

② 在审判过程中,被告人可以拒绝辩护人继续为他辩护,也可以另行委托辩护人辩护。

During a trial, the defendant may refuse to have his defendant continue to defend him and may entrust his defence to another defender.

条款中的"可以"被理解成授权性规定;如果被理解成义务性规定,"可以"就表示必须,译为must。对"可以"的翻译需要严谨对待。

2. "除外"的规定

"除外"指的是将某些行为或者情形另外处理,不适用于当前的处罚,有译者将其翻译成 except,或将 otherwise 和 unless 相结合来实现表达。"除外"结构在很多立法文本中都存在,常写作"法律、法规另有规定的除外"。但其英文翻译并不统一,如《行政复议条例》中有 5 例"法律、法规另有规定的除外"表述。

如第十六条规定:

③ 对法律、法规规定需要上级批准的具体行政行为不服申请的复议,由最终批准的行政机关管辖。法律、法规另有规定的除外。

If an application for reconsideration is filed by a person who does not accept a specific administrative act which, according to the provisions of the laws, is subject to the approval of an administrative body at a higher level, the case shall be under the jurisdiction of the administrative body that makes the final decision <u>unless otherwise provided for by the laws and regulations</u>.

再如第二十九条规定:

④ 公民、法人或者其他组织向有管辖权的行政机关申请复议,应当在知道具体行政行为之日起十五日内提出,法律、法规另有规定的除外。

Where a citizen, a legal person or any other organization files an application for reconsideration with the administrative body that has jurisdiction over the case, he/she or it shall do so within 15 days from the day when he/she or it becomes aware of the specific administrative act, <u>except as otherwise stipulated by the laws and regulations</u>.

"法律、法规另有规定的除外"有时译为 unless it otherwise provides 或 unless otherwise provided by the laws and regulations。《刑事诉讼法》中几例的译法也不统一。

如《刑法诉讼法》第十九条规定:

⑤ 刑事案件的侦查由公安机关进行,法律另有规定的除外。

Investigation in criminal cases shall be conducted by the public security organs, <u>except as otherwise provided by law</u>.

再如第二十条规定:

⑥ 基层人民法院管辖第一审普通刑事案件,但是依照本法由上级人民法院管辖的除外。

The Primary People's Courts shall have jurisdiction as courts of first instance over ordinary criminal cases; however, those cases which fall under the jurisdiction of the People's Courts at higher levels as stipulated by this Law <u>shall be exceptions</u>.

为了保持文本之间的一致性和统一性,本条款的后半句也可以译为 unless it is

otherwise provide by this Law that those cases fall under the jurisdiction of the People's Courts at higher levels。

《刑事诉讼法》中的"……以外"与"……除外"所指一致时,译法与其一样,如第十一条规定:

⑦ 人民法院审判案件,除本法另有规定的以外,一律公开进行。

Cases in the People's Courts shall be heard in public, unless otherwise provided by this Law.

3. ……的案件

《刑事诉讼法》中有42例提及"……的案件",根据在句中的意思不同,"案件"既可译为复数形式 cases, 也可译为 a case。

如第二十六条规定:

⑧ 几个同级人民法院都有权管辖的案件,由最初受理的人民法院审判。

When two or more People's Courts at the same level have jurisdiction over a case, it shall be tried by the People's Court that first accepted it.

在上例中"案件"译为单数 a case, 而下例则不同。

第一百六十九条规定:

⑨ 凡需要提起公诉的案件,一律由人民检察院审查决定。

All cases requiring initiation of a public prosecution shall be examined for decision by the People's Procuratorates.

4. "判决"和"裁定"

在程序法中,"判决"和"裁定"出现的频率相对较高,民事诉讼法中有50多例,刑事诉讼法中也有20例。

为了准确翻译"判决"和"裁定",译者应首先熟悉英文中表示"判决"和"裁定"的词汇。根据不完全统计,大致有 decision, judgment, order, ruling, sentence, adjudication, decree, verdict, opinion, disposition。

decision 的词义最为广泛,指任何类别的判决或裁决,既包括法院做出的判决(judicial decision),也包括仲裁庭的裁决(arbitral decision)以及其他行政机关、委员会做出的裁决。

judgment 是指法庭对案件各方当事人的权利和义务或是否承担责任问题做出的最后决定,基本对应汉语里的"判决"。

order 是法庭针对诉讼中的附属和从属问题做出的命令或决定,它不追究案件的是非曲直(当事人的权利、主张的实质依据等),而是处理一些临时问题或者对诉讼程序上的问题做出指示。因此,译者可以把 order 译为"裁定",也有人将其译为"法庭命令"或"法官命令"。

ruling 是指法官在庭审过程中对证据的可采性、申请是否许可等问题所做出的决定。中国大陆的法律体系通常将法院根据实体法做出的判决和根据程序法做出的裁定进行区分，因此也有人将"裁定"译为 ruling。

sentence 专指刑事判决、科处刑罚，如 a sentence of 20 years in prison 译为"判处20年监禁"。

adjudication 作"判决"讲时意思同 judgment，但其另一重含义是强调一个过程，就是裁决案件的法律程序或者过程。它常常出现在破产案件的语境中，如法院正式宣告某人为破产人的裁决，就可以用 adjudication。在苏格兰法律里，adjudication 更是可以特指扣押债务人的财产以偿债的裁决。

decree 特指法院根据衡平法上的权利所做的裁定。衡平的意思就是"正义，公正"，与普通法相比显得更灵活，是法院根据公平（equity）和良知（good conscience）原则确定诉讼各方权利而做出的裁决或命令。

verdict 是英美法律制度中特有的由陪审团做出的裁决。陪审团就是由各色公民组成的审判团。陪审团做出的裁决仅具有事实认定的效果而非正式判决，法官会据以参酌法律做出判决。

opinion 特指法院或法官阐述其做出判决的理由的书面意见，所以通常译为"判决意见书"。

disposition 是指对案件的裁决，它更多用于刑事案件，尤其是用作对未成年罪犯的判决，指科刑或给予其他所规定的对待和处理。

因此，"判决"可直接译为 judgment，而"裁定"则多译为 order。《刑事诉讼法》中"判决"和"裁定"的翻译难得的高度一致和统一。因此，译者在翻译法律文本遇到"判决"和"裁定"时，可以直接套用。

如第二百四十四条规定：

⑩第二审的<u>判决</u>、<u>裁定</u>和最高人民法院的<u>判决</u>、<u>裁定</u>，都是终审的<u>判决</u>、<u>裁定</u>。

All <u>judgments and orders</u> of second instance and all judgments and orders of the Supreme People's Court are final.

再如第二百七十四条规定：

⑪人民法院应当在收到纠正意见后一个月以内重新组成合议庭进行审理，做出最终<u>裁定</u>。

The People's Court shall, within one month from the date of receiving the recommendation, form a new collegial panel to handle the case and render a final <u>order</u>.

5. 判决书中的时间表达

诉讼文书中的时间表达要精确。因此，在法律文书的中英互译过程中，为了避免互译而产生的偏差，对有关时间的介词的准确理解和使用显得尤为重要。所涉及的常见的时间介词有 after，before，on，by，between，from … to，within，as of。

after 是指如果规定一项行为将在指定的某一天之后的特定期限内履行，则该期限不包括指定的那一天。这是一般规则，但也有例外，须视具体情况而定。

before 是指在时间上先于，但依上下文可有不同义项，如在顺序、重要性、地位上先于。该词不能像 for，during，throughout 等词一样指一段期间，而只是表示某事件或行为的发生早于所提及的时间。同样，一般规则是该期限不包括指定的那一天。

on 包括所指的日期，常用短语 on or after（当期或期后）、on or before（当期或期前）。在某一天有时也用 on or about。

by 表示到某一日期履行的行为可在该日之前或者在当日履行。

between 一般表示以两个指明的日子或日期为界限的时段。若一行为是介于两个特定日期之间所为，则该行为必须是在后一日期开始前实施的，此类案件在计算时间时，两个终端的特定日期都被排除在外，但另有规定的除外。为了避免产生歧义，可以这样处理，如"The appointee may exercise his right after July 1, 2008 and before July 30, 2008."（不包括 July 1 和 July 30）或者"The appointee's right begins on July 1, 2008 and ends on July 30, 2008."（包括 July 1 和 July 30）。

from … to 常表示从某一天或指定的日期开始计算一段时间，开始计算的那个日期要被排除在外，而这一时段的最后一天要被包括在内。例如：

⑫ 合营公司的财务年度为日历年，即从1月1日至12月31日，但合营公司的第一个财务年度应从合营公司成立之日起至该日历年的12月31日止，合营公司的最后一个财务年度应在合营公司解散之日终止。

The fiscal year of the Joint Venture Company shall coincide with the calendar year, i. e. from January 1 to December 31. However, the first fiscal year of the Joint Venture Company shall commence on the date of its establishment and end on the date of dissolution of the JV Company.

within 排除第一天而包括最后一天，它后面也可接 of，after，from 等介词。在每种表述里，所述日期都不被计算在内。例如：

⑬ If any other Party materially breaches this Contract and such breach is not cured within sixty (60) days of a written notice to the breaching Party …

如果另一方实质性违反本合同，且在收到书面通知后六十（60）日内未纠正其违约行为……

as of 可理解为"截止到"，把一件事情定在一个时间而在另一个时间承认这件事情，对当前到以后某个日期的趋势做预测。例如：

⑭ Consultant hereby agrees to indemnify, hold harmless and defend Client from and against any and all claims, liabilities, losses, expenses, or damages asserted against Client by a third party to the extent such Liabilities result from the infringement of the Works delivered on any third party's trade secret, trademark, service mark, copyright or patent issued as of the date of this Agreement.

顾问谨此同意，若因其交付的作品对任何第三方截止到本协议之日发布的商业秘密、商标、服务标记、著作权或专利构成侵权，而导致第三方对客户提起索赔、追究其责任、要求其赔偿损失和费用或支付赔偿金，顾问将向客户做出赔偿，使客户免受损害，并为客户进行抗辩。

第四节　翻译实例分析

本节选取与刑事诉讼相关的段落（如法条、判决书、公诉书等）进行分析，帮助初学者超越短语层面来认识简单的与刑事诉讼程序相关的文本翻译。

1. 陪审团概况

If the jury of twelve cannot reach an agreement, this does not mean that the defendant is not guilty, as it only means there will be a retrial until 12 jurors arrive at a unanimous verdict of guilty or not guilty.	如果12名庭审陪审团成员没有达成一致，庭审宣告无效；但这不意味着被告无罪，而是由法庭重新审判，一般直到有一个12个陪审员构成的陪审团对于被告的罪与非罪达成一致。

本段文字是介绍陪审团的概况，其中涉及 jury, defendant, juror, verdict 等基本术语，内容相对简单。译文直接省略 it only means that 结构，因为此结构本身并无实体含义，意思为"只是意味着"，将其直接翻译出来显得啰唆，同时口语化的表达也会削弱法律文本的严肃性。此外，guilty 为形容词，译文对其进行了词性转换，用作名词简洁明了。

2. 羁押和刑事拘留

（被告人某某）因本案于2017年8月9日被羁押，次日被刑事拘留，2017年9月8日被逮捕，现被押于苏州看守所。	On suspicion of his involvement in this/the present case, the defendant was detained on August 9, 2017 and kept in custody for investigative purposes the next day. He was arrested on September 8, 2017, and now is held in custody in Suzhou Detention Center.

我们要将原文中的"羁押"和"刑事拘留"区分开来。根据刑事诉讼法的有关规定，刑事拘留是保障刑事诉讼顺利进行的强制措施，本身不具有惩罚性，应该理解为一种审判前的羁押；它的适用主要是为了防止犯罪嫌疑人逃跑、自杀或者继续危害社会，以此来保证刑事诉讼的顺利进行。审前的羁押不是独立的强制措施，而是依附于逮捕和拘留，所以原文本中的羁押和刑事拘留是同一种强制措施，译者在翻译的时候需要综合

考虑，以便于外国人理解，在不超越法律规定的情况下改译以实现功能上的对等。因此译文中 detained 和 be kept in custody for investigative purposes the next day 可以看作一种翻译上的突破（张法连、张鲁平，2014）。

3. 搁置判决

If the jury finds the defendant not guilty, the judge may not set aside the verdict, even if he believes that the jury verdict cannot stand as a matter of law. If the jury finds the defendant guilty, but the judge believes that the guilty verdict cannot stand as a matter of law, then the judge can set aside the jury's guilty verdict; but the prosecutor may appeal the judge's holding.	如果陪审团裁定被告无罪，庭审法官不得搁置无罪裁定，即使庭审法官认为无罪裁定在法律上不可能成立。如果陪审团裁定被告有罪，而庭审法官认为有罪裁定在法律上不可能成立，庭审法官可以搁置此有罪裁定；但是这时检察官可以上诉。

set aside the verdict 作为固定短语，意为"搁置判决"；stand as a matter of law 也稍难翻译，应该理解为"在法律上成立"；appeal the judge's holding 可以理解为"检察官可以上诉"（按照中国法律，检察官可以提起抗诉，应根据法律体系的不同选择对应词汇）。

4. 刑事判决书

公诉机关指控，2017年7月初，被告人M与他人合谋通过陈某某走私"冰毒"到菲律宾马尼拉后，被告人M为陈某某办理了签证、机票、酒店住宿等出境事宜，准备让陈某某乘坐2017年7月10日22时15分起飞的广州至马尼拉的航班携带毒品出境。同年7月10日，被告人M纠合被告人Z到被告人Z入住的广州市广园西路的龙安酒店310房，后一起购买一个褐色行李箱返回该房。被告人M、Z和其他同案人在310房内将10包"冰毒"分别用透明塑料袋、黑色胶带、蓝色复写纸层层包裹，藏匿于10只女鞋的鞋底处，再将夹藏"冰毒"的女鞋及陈某某的护照等物放进上述褐色行李箱中。同日	The Prosecution makes the following charges: At the beginning of July 2017, Defendant M conspired with others to smuggle "ice" to Manila, the Philippines through Chen XX. Having arrived at Manila, Defendant M arranged visa, flight tickets and hotel accommodation for Chen XX carrying drugs to take flight at 22:15 on July 10, 2017 from Guangzhou to Manila. On July 10, 2017, Defendant M ganged up with Defendant Z in Room 310, Long An Hotel, West Guangyuan Road, Guangzhou, where Defendant Z checked in, went together to buy a brown luggage case and then returned to the said room, where they and other accomplices used transparent plastic bags, black adhesive tapes, blue carbon papers respectively to wrap 10 packs of the drug "ice" layer upon layer and concealed them in the soles of 10 women's shoes, and then put the shoes with the concealed drug and Chen XX's passport and other articles into the aforesaid brown

20时许，被告人 M、Z 从龙安酒店携带上述行李箱到广州市三元里百壮国际皮具会展中心旁的澄海狮头鹅快餐店和陈某某见面，在准备将该行李箱交给陈某某时被公安人员抓获。公安人员在上述行李箱内 10 只女鞋的鞋底查获白色晶体 10 包。

luggage case. At around 20：00 on July 10, 2017, Defendants M and Z carried the aforesaid luggage case from Long An Hotel to meet with Chen XX in Chenghai Shitou'e Fast Food Restaurant next to Baizhuang International Leather Exhibition Center, Sanyuanli, Guangzhou, where they were captured by the public security officers when about to give the luggage case to Chen XX. The police officers seized ten packs of white crystal in the soles of women's shoes in the aforesaid luggage case.

本段文字选自一份走私毒品案的刑事判决书，描述的是犯罪嫌疑人的犯罪过程和被抓获的场景，其中涉及的法律术语不多。"公诉机关"指的是检察院，所以译为 the Prosecution，首字母 P 大写，强调的是本判决书中所指的检察院。

第一个难点可能是对"纠合"一词的处理。"纠合"是指纠集、聚集、集合等（多用于贬义），英译选择的词语要体现相应的感情色彩，可以译为 ganged up with。

另一个难点是"分别用透明塑料袋、黑色胶带、蓝色复写纸层层包裹"，这句话描述了犯罪嫌疑人如何伪装毒品的过程，翻译时不能遗漏信息。其中"透明塑料袋、黑色胶带和蓝色复写纸张"译为 used transparent plastic bags, black adhesive tapes, blue carbon papers。

5. 检察院的工作

人民检察院以三检刑诉字（2014）第 176 号起诉书指控被告人张永志、潘义海、张春磊、李野、王广龙、冯金超犯故意伤害罪，被告人王广龙、王亚飞、赵建东犯盗窃罪，于 2014 年 5 月 23 日向本院提起公诉。本院依法组成合议庭，适用普通程序，公开开庭审理了本案。

The People's Procuratorate based on (2014) No. 176 San-jian-xing-su-zi Information accuses defendants Zhang Yongzhi, Pan Yihai, Zhang Chunlei, Li Ye, Wang Guanglong and Feng Jinchao of intentional injury, and accuses defendants Wang Guanglong, Wang Yafei and Zhao Jiandong of theft. The Procuratorate instituted a public prosecution to this Court on May 23, 2014. This Court thus constituted a collegial panel in accordance with the law and heard the case in public, applying general procedure.

人民检察院指派检察员芮爽、代理检察员张伟建出庭支持公诉。被告人张永志、潘义海、张春磊、李野、王广龙、冯金超、王亚飞、赵建东，辩护人郑

Procurator Rui Shuang and acting prosecutor Zhang Jianwei were designated by the People's Procuratorate to appear before the court and support the prosecution. Defendants Zhang Yongzhi, Pan Yihai, Zhang Chunlei, Li Ye, Wang Guanglong, Feng Jinchao,

志刚、霍振林到庭参加诉讼。现已审理终结。	Wang Yafei, Zhao Jiandong and their attorneys Zheng Zhigang and Huo Jianlin were present as requested. The trial has concluded so far.

本段文字常见于刑事判决书中对检察院工作的描述，为程式化的结构，前面主要概述人民检察院的起诉书。"人民检察院"译为 The People's Procuratorate，对起诉书的首部中的编号翻译则采用拼音对应，译为"（2014）No. 176 San-jian-xing-su-zi Information"。指控某人犯故意伤害罪使用 accuse sb. of intentional injury，指控某人犯盗窃罪为 accuse sb. of theft。"向本院提起公诉"也是刑事判决书中的常有表达，译为 institute a public prosecution to this Court，"本院"采用首字母大写指代即可。

"本院依法组成合议庭，适用普通程序，公开开庭审理了本案"是程式化的表达，按照固定结构翻译即可，译为"This Court thus constituted a collegial panel in accordance with the law and heard the case in public, applying general procedure."，其中涉及术语合议庭（collegial panel）、普通程序（general procedure）。"出庭支持公诉"是程式化用语，译为 appear before the court and support the prosecution。同样的还有"到庭参加诉讼"，翻译犯罪嫌疑人的到庭参加诉讼，不能照搬 appear before the court，而是强调被要求出庭所以译为 were present as requested。"现已审理终结"译为"The trial has concluded so far."。熟练掌握该段文字的译法后，翻译各种刑事判决书的开始部分的难度就会极大降低。

6. 犯罪过程和受害人损伤描述

Defendant Liu through his words and actions intended to and did confine the Plaintiff within the limousine between Origami and the Pillsbary mansion described in the paragraphs referenced above. The Plaintiff, having being coerced into the limousine under false pretense, was unable to leave either the limousine or Defendant Liu's presence. The Plaintiff was aware of her confinement and the actions taken to preserve that confinement by Defendant Liu and others acting at his direction. As a result of the Plaintiffs' confinement in the limousine, Defendant Liu was able to engage in harmful and offensive touching and manipulation of the Plaintiff. The offensive contact caused the Plaintiff to withdraw from all classes during the Fall 2018 semester at the University of M and to seek ongoing professional counseling, care and treatment.	根据上述段落所描述的，从 Origami 餐厅行驶到 Pillsbary 豪宅的这段途中，被告刘某某通过他的言语和行为企图且确实将原告拘禁在豪华轿车里。被告刘某某借助虚假借口将原告强行带入豪华轿车内，使原告既无法离开豪华轿车也无法离开被告刘某某。 原告觉察到自己处于被限制人身自由的状态，也觉察到被告刘某某以及受其指示的其他人为了限制她的人身自由而采取的行动。由于原告被限制在了豪华汽车内，被告刘某某得以对原告实施了具有伤害性质和冒犯性质的碰触和操控。这些冒犯性质的（身体）接触导致原告退出了其在 M 大学 2018 年秋季的所有课程去寻求专业的（心理和精神的）咨询、照料

As a direct and proximate result of these acts, the Plaintiff has sustained the following past and future damage:
a. Body injury;
b. Physical pain and suffering;
c. Inability and loss of capacity to lead and enjoy a normal life;
d. Mental anguish, humiliation and embarrassment;
e. Loss of or diminution of earning or earning capacity;
f. Emotional anguish and emotional pain and suffering;
g. Medical and related expenses, past and future, incurred in seeking a cure for her loss.
Wherefore, the Plaintiff demands a trial by jury and judgment against Defendant Liu, for an amount that exceeds ＄50,000 plus costs, and for such other relief to which the Plaintiff may be justly entitled.

和治疗，持续至今。
作为被告上述行为的直接和最邻近的后果，原告已经并将继续遭到如下损害：
a. 身体损伤；
b. 身体上的痛苦与折磨；
c. 无力享受正常生活并丧失享受正常生活的能力；
d. 心理上的悲恸、羞辱和难堪；
e. 经济收入或经济收入能力的丧失或降低；
f. 情绪上的悲恸以及情绪上的痛苦与折磨；
g. 过去和将来为弥合其损失而导致的医疗及相关费用。
因此，原告要求陪审团对被告刘某某进行审理，要求超过五万美元的赔偿，其中不包括诉讼成本和利息以及其他原告应得的救济。

  本段文字选自起诉书中对犯罪过程和受害人损伤的描述，defendant 译为"被告"，plaintiff 译为"原告"，首字母大写表明是本案中的原告和被告。having being coerced into the limousine under false pretense 中的 coerce 是"强迫"的意思，false pretense 译为"虚假借口"。seek ongoing professional counseling, care and treatment 中的 ongoing 不能简单地译为"正在进行"，而是强调持续到现在的影响，从而突出犯罪嫌疑人的恶劣行径，因此参考译文译为"专业的（心理和精神的）咨询、照料和治疗，持续至今"。

  另一个值得留意的翻译是 body injury 和 physical pain and suffering，两者并不重复：body injury 侧重身体受到的损伤，更多从医学角度来考量；physical pain and suffering 则强调感知上承受的身体痛苦和折磨。inability and loss of capacity 中的 inability 指的是"现在不能"，loss of capacity 指的是"失去能力"，两者也存在较大差异。mental anguish, humiliation and embarrassment 和 emotional anguish and emotional pain and suffering 也不能被认为是重复，前者译为"心理上的悲恸、羞辱和难堪"，而后者则译为"情绪上的悲恸以及情绪上的痛苦与折磨"。在翻译最后一句话 for such other relief to which the Plaintiff may be justly entitled 时，译文化模糊为具体。such other relief 从字面来看是抽象而不明确的，译文根据司法实践判断补全信息，即"诉讼成本和利息以及其他原告应得的救济"。

翻译练习

练习 1

如不服本判决,可在接到判决书的第二日起十日内,通过本院或者直接向广东省高级人民法院提出上诉。书面上诉的,应当提交上诉状正本一份、副本二份。

练习 2

公诉机关当庭提交相关书证、物证照片、毒品鉴定结论、被告人供述等证据。

练习 3

When another resident of the Plaintiff's secured building arrived at the scene, the officers were able to enter the building without alerting the Plaintiff or Defendant Liu. After locating the Plaintiff's apartment, the officers assumed tactical posting positions outside her door. Two officers were positioned on the left side of her door and one was on the right side. The officer on the right upholstered his taser and placed it at his side, while another officer on the left side upholstered his firearm. One of the officers then knocked on the Plaintiff's door with a flashlight, and the Plaintiff, fully clothed, opened the door a moment later. The foregoing all appears on body camera footage.

练习 4

At approximately 1:39 p.m., on June 9, Zhang sent a text message from her cell phone to a manager of an apartment complex. In the message Zhang said that she was running behind to meet the manager to sign a lease, she thought she would arrive at approximately 2:10 p.m., for her appointment. At approximately 2:38 p.m., the apartment manager sent a text message to Zhang and received no response. Later on June 9, at approximately 9:24 p.m., a University of Illinois associate professor reported to University police that multiple colleagues had tried to reach Zhang by phone and she had not responded.

练习 5

The Court held: In light of the instructions on intent given in this case, the presumptions may be rebutted could reasonably be read as telling the jury that it was required to infer intent to kill as the natural and probable consequence of the act of firing the gun unless the defendant persuaded the jury that such an inference was unwarranted. The very statement that the presumption may be rebutted could have indicted to a reasonable juror that the defendant bore an affirmative burden of persuasion once the State proved the underlying act giving rise to the presumption.

本院认为，被告人虽是肯尼亚国籍，但在中国进行犯罪活动，应适用我国法律。被告人以非法占有为目的，秘密窃取公民财物，数额较大，公诉机关指控其犯盗窃罪成立。被告人犯罪时不满18周岁，依法应当从轻或者减轻处罚。被告人归案后，积极坦白罪行，认罪态度较好，退赔绝大部分赃物，依法可以酌情从轻处罚。

第十章
行政法的基本知识和翻译

行政法是指行政主体在行使行政职权和接受行政法制监督过程中与行政相对人、行政法制监督主体之间产生的各种关系,以及行政主体内部产生的各种关系的法律规范的总称。

在中国,行政法由规范行政主体和行政权设定的行政组织法、规范行政权行使的行政行为法、规范行政权运行程序的行政程序法、规范行政权监督的行政监督法、行政救济法等部分组成。其重心是控制和规范行政权,保护行政相对人的合法权益。行政法可以简单分为一般行政法和特别行政法。一般行政法主要由行政复议法(administrative reconsideration law)、行政处罚法(administrative penalty law)、行政许可法(administrative licensing law)等组成;特别行政法则包含治安管理处罚法、海关法、教育法等。

行政诉讼是指行政管理相对人(a person subjected to an administrative action)不服行政机关(administrative body/agency)所做的处理决定,依法起诉行政机关,人民法院适用行政法,按照行政诉讼法(administrative litigation law)的规定予以审理和裁决的活动。

行政法一般被认为是公法范畴,但是在美国公法和私法之间的区别没有大陆法系国家那么清晰。故而美国行政法案件由受理私法案件的普通法院审判。行政法包括实体法和程序法。美国行政法研究的主要对象是后者。就联邦一级而言,美国的行政程序法可以追溯至1789年的《联邦宪法修正案》,但是实质意义上的行政程序法则始于1887年为处理铁路工业问题而成立的州际商业委员会。该委员会是美国联邦行政部门中最早的独立规制机构(independent regulatory agency)。20世纪30年代,在罗斯福总统推行的"新政"(the New Deal)时期,各种联邦行政机关如雨后春笋般成立,美国的行政程序法也得到长足的发展。美国的行政法是由宪法、法律、判例、行政规章等组成的。其中,最为重要的是联邦宪法第五修正案中的正当程序(Due Process)条款和1946年的《联邦行政程序法》(Federal Administrative Procedure Act)。

英国行政法的重要原则产生于判例,在某些原则上判例之间并非完全一致,学者间的理解也有分歧。英国行政法与美国的行政法较为类似:诉讼由普通法院管辖,没有独立的行政法院系统。普通法院在受理行政诉讼时使用一般法律规则。在英国,国家赔偿责任确立以后，国家的责任也适用一般的法律规则。行政机关和私人签订合同时也适用一般的合同规则。

第一节　常用术语

诉讼法的常用术语见表10-1。

表10-1　诉讼法的常用术语及其英文表达

术语	英译
给予	mete
简章	prospectus
复审法院	review court
行政程序法	administrative procedure law
联邦通讯委员会	Federal Communication Commission
核能管理委员会	Nuclear Regulartory Commission
海事委员会	Maritime Adminsitration
联邦贸易委员会	Federal Trade Commission
证券交易委员会	Security Exchange Commision
国家劳工关系局	National Labour Relations Board
行政单位	administrative unit
批准、不批准或不作为	grant, denial or failure to act
标准程序	paradigmatic procedure
有记录的	on the record
行政法法官	administrative law judge
类似法律的规范	statute-like norm
以行政方式做出决定	decision is taken bureaucratically
司法监督	judicial control
行政职权	administrative power
行政法律规范	administrative legal specifications
行政主体	administrative subject
政令	government decree
依职权	ex officio
行政裁量	administrative discretion
行政法学	administrative jurisprudence

续表

术语	英译
行政救济	administrative remedy
行政听证	administrative hearing
行政诉讼	administrative litigation
复议机关	reviewing body
行政行为	administrative action
具体行政行为	specific administrative act
抽象行政行为	abstract administrative act
行政不作为	administrative inaction
行政处罚	administrative penalty
行政处分	disciplinary sanction
依法行政	administration under the law; law-based administration
行政许可	administrative licensing
行政补偿	administrative recuperation
行政检查	administrative inspection
行政鉴定	administrative appraisal
行政救济穷尽原则	doctrine of exhaustiveness/administrative remedies
行政拘留	administrative detention
行政强制	administrative coercion
行政强制措施	administrative coercive measure
行政强制执行	administrative execution; execution of administrative act
行政裁决	administrative adjudication/ruling
行政主体	administrative subject
行政机关	administrative organ/agency
行政法规	administrative regulation
行政制裁	administrative sanction
行政赔偿	administrative compensation
行政追偿	recourse of administrative compensation
行政责任	administrative responsibility/duty
地方政府规范性文件	normative documents of local government
法治	rule of law
法制	rule by law

续表

术语	英译
法治政府	rule of law government
依法治军	governing the army under the law
总则	general provision
附则	appendix
正当程序	due process
治安管理	security administration
治安条例	security regulation
授权原则	delegation doctrine
豁免	immunity
管理机关	regulatory agency
裁决性听证	adjudicatory hearing
公共行政	public administrative
暂扣/吊销许可证	suspend/revoke administrative license
（国务院的）直属行政机关	bureau
（国务院中的）部门	department
（行政机关的）内设机构	institution
法制办公室	legal affairs office
行政执法人员	（administrative）law enforcement officer
官员负责制	administrative accountability
吊销许可证或营业执照	rescission of a permit or a licence
责令停产停业	suspend production or business operations
扣押、冻结财产	distraint or freezing of property
申辩和质证	defend oneself and make cross-examination
法定职责	statutory functions and duties
全面深化改革	comprehensively deepen the reform
中国特色社会主义法治	socialist rule of law with Chinese characteristics
社会主义法治国家	socialist rule of law country

第二节　核心术语的表达和理解

1. 美国现设主要行政部门和部门主管

美国现设主要行政部门和部门主管的名称及英译见表10-2。

表 10-2　美国现设主要行政部门和部门主管

部门	汉译	部门主管	汉译
Department of State	国务院	Secretary of State	国务卿
Department of the Treasury	财政部	Secretary of the Treasury	财政部长
Department of Defense	国防部	Secretary of Defense	国防部长
Department of Justice	司法部	Attorney General	司法部长
Department of the Interior	内政部	Secretary of the Interior	内政部长
Department of Agriculture	农业部	Secretary of Agriculture	农业部长
Department of Commerce	商务部	Secretary of Commerce	商务部长
Department of Labor	工部	Secretary of Labor	劳工部长
Department of Health and Human Services	卫生和公共服务部	Secretary of Health and Human Services	卫生和公众服务部长
Department of Homeland Security	国土安全部	Secretary of Homeland Security	国土安全部长
Department of Education	教育部	Secretary of Education	教育部长
Department of Energy	能源部	Secretary of Energy	能源部长
Department of Housing and Urban Development	住房和城市发展部	Secretary of Housing and Urban Development	住房和城市发展部长
Department of Transportation	运输部	Secretary of Transportation	运输部长
Department of Veterans Affairs	退伍军人事务部	Secretary of Veterans Affairs	退伍军人事务部长

2. 英国现设主要行政部门和部门主管

英国现设主要行政部门和部门主管的名称及英译见表 10-3。

表 10-3　英国现设主要行政部门和部门主管

部门	汉译	部门主管	汉译
Prime Minister's Office	首相办公室	Prime Minister	首相
Office of the Deputy Prime Minister	副首相办公室	Deputy Prime Minister	副首相
Department for Culture, Media and Sport	文化、媒体及体育部	Secretary of State for Culture, Media and Sport	文化、媒体及体育大臣/部长
Department for Education and Skills	教育与技能部	Secretary of State for Education and Skills	教育与技能大臣/部长
Department for Environment, Food and Rural Affairs	环境、食品及农村事务部	Secretary of State for Environment, Food and Rural Affairs	环境、食品及农村和事务大臣/部长
Department of Health	卫生部	Secretary of State for Health	卫生大臣/部长

续表

部门	汉译	部门主管	汉译
Department for International Development	国际发展部	Secretary of State for International Development	国际发展大臣/部长
Department of Trade and Industry	贸易及工业部	Secretary of State for Trade and Industry	贸易及工业大臣/部长
Department for Transport	交通部	Secretary of State for Transport	交通大臣/部长
Department for Work and Pensions	工作及养恤金部	Secretary of State for Work and Pensions	工作及养恤金大臣/部长
Department for Constitutional Affairs	宪法事务部	Secretary of State for Constitutional Affairs	宪法事务大臣/部长
Ministry of Defence	国防部	Secretary of State for Defence	国防大臣/部长
Foreign and Common Wealth Office	外交及联邦事务部	Secretary of State for Foreign and Common Wealth Affairs (the Foreign Secretary)	外交及联邦事务大臣/部长（外交大臣/部长）
Home Office	内务部	Secretary of State for the Home Department (the Home Secretary)	内务大臣/部长
Northern Ireland Office	北爱尔兰事务部	Secretary of State for Northern Ireland	北爱尔兰事务大臣/部长
Scotland Office	苏格兰事务部	Secretary of State for Scotland	苏格兰事务大臣/部长
Wales Office	威尔士事务部	Secretary of State for Wales	威尔士事务大臣/部长
HM Treasury	财政部	Chancellor of the Exchequer	财政大臣/部长
Privy Council Office	枢密院	Lord President of the Privy Council	枢密院大臣/院长
Law Officers' Department	法务部	Attorney General	总检察长

3. 中国现设主要行政部门

中国现设主要行政部门的名称及英译见表10-4。

表10-4　中国现设主要行政部门

行政部门	英译
外交部	Ministry of Foreign Affairs
发展改革委员会	Development and Reform Commission
国防部	Ministry of National Defence

续表

行政部门	英译
科学技术部	Ministry of Science and Technology
文化旅游部	Ministry of Culture and Tourism
教育部	Ministry of Education
民族事务委员会	Ethnic Affairs Commission
民政部	Ministry of Civil Affairs
公安部	Ministry of Public Security
国家安全部	Ministry of State Security
应急管理部	Ministry of Emergency Management
司法部	Ministry of Justice
财政部	Ministry of Finance
人力资源和社会保障部	Ministry of Human Resources and Social Security
生态和环境部	Ministry of Ecology and Environment
自然资源部	Ministry of Natural Resources
住房和城乡建设部	Ministry of Housing and Urban-Rural Development
交通运输部	Ministry of Transport
工业和信息化部	Ministry of Industry and Information Industry
水利部	Ministry of Water Resources
农业农村部	Ministry of Agriculture and Rurual Affairs
商务部	Ministry of Commerce
卫生健康委员会	Health Commission
审计署	Audit Office
退役军人事务部	Ministry of Veteran Affairs

4. administrative，executive

两个词都可译为"行政"，但存在差异。administrative 多理解为行政事务，为行政机关中的行政，还译为"管理"；executive 泛指行政、立法和司法三权或者三个部门其中之一的行政。例如：

① The Commission sets the pattern for those independent regulatory agencies—functioning outside the excutive departments and regulation some aspects of private activity—that are the most distinctive species of administrative body of the United States.

该委员会为美国行政机构中最具有特色的，在行政部门之外行驶其职能，并为管理个人活动的某些方面的那些独立的管理机关设定模式。

5. penalty, fine

penalty 译为"罚金",fine 译为"罚款"。在中国,虽然二者都是以现金形式实现,但其法律意义截然不同。罚金是刑法的附加刑之一,主要适用于触犯刑法的犯罪分子,并且只能由人民法院依照刑法的相关规定来判决,其他任何单位和个人都无权判处罚金;罚款属于行政法的范畴,是行政处罚方式,由行政单位对违反行政法规的个人或者单位进行处罚,不需要经过人民法院来判决。工商行政管理局依照工商行政管理的具体规定就可以罚款;公安局也可以对违反治安管理处罚条例的个人或者单位按照具体程序处以罚款。

6. criminal detention, detention

criminal detention 译为"拘役",detention 译为"拘留"。两者都有限制人身自由的意思,但有实质差异,不能相互代替,不能混淆使用。

在中国,拘役属于刑法的范畴,是短时间内剥夺犯罪分子人身自由、实施劳动改造的刑罚方法,由公安机关就近执行。

拘留则比较复杂,可以分为三种:刑事拘留、行政拘留和司法拘留。刑事拘留是刑事诉讼法中的一种强制措施,是公安机关、人民检察院在侦查过程中,遇有紧急情况时,对现行犯或者重大嫌疑分子暂时性剥夺其人身自由的一种强制措施。行政拘留是公安机关对违反了行政法律法规的公民所做出的短期限制人身自由的一种处罚。司法拘留是在民事诉讼过程中对严重妨碍民事诉讼活动的当事人及其他诉讼参与人采取的、在一定期限内限制人身自由的强制措施。

第三节 常见句型结构

1. if …

if … 译为"……的",表示前面是条件,后面一般跟结果句。例如:

② If an illegal act constitutes a crime, the administrative organ must transfer the case to a judicial organ for investigation of criminal responsibility in accordance with law.

<u>违法行为构成犯罪的</u>,行政机关必须将案件移送司法机关,依法追究刑事责任。

句子中的 if 就对应"……的"。其中"依法追究刑事责任"的翻译也值得留意,这里的追究并不是直接给予处罚,而是对其犯罪行为和责任进行调查,所以译为 for investigation of criminal responsibility。该句中的"依法"的翻译跟刑法和民法文本中的译法一致,用 in accordance with law 即可。

再如:

③ If a party refuses to accept the decision on administrative penalty made on the spot, he may apply for administrative reconsideration or bring an administrative lawsuit in accordance with law.

当事人对当场做出的行政处罚决定不服<u>的</u>,可以依法申请行政复议或者提起行政诉讼。

2. 依法治国、依法行政和法治政府

"依法治国"译为 govern the country according to law。govern the country in accordance with (the) law 非常正式,但作为固定词组则略显冗长。rule the country in accordance with (the) law 也非常正式,但 rule 有高高在上的统治意味,除非有意传达这一层意思,否则不建议使用。manage state affairs according to law 重在强调依法管理国家事务,用于翻译"依法治国"时,含义偏窄。run the country according to law 非常口语化,不够正式。

"依法行政"作为一个惯用语,administration according to law 是最好的译法。如果强调依法行政,还可用 law-based administration 或者 administration under rule of law;前者更简洁,也更能传达它在中国当下语境中的官方含义。如果描述其动态过程,可以用 handle administrative affairs according to law, perform all duties according to law 之类,但都不属于一个固定词组。

"法治政府"译作 law-based government 或 rule of law government 都可,在官方前者更为通用。government that is ruled by law 显得冗长,不适合作术语使用。

3. establish

establish 在法律文本中一般译为"设立,设定,建立",译者须根据 establish 出现的语境来判断和选择译文所用。例如:

④ Where necessary, the State Council may adopt the form of releasing decisions to <u>establish</u> administrative licenses. After implementation, except for the matters under temporary administrative licenses, the State Council shall timely propose to the National People's Congress and its Standing Committee to formulate laws, or formulate administrative regulations by itself.

必要时,国务院可以采用发布决定的方式<u>设定</u>行政许可。实施后,除临时性行政许可事项外,国务院应当及时提请全国人民代表大会及其常务委员会制定法律,或者自行制定行政法规。

⑤ The regulations and rules shall not make specific requirements for the implementation of the administrative license set down by the upper law, shall not increase administrative license; for the specific conditions of administrative license, they shall not <u>establish</u> any other condition in violation of the upper law.

法规、规章对实施上位法设定的行政许可做出的具体规定,不得增设行政许可;对行政许可条件做出的具体规定,不得<u>增设</u>违反上位法的其他条件。

establish any other condition 中,establish,any other 结合起来译为"增设"。

第四节 翻译实例分析

1. 合法性原则

Legality is the foremost principle of administrative law, which means that administrative subject must implement administrative activities according to lawful authorization, form and procedure, and undertake corresponding legal responsibility for its illegal administrative activities. The basic content of the principle of legality is as follows. Firstly, the administrative authority of administrative subject shall be set or conferred by law. Secondly, administrative activities carried out by administrative subject's activities must comply with administrative legel specifications. Thirdly, administrative subject's activities against law are invalid. Fourthly, administrative subject must undertake corresponding responsibility for its illegal administrative activities.

合法性原则是行政法的首要原则，是指行政主体必须按照法定授权、形式和程序实施行政行为，并对其违法行政行为承担相应的法律责任。合法性原则的基本内容是：第一，行政主体的行政职权依法设定或被授予；第二，行政主体的行政行为必须符合行政法律规范；第三，行政主体的违法行为无效；第四，行政主体必须对其违法行政行为承担相应的法律责任。

本段文字属于行政法学研究文本，对合法性从四个角度进行深入剖析，即授权法定、行为法定、违法无效和违法追责。本段文字的逻辑性强，层次清晰，译者在翻译的时候也要将此体现出来，其中有不少前面讲解过的专业术语，如行政主体（administrative subject）、行政行为（administrative activities）、行政法律规范（administrative legal specifications）和行政职权（administrative authority）。

本段中有两个地方需要注意。首先，implement administrative activities 不能简单译为"推行行政活动"，这样的表达不符合现行法言法语，可以调整为"实施行政行为"。反之亦然，译者在翻译"实施行政行为"时，应采用 implement administrative activities，而不是 carry out the administrative activities。

第二个需要注意的是 the administrative authority of administrative subject shall be set or conferred by law 中对 set, confer 的理解。set 指的是"授权"，即根据具体的法律规定所享有的权利，confer 指的则是"授予"，是一种授权关系。

2. 法治思想和行政法发展

Legal ideas and doctrines sometimes provoke social change, but more often they follow a safe distance behind. Administrative law fits this general pattern. The great social and economic transformations of the 20th century have only recently begun to be reflected in

有时法治思想和理念能够引发变革，但这种变革往往是有适宜的滞后性。行政法恰恰适应这一总体格局。20世纪伟大的社会和经济转型最近才开始反映在行政法领域。福利

administrative law. The rise of the welfare and the regulation of social and economic activity have meant a substantial expansion of government in the middle and later years of the 20th century. New and wild-ranging legislative programmes have been developed, a host of new authorities have been created, and the lives of citizen have been much controlled and regulated. As the close of the century approaches, administrative law continues to develop and mature as it strives to find the doctrines and values, the ideas and institution's, necessary to bring the administrative state within a framework of law.

国家的兴起以及社会和经济活动的监督意味着20世纪中后期政府的大幅度扩张。新型而广泛的立法程序蓬勃发展，新型行政主体不断涌现，人们的生活受到了更多的制约和规制。在本世纪（20世纪）即将结束的时候，行政法在探寻法律理念和价值观念、思想和制度的过程将继续发展和成熟，最终必将在法治的框架里建立起行政国家。

本段文字描述了法治思想和行政法发展的关系，而非诉讼文本。涉及的术语不是太多，如 legal ideas and doctrines（法治思想和理念）、legislative programmes（立法程序）、control and regulate（制约和规制）和 institution（制度）。

在句式结构处理层面，值得注意的有：more often they follow a safe distance behind 强调的是法律的滞后性，safe 体现了作者的感情色彩，其认为这种滞后性是积极可取的，译文要体现这种情感倾向；necessary to bring the administrative state within a framework of law 承接前半句，强调发展的结果，necessary 译为"最终必将"较合适。

3. 公证书翻译

商标注册公证书

（　　）第_____号

兹证明我国_____公司生产的_____的_____商标注册证（登记号为_____号）系我国工商行政管理总局出具。该商标的专有权属于我国_____公司。

中华人民共和国_____省_____市公证处

公证员：_____
_____公证处：_____
_____省
中华人民共和国

NOTARIAL CERTIFICATE OF
REGISTRATION OF TRADEMARK

(　　) No. _____

　　This is to certify that No. _____ Trademark Registration Certificate, identifying the _____ Trademark on _____ (the name of the goods) produced by _____ Company, is issued by the General Adminsitration for Industry and Commerce of the People's Republic of China. The patent right of the Trademark Registration belongs to _____ Company.

Notary: _____

_____ Notary Public Office (seal)

_____ Province

The People's Republic of China

　　公证是公证机构根据自然人、法人或者其他组织的申请，依照法定程序对民事法律行为、有法律意义的事实和文书的真实性、合法性予以证明的活动。公证文书的译文优劣对自身文书效力的发挥和公证行业和机构的形象有着重要影响，因为译文质量问题还曾引发过公证赔偿纠纷。司法部在2000年就英文质量问题曾发布过相关专门的通知文件。

　　公证书是法律文书的一种，译者在翻译时要注意规范、准确、严谨、一致等，比如要将标题放在正文上方的中央，不用引号，将所有单词全部大写或者每个单词的首字母大写。以准确为例，"婚姻状况公证书"若译为 Notarial Certificate of Marital Status，就不如按照实际情况，分别译为 Notarial Certificate of Marriage，Notarial Certificate of Divorce，Notarial Certificate of Being Single。因为篇幅限制，公证书的翻译还要注意简洁和精练，如"毕业证书"虽可以译为 Graduation Certificate，但 diploma 更合适。

　　本例是商标注册公证书，标题居中全部大写，套用固定结构"this is to certify that …"。"证明"常见的对应单词有 prove, testify, certify, 三者之间有细微差别：

　　testify 指的是 make a formal statement of what is true, especially in a court of law；

　　prove 指的是 show that something is true by providing facts, or information etc.；

　　certify 指的是 state that something is correct or true, especially after some kind of test。

　　比较起来，显然 certify 更符合语境的要求。

4. 判决书

United States Court of Appeals, Ninth Circuit
FRIENDS OF ANIMALS; Predator Defense, Plaintiffs-Appellants, v. UNITED STATES FISH AND WILDLIFE SERVICE, an agency of the United States, Defendant-Appellee
No. 15-35639
Decided: January 10, 2018

…

This case arises from efforts by the United States Fish and Wildlife Service ("Service") to balance the interests of two types of owls who compete for the same territory. The first is the northern spotted owl, whose range is from British Columbia to California but the majority of which are "found in the Cascades of Oregon and the Klamath Mountains in southwestern Oregon and northwestern California". See Endangered and Threatened Wildlife and Plants; Determination of Threatened Status for the Northern Spotted Owl, 55 Fed. Reg. 26,114, 26,115 (June 26, 1990). … The principal reason for the decline in the population was the loss of old-growth forest habitats on which the species relies. Id.

A second factor in the northern spotted owl's population decline, however, involved another species of owl at issue in this case: the barred owl. The barred owl's "adaptability and aggressive nature appear to allow it to take advantage of habitat perturbations", and it has spread from its native habitat in the eastern United States to the Northwest, where it has come greatly to outnumber the native northern spotted owls. Barred owls' diets can overlap with spotted owls' by as much as 76%, and the more aggressive barred owl may displace spotted owls and may even physically attack them.

美国第九巡回上诉法院
动物之友、捕食者保护协会（原告和上诉人），起诉美利坚合众国的一个政府机构美国渔业与野生动物动物保护局（被告和被上诉人）
编号：15-35639
裁决日期：2018年1月10日

…………

此案件源于美国渔业和野生动物动物保护局（以下简称"动物保护局"）为了平衡在同一个区域竞争的两种猫头鹰的利益所做出的努力。第一种猫头鹰是北方斑点猫头鹰，它的活动范围从不列颠哥伦比亚一直到加州，但绝大部分"被发现在俄勒冈州的卡斯卡德、俄勒冈西南的克拉马斯山脉，以及加州西北部"，见《濒临灭绝的野生动植物》及《有关北方斑点猫头鹰濒危状态的决定》，《联邦公报》第55卷，第26115-26115页（1990年6月26日）。……其数量下降的主要原因是其赖以栖息的原始森林数量的减少。

数量下降的第二个主要原因与本案中所涉及的另外一个猫头鹰的品种相关：斑纹猫头鹰。斑纹猫头鹰的"适应性和攻击性似乎允许其适应栖息地的变化"，而且它已经从其原始栖息地即美国东部蔓延至西北部，在那儿它的数量远远超过了本土的北方斑点猫头鹰的数量。两种猫头鹰的食物约有76%的重叠，更富攻击性的斑纹猫头鹰有可能在当地取代斑点猫头鹰，甚至可能攻击斑点猫头鹰。

本段节选自民告官案件,是2018年美国上诉法院判决书的一部分,其中保留了判决书抬头,以向读者介绍美国判决书的基本格式。通读判决书的正文部分会让人产生一种错觉:这不是判决书文本,更像是生物教材的节选内容。

其中对法条的引用会让读者感到困惑,如 Fed. Reg.,指的是 Federel Register(《联邦公报》),后面的数字是起始页和出版年代。再以 7 C.F.R. §319(2004)为例,译为"《美国联邦行政法典》(Code of Federal Regulation)2004版第7篇第319条"。再如 Mo. Rev. Stat,§400. 2-207(2004),其中 Mo. Rev. Stat 的全称是 Missouri Revised Statute,译为"《密苏里州修正法典》2004版第2篇第207条第400页"。

与国内判决书重罗列事实和证据、说理部分稍弱的模式不同,美国判决书的撰写重道理,为说明一个观点,引经据典,援引许多制定法或案例中的原文(因此判决中充满了各种引用符号),不仅从成文法律中寻找支持观点,也保留了遵循先例原则。

5. 复审裁定公告

商务部决定对原产于美国的进口干玉米酒糟所适用的反倾销和反补贴措施进行复审。经过调查,根据《中华人民共和国反倾销条例》和《中华人民共和国反补贴条例》的规定,商务部做出复审裁定。现将有关复审事项公告如下:

(1) 裁定

根据调查结果,商务部裁定有必要继续对原产于美国的进口干玉米酒糟征收反倾销税和反补贴税。

(2) 反倾销和反补贴措施

根据《中华人民共和国反倾销条例》和《中华人民共和国反补贴条例》的规定,进口经营者在进口原产于美国的干玉米酒糟产品时,继续向中华人民共和国海关缴纳相应的反倾销税和反补贴税。

Ministry of Commerce decided to review the applied anti-dumping and countervailing measures against imports of dried corn distillers' grains originating in the United States. After Ministry of Commerce completed its investigation, it made a ruling on the review according to the Anti-dumping Regulations of the People's Republic of China and the Countervailing Regulations of the People's Republic of China. The relevant matters on the review are hereby announced as follows:

(1) Ruling

According to the investigation results, Ministry of Commerce has ruled that it is necessary to continue to impose anti-dumping duties and countervailing duties on imports of dried corn distillers' grains originating in the United States.

(2) Anti-dumping and countervailing measures

In accordance with the Anti-dumping Regulations of the People's Republic of China and the Countervailing Regulations of the People's Republic of China, any person or organization that refuses to accept the review may apply for administrative reconsideration or initiate litigation to a people's court according to the law of the People's Republic of China, when an import operator imports dried corn distillers' grains originating in the United States, the operator shall continue to

（3）行政诉讼和行政复议
根据《中华人民共和国反倾销条例》第 53 条和《中华人民共和国反补贴条例》第 52 条的规定，对本复审决定不服的，可以依法申请行政复议，也可以依法向人民法院提起诉讼。

pay the corresponding anti-dumping duties and countervailing duties to the Customs of the People's Republic of China.
(3) Administrative litigation and administrative reconsideration
According to Article 53 of the Anti-dumping Regulations of the People's Republic of China and Article 52 of the Countervailing Regulations of the People's Republic of China, any person or organization that refuses to accept the review may apply for administrative reconsideration or initiate litigation to a people's court according to the law.

本段文字节选自复审裁定的公告，其中有不少反复使用的术语，结构清晰，句式也不复杂。第一段是背景介绍，后面几段文字的程式固定，分别为裁决、反倾销和反补贴措施、救济手段的具体内容。

第一段三句话概括原因、行动和结论，涉及的术语有"反倾销""反补贴""复审裁决""复审事项"等，都有官方表达可参照。稍有难度的要算"原产于"，有人可能会用 be made in 来翻译。但 be made in 并不能体现"原"意思，只译出"产于"。译文中的 originate in 则两个含义兼而有之，更合适。

第二段阐述裁定结果，标题中的"裁定"的翻译应该和后面两个标题整体考量，都属于名词性质，所以译为 ruling 较为合适。

第三段具体强调进口经营商需要缴纳两种税。这里的"根据"与上一段的"根据"功能一致，可以译为 according to 或 in accordance with。本段容易被疏忽的是"继续向中华人民共和国海关缴纳相应的反倾销税和反补贴税"的翻译，译者要理解到"继续"的义务性，它是必须要做的事情，所以在翻译时须加入情态动词 shall。

第四段是告知复审裁定结果的救济手段。原文并没有点明谁对本复审决定不服，英译需要遵循表达逻辑来补充信息，即 any person or organization。其中，"对本复审决定不服""申请行政复议""向人民法院提起诉讼"的英译程式化表达值得借鉴。

翻译练习

练习 1

行政执法主体违反本规定的，由本级人民政府法制机构建议改正；拒不改正的，由本级人民政府给予通报批评；情节严重的，由监察机关依法追究有关负责人和直接责任。

练习2

拆除房屋应经国土管理部门批准并领取拆除房屋许可证。未经批准许可，任何单位或个人均不得擅自拆除房屋。

练习3

下列旧机动车辆禁止交易：走私车辆；来源不明的车辆；手续不全的车辆；按规定报废的车辆；擅自拼装组装的车辆；其他按规定禁止转让的车辆。

练习4

坚持依法治国、依法执政、依法行政共同推进，坚持法治国家、法治政府、法治社会一体建设，实现科学立法、严格执法、公正司法、全民守法，促进国家治理体系和治理能力现代化。

练习5

美国谷物协会向商务部提交了《关于对进口至中国的美国干玉米酒糟终止征收反倾销税及反补贴税的请求》，请求商务部考虑中国市场发生的重要变化以及中国的公共利益，申请对原产于美国的进口干玉米酒糟所适用的反倾销和反补贴措施进行复审调查，终止征收反倾销税和反补贴税。

翻译练习参考答案

第一章 法律翻译职业现状

马克·杰纳斯是伊利诺伊州卫生保健和家庭服务部的一名儿童护理专家。美国州县与市政工人委员会第31分会（以下简称"分会"）经投票表决，成为包括杰纳斯在内的35 000名公职人员的集体谈判代表。由于不认同分会提倡的许多公共政策立场，包括它在集体谈判上的立场，杰纳斯拒绝参加该分会。杰纳斯认为，分会在谈判中未重视伊利诺伊州的财政危机，也未反映出他或伊利诺伊州公民的最佳利益。因此，杰纳斯也拒绝缴纳任何费用和提供任何资助。然而，按照集体合同的约定，他每月要缴纳44.58美元的工会费，一年共计535美元。

杰纳斯对州当前财政状况的担忧得到州长的认同。伊利诺伊州州长向联邦地区法院提起诉讼，州司法部长作为被告的辩护人参加诉讼，州长请求宣告上述《劳动关系法》中关于强制缴纳"代理费用"的规定违宪。地区法院认为州长不具有诉讼资格，驳回了州长的诉讼请求。但是，由于杰纳斯和其他两名劳动者因为代理费明显伤害了他们的权益而在诉讼过程中参与进来，为了节省司法成本，地区法院允许他们基于重新提交的诉状继续进行诉讼程序。

苹果公司提出抗辩，主张Illinois Brick一案的规则是仅允许消费者起诉负责定价的一方当事人，无论该方是否直接向消费者出售商品或服务。联邦高院则认为，苹果公司提出的这一观点存在三个主要问题。

第一，这一观点与法条和先例相违背。如果要支持该观点，联邦高院须改写在Illinois Brick一案中的观点，并抛弃长期以来的明线规则——直接购买者可起诉，非直接购买者不得起诉。

第二，从经济和法律来看，苹果公司的观点说服力不足。根据苹果公司的观点，是否允许起诉将根据零售商与其生产商和供应商的财务安排来决定，这种规则过于随意。同时，按照该观点，如果零售商的零售价格是以其向制造商或供应商支付的价格为基础往上增加确定，消费者可以起诉垄断零售商；但如果零售价格是由制造商或供应商决定，而零售商仅收取佣金，则消费者不得起诉垄断零售商。

第三，苹果公司的观点会引导垄断零售商与制造商、供应商通过构建交易来逃避消费者的反垄断诉讼，进而阻碍有效的反垄断执法。

练习 4

首先，苹果公司提出，仅允许上游的应用开发商起诉苹果公司，不允许下游的消费者起诉，就意味着更为有效的反垄断执法。但这一说法站不住脚，与反垄断的长久目标——有效的私人执法及消费者保护相悖。

其次，苹果公司认为在消费者提起的反垄断诉讼中计算垄断零售商的损害赔偿金额可能是复杂的。但联邦高院认为，Illinois Brick 规则不是护身符，不能仅因为赔偿金额计算可能很复杂而让垄断经营者免于诉讼。

最后，苹果公司还主张，已确定应用开发商可起诉零售商，若再允许众多消费者起诉零售商，会导致重复索赔。但是本案不属于一条分销链上不同层级的多方当事人都向最上游的制造商主张偿还由后者超额收费的部分，将导致最上游的制造商重复赔偿的情形。

第二章　法律语言的特点

练习 1

除下文所述事项外，保荐人无责任监督或确保公司持续遵守《创业板上市规则》和适用于公司的其他有关法律和法规。

练习 2

本条规定的距离应该按照《健康与安全法》第 11362.768 条第 c 款的方式衡量，除非法律另有规定。

练习 3

投资方特此依照纽约州法律设立合资公司，以实现本合同规定的合资公司的经营目的。

In the course of dispute resolution, the parties to a joint venture shall continue to perform the provisions of the joint venture agreement, contract and articles of association, except for matters in dispute.

The shareholders of a company shall abide by laws, administrative regulations and the articles of association of the company and exercise shareholder's rights according to the law, and may not abuse shareholder's rights to harm the interests of the company or other shareholders, or abuse the independent status of the company legal person and the limited liability of shareholders to harm the interests of the creditors of the company.

No party shall have the right to withdraw his capital contributions or demand or receive the return of his capital contributions or any part thereof, except as otherwise provided in this Agreement.

第三章　法律职业和法院结构

大型律师事务所雇佣少数族裔律师的百分比不足以说明全部问题。能够获准成为有名气的律师事务所合伙人的少数族裔律师的比例更低。1982年《美国法律杂志》的调查发现：在106个律师事务所中没有一个黑人合伙人；在133个律师事务所中没有拉丁裔合伙人。大门可能已经敞开，但是少数族裔仍处于权力、名气和报酬的较低位置。

练习 2

法律职业管理是各州主要需要考虑的问题，各州对其准入职业都有自己的要求。大多数州都要求有3年以上的大学本科教育以及获得法学学位。每个州都有自己的针对申请进入法律职业的申请者举办的书面考试。但是几乎所有的州都会使用"跨州律师考试"，这是一项为期一天的考试，都是多项选择题。各州还会再加一天针对本州法律规定的写作考试。

练习 3

In the federal court system, there are 13 U. S. Courts of Appeal—also referred to as U. S. Circuit Courts of Appeals. The Federal Courts of Appeal have for 12 circuits, including the U. S. Court of Appeal for the District of Columbia Circuit, hear appeals from the Federal District Courts located within their respective judicial circuits. The Court of Appeal Thirteen Circuit, called the Federal Circuit, has national appellate jurisdiction over certain types of cases, such as cases involving patent law and cases in which the U. S. government is a defendant.

练习 4

The Supreme People's Court conducts trial of the following cases: ① first-hearing cases placed with the SPC by laws and regulations and those the SPC deems within its jurisdiction; ② appeals or protests against trial decisions or verdicts of the higher people's courts and special people's courts; ③ appeals against court judgments lodged by the Supreme People's Procuratorate according to trial supervision procedures; ④ giving approval to death sentence.

第四章 民法的基本知识和翻译（上）

练习 1

A person who causes harm to another person in self-defense assumes no civil liability. A person who, when acting in self-defense, exceeds the necessary limit and causes unreasonable harm to another person shall assume appropriate civil liability.

练习 2

If a person, when seeking to avoid peril in response to an emergency, causes harm to others, the person who created the peril shall assume civil liability. Where the peril is caused by natural forces, the person who causes harm by seeking to avoid the peril assumes no civil liability, but may give appropriate compensation. If a person adopts improper measures or exceeds the necessary limit in seeking to avoid peril in response to an emergency and causes unreasonable harm to others, such person shall assume appropriate civil liability.

练习 3

An act conducted by a person without authority, exceeding the authority, or after the authority is terminated is not effective against the principal who has not ratified it.

A counterparty may urge the principal to ratify the act within one month after receipt of the notification. Inaction of the principal is deemed as refusal of ratification. A bona fide counterparty has the right to revoke the act before such act is ratified. Revocation shall be made by actual notice.

When the act is not ratified, a bona fide counterparty has the right to request the person who conducts the act to perform debt obligations or compensate for loss thus incurred, provided that the scope of compensation shall not exceed the benefit the counterparty would have received when the principal ratified the act.

Where the counterparty knows or should have known that the person conduting the act has no authority, the counterparty and such person shall assume liability in proportion to their fault.

现在最普通的一种财产所有权是无条件继承不动产权,通常来说该术语用来指绝对无条件继承不动产,这种不动产所有人具备一切可能的权利、特权及能力。无条件继承不动产只限于个人或继承人,并且它的权利分配永远没有任何限制和条件。进一步来说,所有权人对该财产具有排他性的占有和使用权利。无条件继承不动产的存续期限可能是无期限的,它可以被出售或者赠送。如果没有遗嘱,这种不动产权将由权利人的法定继承人继承。

附属物有各种不同的定义。有的定义为:原为动产,因依附于不动产的使用而成为不动产的一部分;有的定义为:作为动产,因长期附着于不动产而成为其一部分的动产。还有的定义为:作为动产,紧密地附着于不动产上至不损及财产的完好不能将其分离。然而,没有任何一个定义能适用所有情形。决定某物是附属物的主要意义是它将被视为土地的一部分,除不动产的所有人,一般不允许将它移走。

第五章 民法的基本知识和翻译(下)

除非另有明确表示,由于执行本协议所引发的或与本协议有关的协议双方的所有争议、纠纷或歧义,以及任何违约及过失(包括但不限于有关本协议存续的争议、仲裁条款有效性的争议),如不能以友好协商的方式解决,则提交仲裁。

练习 2

借款人应按照本协议和票据完成所有支付义务。向银行的偿付应不附带其他费用并且是免税的,而且银行所收到的偿付款项不含任何税收。借款人应按本协议承担全部本协议规定的税收。

练习 3

Party B must provide a duplicate copy of the construction designs and drawings, and both copies should be signed by both parties.

If materials provided by Party A for the construction do not meet the necessary requirements, Party A shall bear responsibility for any resulting delays in the completion in the project.

If the quality of Party B's work results in any accidents, the liability for such accidents shall be the responsibility of Party B.

If, during the construction, Party A wishes to propose a change to the design, he should sign a "Change of Project" with Party B and must assume responsibility for resulting delays or increase in costs. If Party A secretly attempts to change to design directly with the construction personnel and this action causes loss to Party B, then Party A must compensate Party B for this loss.

The standard of work. It is the responsibility of Party B to make sure that all construction works are carried out to the requirements of the design and to make sure that all internal walls and hidden construction parts are to the required standard.

Project completion. Party B must notify Party A when the project is complete and ready for inspection by Party A. After inspection both parties must sign an "Engineering Quality Acceptance" document. If Party A is not available to inspect the construction site on the completion date, he must notify Party B of the soonest available date. Where Party A is not available on the completion date to retake custody of the location, he must pay any extra costs incurred by Party B.

One-year warranty. After completion of the work and signing of the "Single Warranty", there shall be a one-year warranty on the construction.

练习 4

(1) Rights and Obligations of Party A

a. Party A has the right to supervise and manage the use of freezer. And Party A has the obligation to inform Party B of the corresponding results after each inspection.

b. Where Party B's freezer is not put into the designated market or is not put into the terminal, Party A has the right not to pay all the remaining subsidies and Party A has the right to terminate this contract.

c. During the term of validity of the contract, if Party B violates the contract by displaying products other than Party A's products and putting up posters of other manufacturers for a total of two times, Party A has the right not to pay all freezer rental fees for the second current quarter. If Party B violates the contract for more than three times (including three times), Party A has the right not to pay all remaining rental fees.

(2) Rights and Obligations of Party B

a. The refrigerator purchased by Party B (used for Party A's cold drink products) shall be owned by Party B. All direct or indirect expenses or losses arising from the freezer shall be borne by Party B alone.

b. Party B shall ensure that other products shall not be displayed, the posters of other manufacturers shall not be posted in Party B's freezer, and the freezer shall not be leased, sold or lent to others. The freezer shall be kept clean and in good appearance during use and the image of Party A shall not be damaged.

c. Party B shall be responsible for the delivery, daily management, service and product supply of the freezer. Party B shall establish a freezer management account after the freezer is put on the market, and use the asset management system to establish terminal information and update it in time. Party B shall provide the freezer management account to Party A's business personnel every week to facilitate Party A's checking and management.

d. After the expiration of the term of the main contract, if Party B continues to operate Party A's cold drinks, Party B shall have the right to continue to use the unified image of Party A with the consent of Party A; if Party B doesn't operate Party A's cold drink business, Party B shall not use Party A's unified image.

第六章 民事诉讼法的基本知识和翻译

The Appellant declines to accept the No.12 Civil Judgment, in respect of the lease contract case, and hereby files the appeal in accordance with law.

Facts and reasons:

Firstly, the Appellant's basic and leading opinions about the case as follows:

The Appellant holds that in accordance with the mentalities of highly autonomous expression of intentions and contract freedom advocated in the Contract Law, as well as the mainstream law-enforcing mentalities in judicial practice at present, there exist three contracts between the Appellant and the Appellee, which shall be deemed to be valid. The subjects, matters and considerations involved in the three contracts are basically identical.

① The first-instance court ascertained that the house lease contract executed between the Appellant and the Appellee was invalid. This ruling has no legal basis.

② The court ascertained that the Appellant's exercise of the right to avoid performing the contract as a defense against the Appellee's breach by reason that the Appellee has performed a majority of the contractual obligations and the Appellant was using the lease house when the parties entered into the contract. This ruling is in material violation of the provision of the Contract Law in respect of the defensive refusal to perform the contract.

Secondly, the following are some defenses of the Appellant based on the first-instance judgment, which cannot be fully accepted.

① The ruling of the first-instance court ordering the Appellant to pay the rental according to the rental standard prescribed in the contract of 2016 by reason that the Appellant was in an actual lease relationship with the Appellee subsequent to 2017 is not law-based.

② The first-instance judgment on the 13 square meters in respect of which the Appellant failed perform the contract is explicitly wrong in law enforcement.

③ Given the isolated law enforcement by the first-instance court (i.e. it only considered the contract of 2016), the Appellant has paid more than RMB20,000 in rental following 2016.

④ Even under the circumstance of only handling the contract of 2016 by the first-instance court, no compensation has been given to decoration, which is unfair either.

In summary, the Appellant maintains that there have existed three contracts between the Appellant and the Appellee. The Appellee and the first-instance court has intentionally isolated the complete set of civil juristic relationships between the parties, thereby leading to one-sided judgment in the first instance and imposing burden of the parties' litigation efforts. Meanwhile, the criteria for law-enforcement were unbalanced and unharmonious in the first instance, together with other problems including entitled law application and illegal ruling. Therefore, the Appellant requests second-instance court to make a fair judgment on the basis of ascertaining all facts of this case.

原被告夫妻关系不和，为此原告请求法院做出如下判决：

① 准许原被告离婚，解除双方夫妻关系，解除当事人相互间的所有义务；

② 请求法院判断属于原告个人的单独财产包括他婚前的全部财产，这些财产包括位于密西西比州兰金县老芬宁路420号的住宅，以及他的个人珠宝、私人汽车和财物。请求法院判定被告个人的单独财产包括她婚前全部财产和个人珠宝、所有物和财物。

③ 法院认为合理及适当的其他和进一步补偿。

练习 3

Entrusted Matters: to prepare the answer and appear before the competent court hearing; to counter claim, to investigate, collect and deliver to the relevant court and related evidence; to make compromise; to accept any mediation presided over by court; to admit, waive or modify the claims; to prepare the statement of appeal and file an appeal; to apply for retrial; to apply for measures of evidence preservation and measures of property preservation during or before the proceedings; to apply for enforcement of the valid court documents; to accept service of court documents; to sign and receive verdicts, judgments, summons, decisions and any other court documents; to handle all other issues in connection with the said matter.

练习 4

法院分析的第一步是确定被告是否应当合理预见被告已故妻子所遭遇的伤害。原告认为,被告对杰克逊有一定程度的了解:有过犯罪前科;曾被指控犯有三级入室盗窃罪、盗窃罪以及行为失常;曾吸食大麻;企图自杀;有暴力、自虐行为。然而对于一个被指控犯有入室盗窃以及行为失常的人,他人无法合理预见到他会实施伤害、殴打以及谋杀行为。同样对一个曾吸食大麻或试图自杀的人,他人也无法预见到他会有这种残忍的暴力行为。

第七章 仲裁的基本知识和翻译

练习 1

凡因执行本合同所发生的或是和本合同有关的一切争议,双方应通过友好协商解决。协商不能解决时,应提交中国国际经济贸易仲裁委员会,根据其仲裁规则进行仲裁。仲裁的判决是终局性的,对对方都有约束力。

练习 2

仲裁。因履行或终止本协议而产生的任何纠纷、争议或索赔,应依据当时的美国仲裁协会之规则,提交马萨诸塞州仲裁解决。仲裁裁决对各方均为终局,具有约束力和决定性,且所做判决可由任何有管辖权之法院予以登记。

练习 3

The parties may agree to submit their disputes to CIETAC or a sub-commission/arbitration center of CIETAC for arbitration. Where the parties have agreed to arbitration by CIETAC, the Arbitration Court shall accept the arbitration application and administer the case. Where the parties have agreed to arbitration by a sub-commission/arbitration center, the arbitration court of the sub-commission/arbitration center agreed upon by the parties shall accept the arbitration application and administer the case. Where the sub-commission/arbitration center agreed upon by the parties does not exist or its authorization has been terminated, or where the agreement is ambiguous, the Arbitration Court shall accept the arbitration application and administer the case. In the event of any dispute, a decision shall be made by CIETAC.

Where the parties agree to refer their dispute to CIETAC for arbitration but have agreed on a modification of these Rules or have agreed on the application of other arbitration rules, the parties' agreement shall prevail unless such agreement is inoperative or in conflict with a mandatory provision of the law applicable to the arbitral proceedings. Where the parties have agreed on the application of other arbitration rules, CIETAC shall perform the relevant administrative duties.

高等法院的裁定

Davis QC（作为高等法院副法官）不同意仲裁员的裁定，即第2（i）条的争议不在最初提及的仲裁范围之内。法庭指出，仲裁员裁决背后的原因难以理解，法庭基本上是在重新审理管辖权问题。在这方面，主要问题似乎是根据第2（i）条提出的争议是否不在提交仲裁员的事项范围之内，因为仲裁最初是根据《BG契约》不同条款引起的争议进行的。法官不同意这种做法。相反，他认为，法庭在确定所提及的事项时，应当采取"语境的广义解释"，包括更广泛的事实背景，如指定仲裁员和接受指定的信函。

在这种情况下，法官接受了申请人的论点，即提交仲裁员的事项被正确地视为"赔偿"请求，"无论是否根据第2（i）条、第5或第6条"。因此，对第2（i）条违反的事实没有从一开始就被提及，并不意味着它不在仲裁员的管辖范围内。

第八章　刑法的基本知识和翻译

原本惩罚是由罚金、伤害肉体的处罚和死刑组成。肉刑的主要形式有烙印、鞭笞和断肢。还有一种早期处罚称为流放——让罪犯离开所熟悉的社区。这些早期的刑罚流传到现代社会,至今在世界上一些地区还能见到,然而在我们所处的社会中,那些刑罚大部分已经被摒弃,由新的刑罚方法代替。

放火烧毁他人所有但无人居住的住宅,或他人所有但无人居住的建筑物、矿坑、火车、电车或其他供水、陆、空公共交通运输的船、车、飞机者,处三年以上十年以下有期徒刑。

放火烧毁前项自己的所有物、威胁公共安全者,处六个月以上五年以下有期徒刑。

失火烧毁第一款所有物,处六个月以下有期徒刑、拘役或三百元以下罚金;失火烧毁第二款所有物、威胁公共安全者,处六个月以下有期徒刑、拘役或三百元以下罚金。

The punishment of a criminal sentenced to public surveillance, criminal detention, fixed term imprisonment or life imprisonment may be commuted if, while serving his sentence, he conscientiously observes prison regulations, accepts education and reform through labor and shows true repentance or performs meritorious services; the punishment shall be commuted if a criminal performs any of the following major meritorious services:

① Preventing another person from conducting major criminal activities;

② Informing against major criminal activities conducted inside or outside prison and verified through investigation;

③ Having inventions or important technical innovations to his credit;

④ Coming to the rescue of another in everyday life and production at the risk of losing his own life;

⑤ Performing remarkable services in fighting against natural disasters or curbing major accidents;

⑥ Making other major contributions to the country and society.

Though the concept of a criminal offense is well established today, this was not always the case. The recognition of a class of illegal acts known as crimes was a product of a gradual historical development. Society made several crucial determinations in accepting the concept of crime, some of which are still being reexamined today. The society had to determine that there were some actions that should be viewed as injuries to the public as a whole rather than just to the individual victim.

同很多州一样,密苏里州不断改进死刑执行方法。在20世纪初期,该州用毒气室取代了绞刑,后又以注射替代了毒气室。在巴克鲁的定罪后程序终结前,密苏里州的"致命注射方案"规定的致死药剂包含三种成分:硫喷妥钠、泮库溴铵和氯化钾。那时,众多罪犯在美国提出了关于"致命注射方案"的合宪性诉讼,引发了一场"致命注射诉讼潮",巴克鲁也加入其中。

美国联邦最高法院最后以Baze v. Rees案(2008)平息了这场诉讼潮。在该案判决中,首席大法官罗伯茨以及阿利托、肯尼迪大法官指出,只有存在一种可行的、已然实施的、能够显著减少犯人承受剧痛的替代行刑方式时,州拒绝修订致命注射方案才会构成对宪法第八修正案的违反。

第九章 刑事诉讼法的基本知识和翻译

If the Defendants refuse to accept the present judgment as final and binding, they may appeal to the Higher People's Court of Guangdong directly or through this court within ten days commencing on the day following the date of receipt of this written judgment. In the case of lodging a written appeal, the original petition for appeal and two duplicates thereof shall be submitted.

练习2

In order to prove the aforesaid facts, the Prosecution presented the following evidence in court: inter alia, documentary evidence, photographs of the physical evidence, the drug laboratory test report and the defendant's confession.

练习3

当原告所处的这栋有门禁的大楼里的另一位居民到达大门口时,警方得以在没有告知原告或被告刘某某的情况下进入大楼。在找到原告的公寓后,警方在她门口做出警力布控。两名警察在门左边,一名警察在门右边。右边的警察取出他的泰瑟电枪放于身旁,左边的另一名警察取出了手枪。其中一名警察用一枚手电筒敲原告的门,片刻后,穿着整齐的原告开了门。上述情况都被记录在执法记录仪里。

练习4

6月9日大约下午1:39,章某某用手机给租房经纪人发了一条短信。章某某告诉租房经纪人说她可能要迟到,签约的时间改在下午2:10。约下午2:38分,和章某某约好看房的租房经纪人给她发了一条短信,但没有收到回信。晚上9:24,章某某所在的伊利诺伊大学的一名副教授向校园警方报案,并说很多同事尝试联系章某某但她都没有回复。

练习5

本院认为:根据初审法官所给予陪审团的关于犯罪意图的指示,"可予以反驳"的假定可合理地解读为法官告诉陪审团把故意杀人推断为开枪行为的自然及合理的后果是必须的,除非被告能说服陪审团这样的推断是没有根据的。初审法官有关"可以反驳"之假设的陈述,对一个理性的陪审员来说,一旦州检察官证明了是这一根本的开枪行为引出该假设的,则可能意味着要被告负起积极说服陪审团的责任。

练习6

This court finds that even though the accused has the nationality of Kenya, he had committed crime in the territory of China; therefore this case shall under the jurisdiction of China. The accused has stolen a relatively large amount of private property for the purpose of unlawful seizure and the charge of commiting larceny is well founded. As the accused was under the age of 18 while committing the crime, he shall be given lighter sentence. After the accused was brought to justice, he had a good attitude and confessed his criminal acts frankly; besides, most of the stolen property was also returned to the owner; consequently, the accuse may be given a lighter punishment.

第十章 行政法的基本知识和翻译

练习1

Should any administrative enforcement body violate these Provisions, the legislative affairs agency under the people's government at the same level shall suggest correction; should the administrative enforcement body refuse to make correction, the people's government at the same level shall circulate a notice of criticism; if the circumstances are serious, relevant persons-in-charge and directly responsible persons shall be investigated for liability by the supervisory organ, according to the law.

To demolish a house, an approval from the land department shall be required and the permit for house demolition shall be obtained. Without such approval and permission, any unit and individual shall not be allowed to demolish any house without authorization.

It is forbidden to trade any one of the following used motor vehicles: smuggled vehicles; vehicles of unknown origin; vehicles without complete documents; vehicles scrapped as required; vehicles pieced together or assembled without authorization; other vehicles that are forbidden to be transferred as required or prescribed.

Persisting in promoting governing the country under the law, governing under the law and administrating under the law together, persisting in the united construction of a rule of law country, a rule of law government and a rule of law society, realizing scientific legislation, strict law enforcement, judicial justice, and respect for the law among the entire population, and moving forward the modernization of the national governance system and governing ability.

The US Grains Council submitted to the Ministry of Commerce The Request for Terminating the Imposition of Anti-Dumping Duties and Countervailing Duties on Exports of American Dried Corn Distillers' Grains to China, requesting the Ministry of Commerce to consider the important changes in the Chinese market and the public interests of China, carry out review investigation into the applicable anti-dumping and countervailing measures against imports of dried corn distillers' grains originating in the United States and terminate the imposition of anti-dumping duties and countervailing duties.

参考文献

陈秋劲. 2013. 实用法律翻译教程[M]. 武汉：武汉大学出版社.

陈忠诚. 2000. 法范译谭[M]. 北京：中国法制出版社.

高凌云. 2017. 中华人民共和国民法总则（中英对照）[M]. 上海：复旦大学出版社.

何海波. 2011. 中国行政法若干关键词的英文翻译[J]. 行政法学研究（3）：18-27.

何家弘. 2008. 法律英语——美国法律制度[M]. 北京：法律出版社.

胡兆云. 2006. Administration 与 Government 文化语义辨析及其翻译[J]. 外语与外语教学（9）：40-43.

金晓燕. 2013. 法律术语的英译问题探究——以《中华人民共和国刑事诉讼法》为例[J]. 常州工学院学报（社会科学版）(2)：68-73.

李克兴. 2007. 法律翻译理论与实践[M]. 北京：北京大学出版社.

李克兴. 2011. 英汉法律翻译案例评述[M]. 北京：外文出版社.

李克兴，张新红. 2006. 法律文本与法律翻译[M]. 北京：中国对外翻译出版公司.

刘方权，黄小芳. 2008. 刑事诉讼文本中的"可以"[J]. 昆明理工大学学报（社会科法版）（1）：92-97.

聂玉景，王国新. 2010. 刑法文本中的模糊语现象分析[J]. 中州大学学报（4）：6-8.

屈文生，丁沁晨. 2017. 裁判类法律术语英译研究[J]. 中国翻译（6）：92-99.

冉诗洋，李德凤. 2019. 翻译律令"译讯人诈伪"的历史变迁及其启示[J]. 中国翻译（4）：59-65.

王辉. 2007. 英文合同解读语用、条款及文本范例[M]. 北京：法律出版社.

辛全民. 2011. 中国翻译史的分期新探[J]. 广东外语外贸大学学报（2）：84-88.

辛全民，高新华. 2010. 中国古代翻译立法及其现代启示[J]. 湖北广播电视大学学报，30（3）：77-78.

杨俊峰. 2005. 法律英语综合教程[M]. 北京：清华大学出版社.

张法连. 2009. 法律英语词汇双解[M]. 北京：中国法制出版社.

张法连. 2016. 法律英语翻译教程[M]. 北京：北京大学出版社.

张法连，张鲁平. 2014. 谈语用充实视角下的刑事判决书翻译[J]. 中国翻译（3）：93-97.

郑曦. 2019. 英国检察官选任、惩戒制度及其启示[N]. 检察日报，2019-5-11（3）.